THE MISSING FAMILY OF JESUS

Also by Tobias Churton

Invisibles – The True History of the Rosicrucians
Kiss of Death – The True History of the Gospel of Judas
Freemasonry – The Reality
The Magus of Freemasonry – The Mysterious Life of Elias Ashmole
Gnostic Philosophy – from Ancient Persia to Modern Times
The Golden Builders – Alchemy, Rosicrucians and the first Free Masons
The Fear of Vision
Miraval – A Quest
The Gnostics
Why I am still an Anglican (ed.)

Tobias Churton studied theology at Brasenose College, Oxford, where the light of his imagination was kindled by discoveries of long-lost manuscripts in Egypt and the Holy Land. He is now an Honorary Fellow of Exeter University and Faculty Lecturer in Freemasonry and Rosicrucianism at the university's Centre for the Study of Western Esotericism which offers Britain's only Master's degree in that subject.

Tobias worked in British television 1982–93 as a writer, researcher, composer, director and presenter. Following the success of his book *The Gnostics*, based on the Channel 4 TV series, he devoted himself to writing, composing and independent film-making. In 1997, he became founder editor of the international journal, *Freemasonry Today*. Since then he has been invited to lecture on spiritual and Masonic themes across the world. He is the author of *Gnostic Philosophy – from Ancient Persia to Modern Times*; *Miraval* (a novel); *The Golden Builders*; *The Fear of Vision* (poetry); *Kiss of Death: The True History of the Gospel of Judas*; *Freemasonry – The Reality*; *The Invisible History of the Rosicrucians*, and a biography of Elias Ashmole (1617–92), *The Magus of Freemasonry*. Tobias Churton's ground-breaking biography of mage, mountaineer and poet Aleister Crowley is due to appear in 2011.

THE MISSING FAMILY OF JESUS

An Inconvenient Truth –
How the Church erased Jesus's
brothers and sisters from history

TOBIAS CHURTON

WATKINS PUBLISHING

LONDON

This edition first published in the UK and USA 2010 by
Watkins Publishing, Sixth Floor, Castle House,
75–76 Wells Street, London W1T 3QH

1 3 5 7 9 10 8 6 4 2

Designed and typeset by Jerry Goldie

Printed and bound in China

British Library Cataloguing-in-Publication Data Available

Library of Congress Cataloging-in-Publication Data Available

ISBN: 978-1-907486-02-9

www.watkinspublishing.co.uk

Distributed in the USA and Canada by Sterling Publishing Co., Inc.
387 Park Avenue South, New York, NY 10016-8810

For information about custom editions, special sales, premium and
corporate purchases, please contact Sterling Special Sales
Department at 800-805-5489 or specialsales@sterlingpub.com

I dedicate this book to the memory of my beloved mother,
Patricia Churton, who was with me at the beginning,
but just missed the end – too suddenly.

ACKNOWLEDGEMENTS

This has been something of a solo voyage, undertaken in a vessel made not of second-hand but of primary sources seen again after a lifetime's overfamiliarity. It was, as it were, myself against – and with – the elements.

I should especially like to thank publisher Michael Mann, without whose faith and insight this book would have remained just an idea, unwritten. Ideas have to be cracked open, and only sympathetic publishers can make this happen.

My agent Fiona Spencer Thomas deserves a pedestal of her own for her patient, steadfast and intuitive support throughout a project undertaken in difficult circumstances.

My wife Joanna and daughter Mérovée have been everything a husband and father could wish for throughout the tempest.

CONTENTS

Introduction

The devil is in the detail; the angels too. Historically speaking, the issue of Jesus's family has never been a matter of much concern either to the Christian Churches or to the history of religion in general. Jesus's family really was left behind. Occasionally there would be an outbreak of curiosity; in the late Middle Ages there was a need to know something about Jesus's background, evinced in the popularity enjoyed by the 13th-century text, *The Golden Legend*. Lovers of religious art and mythology were introduced to St Anne and St Joachim and other persons venerated with haloes and fascinated awe through legend, not doctrine. It would have been considered at least very strange, but more probably utterly unthinkable, that Jesus's nearest kin (just *how* near was always an issue) could be used as weapons against orthodox Christian belief. Jesus's 'own' were either friendly or, alternatively, part of the prophet's own country-kindred among whom the prophet had no honour. This double identity – both with Jesus and against him – runs through the New Testament in a most mysterious fashion.

To avoid confusion, and to maintain Jesus's exalted and dogmatic status, representations of Jesus's family have been in the main strictly nuclear, often *single-parent* in orientation. Madonna, Child, absent father: like so many celebrity families today, but for very different reasons. Of course we know what the main reason was. He wasn't absent, so much as, well, *everywhere*, in a sense, but mostly in heaven above: an absent Father incarnate! Whereas, to begin with, Mary was the pregnant embarrassment to Joseph, by the time the Gentile Church overcame her Jewish heritage, it was the Jewish Joseph who was an embarrassment to Jesus and his spotless mother. Anyhow, practically speaking, painting Madonna and Child was always a safe bet; it was hard to get sitters for the complete Trinity.

During the last 30 or 40 years, all this has changed. The boat, if not the sacred cradle, has been rocked, and it is still rocking. Interest in the *historical* Jesus has coincided with interest in the *mystical* message, the secret *gnosis* of Jesus. At first sight, this might appear a contradiction, the one interest evincing a concern for realism, authentic history and science, the other idealism, surrealism and mysticism. Do not most people consider science to be at odds with most inherited beliefs? But to many today, religion is not an inherited belief; it might be a new thing you discover at school or on the internet, or on TV, or in a book or magazine. The prevailing *Zeitgeist* has brought a radical realism and a radical spiritualism. Divinity has been brought down to earth and earthiness reaches toward heaven.

Much of this psychological transformation has centred on the ubiquitous figure of Mary Magdalene, a woman for our times, saint and whore. In a number of books, a Gnostic, mystical Jesus and Mary generate a real dynasty of Gnostic, spiritual and magical offspring. There is surely more to this intriguing development than meets the eye.

My life's work in the Gnostic, Masonic, Rosicrucian, Hermetic and magico-esoteric fields is fairly well known among those concerned with such obvious superstitions, but few of my friends and readers realize that all of this vital interest comes to little more in my own mind than a continual commentary on that stubborn old root-system known as the Bible, a collection of largely unread works that deserve something better than their long-term fate as petrified objects of hysterical idolatry. Some might assert that more copies of the Bible are sold each year than condoms, but it remains arguable as to which has provided the most effective birth-control. As my ancestor, Archdeacon Ralph Churton, wrote two centuries ago, 'The only thing worth contending for is the truth.' A few words – but a lifetime's effort! – for the contention never ends; there is no end to the nonsense that the ill-willed, mis-informed or under-informed imagination may create. Those who most favour expressionism may have little to express. The liberty of Mr Speaker is often at the expense of the Mr Wise-to-be-silent.

But paradoxically, and by some marvellous providence – for all things work toward God in the end – the nonsense is often the stimulant for important revelations of the truth.

It occurred to me that there has long been a largely unspoken curiosity to know what happened to Jesus's family. This question set me on my way. I thought, 'all right; let's investigate every shred of contemporary evidence regarding Jesus's family with a completely open, if not empty, mind', by which I mean a refusal to be bound by my own prejudices, or rather post-judices. Whatever came of this I would relate to the reader with as much sense as I could muster. It's an important subject and I don't want to miss anything important, or be seen to be manipulating the material to make some fatuous 'explosive theory' or even to appear as one more cynical debunker in an age which has debunked itself so far as to have toppled backwards rather quickly.

Well, it turned out to be a very surprising adventure. When I embarked, I thought this journey into the past would generate a fairly straightforward guide for those interested in solving the question, an objective analysis and user-friendly investigation of not only the primary evidence but also the historic interpretations of that evidence. I imagined a fairly sober conclusion that might clarify things for the seekers 'out there' but which would leave me secure in my former state of general scepticism about the possibility of learning very much more about the subject.

Maybe it was the time I embarked on this voyage – I know I could not have undertaken it 10 or 20 years ago – but this circumnavigation opened my eyes in a way I would never have dreamed possible. I thought I was looking for the historical family of Jesus; what I found was the elusive historical Jesus as well.

Tobias Churton
England

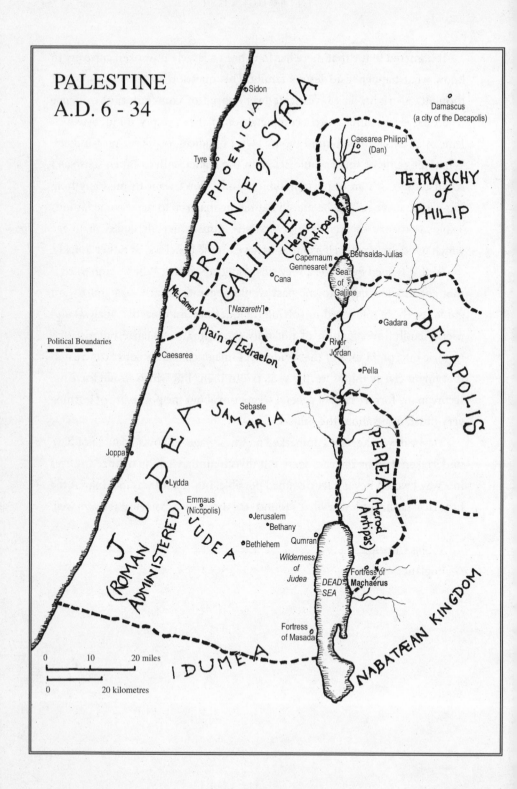

PALESTINE
A.D. 6 - 34

Sidon

Damascus
(a city of the Decapolis)

PROVINCE of SYRIA

PHOENICIA

Tyre

Caesarea Philippi
(Dan)

TETRARCHY
of
PHILIP

GALILEE
(Herod
Antipas)

Capernaum
Gennesaret
Cana

Bethsaida-Julias

Sea
of
Galilee

Mt. Carmel

['Nazareth']

Gadara

DECAPOLIS

Political Boundaries

Plain of Esdraelon

River
Jordan

Caesarea

Pella

Sebaste

SAMARIA

PEREA
(Herod
Antipas)

Joppa

Lydda

Emmaus
(Nicopolis)

Jerusalem
Bethany

Bethlehem

Qumran

Wilderness
of
Judea

DEAD
SEA

Fortress of
Machaerus

JUDEA
(ROMAN ADMINISTERED)

JUDEA

Fortress
of Masada

IDUMEA

NABATÆAN KINGDOM

0   10   20 miles

0   20 kilometres

The Missing Family

The New Testament is a battleground. What kind of religion is it that presents as its 'holy books' such a catalogue of conflict, bickering, sarcasm, hatred, contradiction and political confusion? Of course, this perception is seldom apparent to people who study set texts in Bible study groups or who have long heard the collect, epistle and gospel of Catholic church practice, whether Anglican or Roman, or their many derivatives and antecedents. We remember a number of golden phrases, some parables, a saying or story here and there, or a sequence of potent texts designed to reinforce theological dogmas, such as 'Jesus is the son of God' or 'we are justified by faith' or 'Jesus was crucified but rose again'. At Christmas and Easter, Christian congregations receive a collection of carefully sifted texts that build up a narrative with built-in moral and spiritual lessons. Interpretation is controlled.

What astonishes the objective observer is how it ever proved possible to get such coherence and apparent unity of doctrine from a collection of texts which themselves testify to so much internecine bitterness and public rancour. The answer to that is simple enough. The apparent unity did not come directly from the texts themselves, but from the *interpreters* of the texts. Unity was imposed; it still is. Christianity was not created by someone looking at the New Testament and deciding to form a religion based on it. Nor is the New Testament a religious system. Christianity is not a tree; it is a forest, and sometimes it is difficult to see the wood for the trees, as anyone soon finds out who poses the question, '*What is Christianity?*' and then goes to the New Testament for an answer.

What is all this about conflict? you say. It's all about love and brotherhood, isn't it? Look again. Jesus hates the high priests, Pharisees, scribes and hypocrites everywhere. He shows disdain for Hebrew law in one place while asserting perfect adherence to the Law as the only way to salvation in another. His disciples fight over who should be in charge under him while twisting their commander's words to suit themselves. Jesus's purse-holder argues with his 'master' over how best to employ wealth. The Master advocates poverty as a cure for the rich, not riches as a cure for the poor, thus confounding expectations on all sides, and annoying practically everybody. And all sides are up in arms. Disciples enter the Garden of Gethsemane with swords. Peter swipes off the high priest's servant's ear with one. Galileans do not get on with Judeans. Everyone hates the Herodians. Nobody seems to like the Samaritans. Gentiles are despised. Paul rebukes Peter; Peter rebukes Paul. Paul says he knows better than Jesus's own family. Jesus's brother James writes a letter saying that salvation relies on good works. Paul writes that works cannot save, only faith. Some followers of Jesus want to kill Paul. Paul says anyone who preaches differently to him is 'accursed'. Parable after prophecy declares most people will die eternally anyway; come the apocalypse, it's curtains for sinners. It will be too late to repent once you're in hell.

It's a nightmare. And the reason for the nightmare is that contrary to what many have opined, New Testament texts *reflect* real historical conditions in 1st-century Palestine. Not in every respect, mind you, nor do I mean that the New Testament is strictly historical, but carefully examined, the texts are not 'fairy stories'. They reveal, both on and between the lines, a religion in torment and people caught up in the belief that the apocalyptic 'end times' have dawned. The Messiah has come, or will come soon, or will come back soon. Prophecy leads to war. Had there been no revolt against the Romans, there would have been civil war anyhow. And curiously, the only villains to get off lightly in the New Testament boiling pot are the Romans. There are reasons for that, of course.

It *was* a nightmare, and we should not be surprised that many other facts got lost in the maelstrom: Jesus's family for example. But they were there. They played their part in the history of 1st-century Palestine, and yet, by the middle of the 2nd century, after the crises that tore Judea apart had finally subsided, the family appeared to have vanished. Theologically speaking, they had already become placeless persons.

What happened to them? Who were they?

Confession is good for the soul, but bad for the reputation. Still, I must confess, I did not come to ask these questions after an 'objective' study of the New Testament. Nothing so grand! The questions arose in my mind after sitting down one night to watch the movie, *The Da Vinci Code*, starring Tom Hanks as Dan Brown's fictional symbol-sleuth, Robert Langdon. As I watched, I asked myself, 'Why are so many people fascinated by this story – a tale of the Grail in a modern setting with a couple of nice Gnostic twists?' I concluded that the answer boiled down to a single natural question:

WHATEVER HAPPENED TO JESUS'S FAMILY?

A simple question, one might think, but there is something about this question that sets a whole line of bells a-ringing.

Many today are actively looking beyond the unity of doctrine imposed by religious authorities for many centuries. Many are suspicious that the Churches have obscured or distorted deeper or higher truths than the stark commands of righteousness offered with threats to faithful and faithless alike for two millennia. Social and psychological changes, archaeological discoveries, science and free-thinking scholarship have loosened the bonds of dogma and opened up new vistas. No ecclesiastical Moses has appeared on the peaks to point the way. People have had to find ways by themselves. Popular culture has become a significant organ of prophecy and guidance; so has science. For some the choice is stark: belief or atheism; for many more, new knowledge has set off a process of inner intuition. That is, we do not have to accept everything the Churches preach, but there is, or *perhaps* there is, *something in it*. Is there a secret, or set of secrets, behind the dogma?

This secret might be some astonishing fact that authority does not want us to know about, something that might imperil 'faith' or loosen the hold institutions have on our will and imagination. On the other hand, it might be a key to understanding, a divine key or door to the mystery of our being: a *gnosis*, or spiritual knowledge, a higher reason. Conversely, this very key might be what religious authorities, or political powers, most fear: a way out of the 'Matrix' of a fatal world. Supporting these suspicions and intuitive processes, a revival of magick has occurred.

The revival of magick is reflected in a popular culture of sounds and images that suggest mystical and spiritual dimensions of perception may be accessed through the embrace of mythology and personalized self-discipline of one kind or another. Arguably, 'New Ageism' may not constitute complete spiritual salvation but Carl Jung, for one, would have been pleased to see a remnant of the world 'saved' at least from becoming mere numbers in a materialist ant-colony, brainwashed through TV and the media by the power-hungry: those hungry for *our* power, that is. The materialist world is constantly advertising itself to us in forms many and subtle and it is hard to resist its juicy fruits. And while we are on the subject, it is interesting to note that the way some New Ageists think of our material world corresponds to what Judean 'radicals' thought of Rome: a polluting, distorting force.

What did the Romans do for them? The Romans offered sweeteners to help the conquered forget their former identity: baths, games, privileged member-ships and so on. Take them, the conquered were told, or perish. And of course, there was religion. Worship the emperor, then believe what you like. After 300 years of in-fighting and martyrdom, the Christian Church *triumphed*, according to orthodox history, when the Emperor Constantine *told the bishops* to settle their doctrines at a council convened at his pleasure. *In hoc signo vinces*, by the sign of the Cross, said Constantine, allegedly, he would conquer. And he did. He conquered the Church. But the Church knew it had conquered the Empire.

For a time.

Suppose they gave a religion, and nobody came. Where would all the priests, ministers, mullahs, swamis, gurus and pundits be *then*? Is there life after religion? *Eternal life?*

It is odd, is it not, that the question about what happened to Jesus's family seems to tap into many of our contemporary disquiets in a most curious way.

Controversy about the family appears when the top is threatened.

Now, Dan Brown's story, or rather his use of an older story, was not concerned with the historical family of Jesus. *The Da Vinci Code* presented a series of legends coalescing about a supposed 'fact', a suppressed fact of unknown, or alternative, history. The only family of Jesus that mattered in this story was the one he 'sired' himself, supposedly upon a willing Mary Magdalene who, according to Tim Rice, did not 'know how to love him'. According to Dan Brown and Lincoln, Baigent and Leigh's *The Holy Blood and The Holy Grail*, she did – and how. It is curious that in Dan Brown's telling, the 'new' myth of Jesus's family falls into the same trap, if I may say so, as the one that overtook the Catholic Church's assessment of Jesus's attested family.

The 2nd-century western Church centred on God the Father's 'only begotten' Son: the family – save the Virgin Mum – was either peripheral or non-existent. Likewise, the Brown-Grail narrative centres on Jesus's *own* offspring, so that Jesus becomes the divine Father of his 'only begotten' Grail dynasty, born to reign over an imaginary secret society that transfigures into an authoritative father to real ones, such as the Freemasons, Templars and Rosicrucians, in the fullness of time. This is all thrilling stuff. Indeed, I hope that readers find an historical approach to all of this as thrilling as the fictional one.

In these pages, you will find an investigation into the evidence for Jesus's real family. Will we find myths confirmed or myths denied? Will we find something better? Unlike a novelist, I cannot fill in the plot where there is no plot, but that does not mean there is no place for the imagination in this investigation. However, we have no right to impose a unity of interpretation on this material if there is no unity inherent in the evidence. Nevertheless, we are not simply scouting for 'facts'; *meaning* is vital too, and we must consider as many interpretations as appear significant.

I have hinted at the violent conflicts that characterized Judea and Galilee in the 1st century of the Christian era. Somewhere in all that furnace of hopes and dreams, that long holocaust of the prophetic, self-vindicating, self-loathing visions of ancient Israel, were the members of Jesus's family: mother, father, brothers and sisters, cousins and grandparents, aunts and uncles. They were there.

But funny things happen on the road to meta-stardom. When a concerted effort is made to re-present an individual to the public consciousness, embarrassing family ties are frequently jettisoned. This goes with a corresponding decline in *reality* as the glamour-factor around the 'chosen one' rises. Two fairly recent examples spring to mind. When the Beatles broke through into public consciousness in 1963, the management and marketing boys were concerned about the fact that John Lennon was married. Marriage was considered detrimental to his attractiveness or market-value. John was already 'taken'. The fact of marriage was, initially, suppressed as a policy. John had to appear *available*; the *image* demanded it, whatever the reality. Luckily for the Fab Four, the Beatles' music was strong enough to overcome the inevitable dawning of fact upon the dreams of girls who had set their hearts on their idol.

The second example is that of Adolf Hitler. Even now it seems odd to us that the apparently hysterical orator with his self-begotten '*kampf*' of messianic dictatorship was once an ordinary child with ordinary family members about him. As his political star rose by manipulations clever and crude, Hitler and his henchmen determined to conceal the existence of his living relatives and past relationships. Reality threatened to destroy or dilute the myth. The myth of Hitler as Lone Saviour was a political tool. Knowledge of the family was suppressed; the *Führer* must not appear as other men. Many believed he had been sent by God, that he was an incarnation of the German *Geist*, object of mass veneration, worship: Germany's only-begotten, even though he was an Austrian. The image was fake but powerful. You may say he was a dreamer, but he was not the only one.

There are of course other ways of dealing with the 'family' problem. One alternative to the actual assassination of inconvenient relatives is to transform *the family itself* into the myth. You may think of your own examples, some royal perhaps. In the case of Jesus's family, both concealment and mythic inclusion have been employed by apologists for the mythic being. First, a denial of the existence or significance of Jesus's siblings is discernible as the

Gentile Christian Church pulls itself away from its Galilean and Judean political roots. Second, the family is completely redrawn, mythologized.

Enter: 'The Holy Family'.

Exit: the real one.

———

We have all seen paintings of 'The Holy Family'. It's a pretty nuclear affair. We might see Joseph leading a donkey on which Mary sits, holding the baby Jesus. Otherwise, we might see Mother Mary and baby Jesus, but no daddy at all. During the 13th century and after there was a lot of polite interest in some of Jesus's closest relatives. A book called the *Protoevangelium of James* spoke about Mother Mary's own mother, Hannah or Anna: the Catholic and Orthodox St Anne. Readers were informed that St Anne was married to one Joachim, retroactively canonized as St Joachim. His name became popular in Europe and remains so. Giotto painted a fabulous meeting scene of St Anne and St Joachim. If Mary was blessed by the Lord in Jesus, so was Anne blessed by the Lord with her little girl dedicated to God, Mary. According to the apocryphal story, Mary served the priests at the Temple in Jerusalem; she was a kind of nun, though it was understood she would marry when the time came.

St Anne, the Virgin's mother, appears in numerous works by Renaissance artists, most famously in Leonardo da Vinci's *St Anne, the Virgin and the Infant Christ with a Lamb*. It took the genius of Nicolas Poussin to add some extra spice and dimension to long familiar Holy Family settings, producing a composite family in *The Holy Family with Ten Figures*, painted in 1649. This grouping looks like it popped out of a – admittedly very expensive – family album. It shows Mary and the infant Jesus, St Elizabeth (Mary's cousin) with her son St John the Baptist, while two older 'guests' stand and watch over the gathering with pride: Mary's husband St Joseph, and Joseph's mother-in-law, St Anne.

Poussin's work of genius *The Holy Family on the Steps*, painted a year earlier, is innovative. This time St Anne is not present, but Elizabeth and son John sit on a step below the Holy Mother. Meanwhile, most intriguingly, with his back to the well-lit group, is father Joseph, covered in shadow. Was he, like an imaginary 'Rosicrucian Brother' in the shadow of Jehovah's saving wings? Poussin must have known that the Greek word *tektōn*, usually translated as 'carpenter', also denotes an architect, technician or craftsman in stone. Joseph is engrossed in his drawings. He holds a set of compasses. Propped up on the Temple's steps before him, is a large set square; he is a freemason, a builder. Perhaps he is working on the Temple itself. Twin pillars of the Temple rise up behind Mother and Son, and a look in the book of Kings will soon tell you what the names of those pillars denote, unless you are a Freemason and will know at once.

Don't get carried away! For all the artistic genius and symbol-games employed by imaginative painters of conventional subjects, *real* families were just not like that in those days! A family was more like a clan, and very greatly extended; family was social security. What we have in this genre of religious art, usually commissioned by patrons closely connected to the Church, is a series of ideals, almost abstractions. These holy families do not serve the family, as families did, they serve God; they serve the Church. While the artists concerned tried to work in as much newness as was permissible, the Holy Family itself was a closed shop. You couldn't include just *anyone*. And here we come to a very important point.

After the 5th century AD, Catholic doctrine was rock solid on practically every spiritual and governmental issue; it had to be: it supported an edifice, an edifice both visible and invisible, 'the Body of Christ': the new Temple. What was held true in Rome was supposed to hold true everywhere. That is what 'catholic' means: something believed universally. And the moment I think of what 'catholic' means I immediately think of the famous Cardinal Newman's early trip to Rome, undertaken long before he converted to the Roman Catholic faith in 1845. Rome sent young John Henry Newman into a romantic ecstasy. He was unconsciously seduced by what he saw of the consistency of faith, time, architecture and religious practice he found celebrated in the 'Eternal City'. *This*, he famously declared, was a *religion*.

Out of all the disparate sources, contentious doctrines and old battles of long ago, had emerged a *religion*, a complete system, a binding together of doctrine and practice: a way of life. One might argue that the price for having a unified religion was paid for in historical veracity, not to say doctrinal petrification, ideological sterility and scientific paralysis. But it could still inspire artists and armies, mystics and merchants, peasants and popes. Mere history cannot do this, and was not Henry Ford right when he declared that 'History is more or less bunk'? Who can you trust? Bare records can be tampered with. Books go missing. Testimonies are retracted, modified, forgotten. No, anyone who thinks clever challenges to time-honoured historic markers can topple a religion is very optimistic. People need religion more than history, more perhaps, than what we are disposed to call *truth*. The religion got here before the tools of analysis did. The religion was here before the archaeologists got to the site. Nevertheless, not everyone wants the religion, and not everyone has made their mind up about it, and even those so convinced by their experience of religion that they feel compelled to follow it, still like to think about it all from time to time. Besides, something may emerge from history that makes better sense of religion and may even deepen, restore, or even help to create faith. Knowledge can be very persuasive and a personal faith that resists it on principle may become brittle and some day break.

The point is that religion requires certain images to be respected; history does not. History might wonder, for example, why neither Poussin, nor Leonardo, nor Raphael, nor Giotto included any of Jesus's brothers or sisters in their designs on the Holy Family. Were they not holy *enough*?

Under the rule of Joseph Stalin, senior politicos who fell out of favour were photo-lithographically rubbed out of official propaganda. Wiped from the political scene, their image obliterated, it was as if they had never existed. In the case of the family of Jesus, offending, ambiguous or inconvenient figures did not have to be removed from official iconography. The Missing Family had been missing long before widespread image-making began.

Indeed, one may wonder how it came to be that references to inconvenient figures were not excised from the canonical writings that preceded the image-making. Well, we cannot be sure that this did not happen. However, surviving versions of Matthew and Mark's gospels do give us something to go on. Perhaps these passages were too well known throughout the Empire to disappear quietly; perhaps a bishop could be relied on to explain the references in ways that nullified their value to critics. Paul's letter to the Galatians 2:9, for example, very clearly indicates his run-in with James, the brother of the Lord, so it might have proved unwise to imagine that such a 'pillar' of the Church, as Paul describes James, never existed at all. The point was that Paul saw James as a pain and the Church agreed with Paul. Without Paul, the Gentiles would never have joined the great army of God, advancing *en masse*.

Mark 6:3 tells us that Jesus (Yeshua or 'Joshua') had brothers: James (properly 'Jacob'), Joses (Joseph or 'Yusef'), Simon ('Shimon') and Juda (called 'Judas' in Matthew). Unnamed sisters are also mentioned. But after the establishment of Christianity in the Roman Empire, 300 years later, believers were discouraged from dwelling on questions like: 'Whatever happened to Jesus's family?' Even today, in Catholic encyclopaedias of the saints, St James the Just (the 'Zadokite'), while regarded as Jesus's brother by the majority of Church Fathers, is instead called the 'son of Alphaeus', deliberately obscuring any theologically compromising family relationship.

The Jesus of the Church jumps out as an only child from the pages of dogma. He is God's 'only begotten son'. This is a theological point, but we know now that Jesus was a part of history, and like everyone else, he came from a family. Indeed, his family was important to his work.

The first 'bishop' of the 'Church' in Jerusalem after the Crucifixion was James the Righteous (the '*Zaddik*'), brother of Jesus, a tradition heavily obscured, if not perverted, in the Pauline Acts of the Apostles, as we shall see. James apparently continued his more famous brother's hostility to the more dominant priests, scribes and Pharisees. According to Church historian Eusebius, High Priest Ananus had James stoned close to death then finished off with a fuller's club in AD 62. Brother James was succeeded as second 'bishop' of Jerusalem by Jesus's relative, 'Simeon, son of Clopas'. According to the 2nd-century AD Jewish historian Hegesippus, Simeon was also martyred, like his kinsman James, in AD 106 or 107. Relying heavily on Hegesippus, Eusebius stated that the grandsons of Jesus's brother Judas survived until the reign of the

Emperor Trajan (AD 98–117). One presumes that the 'missing family' knew precisely who they were, and were not missing to themselves.

So, the earliest 'Church' in Jerusalem was apparently a family affair, perhaps even a 'dynasty'. As with all families, there were problems, jealousies.

Jesus did not need children of his own; his family provided man – and woman – power. And, contrary to all those who say Jesus *must* have been married as a religious as well as social duty, sexual continence was seen in his time as an exceptional path to holiness for the exceptionally righteous. Much of that cold bathing that went on in holy communities – what we know as 'baptism' – had a definite purpose. Any man can speak of the suppressant effects of a cold shower.

Why are these facts about Jesus's family so little known? Why for so many people is Jesus an 'unreal' character? The answer is simple. The Roman Church was not particularly concerned with a 'real' character; for catechetical purposes it might have been nice to tell the children and adult catechumens that Jesus lived in the country and knew about sheep, flowers, carpentry, that he cared for little children, the poor, and was friendly with shepherds, but when it came to the doctrine, Jesus was hardly someone you would meet carrying a back-pack in the Peak District. He was right up there on the Right Hand of God and had command of angels. He was the Law. He was a principle whose Word or Wisdom was writ in every ring and round of the cosmos.

The Roman Church wanted a *super*-real character, preferably with no character at all: an *object of worship*. The ancient world was used to worshipping objects, the more fantastic the better. If Christ was human, his humanity (the Jesus part) was bounded and illuminated by Christological event-theology. The 'event' was salvation through incarnation. In him, as St Paul wrote, was 'all the fullness of the Godhead bodily' (Colossians 2:9). Whatever that may indicate, he was unique, the 'second Adam', the first son of God having got us into this mess, the second equipped by Mission Control to get us out. 'Christ Jesus' was also God the Son whose destiny was strictly theological; he had come to redeem 'humanity', as St Paul taught. For this purpose, went the theory, God the Son could not simply materialize full-grown like the *Terminator* of science-fiction. He had to come through the humanity-imparting Virgin's womb, and that womb had to be 'perfect' lest God the Son be polluted by Adam's sin, passed on to all human beings congenitally, according to Paul. Of course, this twist around the pure womb needed something Paul could not provide. Paul taught that *everybody* – save Christ – had been marked by Adam's sin – Eve especially. He made no exceptions for Jesus's mother; virgins were not exempt.

This issue was long disputed. Only in 1854 with Pope Pius IX's Bull *Ineffabilis Deus* were Catholics required to 'firmly and steadfastly' believe in the doctrine of the 'Immaculate Conception'. This allegedly *revealed* doctrine covered the anomaly thrown up by the requirement that God the Son could only enter the world through a perfect vessel: a miracle for sure, to be accepted on faith. The doctrine of the Immaculate Conception was not, as many suppose, the doctrine of Mary's perpetual virginity, that is, that Jesus's conception was immaculate. *That* was already understood. No, the problem was *Mary's* conception. Immaculate Conception meant that Mary's *own* conception in St Anne's womb had to be immaculate so that Adam's sin, Original Sin, by-passed the usual congenital process. Thus, for example, in the *Protoevangelium of James*, it appears that Mary's mother became pregnant while husband Joachim was elsewhere. Precisely how Mary's mother became pregnant is not gone into, though it was accepted as being a miracle granted in answer to a prayer. While the doctrine did not become official, infallible Catholic doctrine for 1,800 years, it had long been accepted in orthodox circles that something of the kind had preserved Jesus from the sin of the world. Once it was accepted that Mary (properly 'Mariamme') had been party to such a miracle, that her surrender to the Holy Spirit had been absolute, Mariamme became a very special lady indeed, almost a goddess. *Almost.* You cannot have goddesses in Christianity, but you can have a 'Mother of God'.

Back in the Middle East, these Roman and Asiatic ideas did not go down well with everyone who had upheld Jesus's Messiahship through thick and thin. By the late 4th century, Christian Jews and others who followed traditions established first in Jerusalem – where they were nicknamed 'the Poor' – were regarded by Catholics as *heretics*, outside of the care of 'the Church'. The 'Poor' did not have the right ideas about Jesus; they failed to see that he was God.

Was it then the case that the Roman Church had effectively usurped the family altogether and become self-appointed executors of Jesus's will and testament, taking the 'Holy Family' with them?

How could they do this?

It wasn't difficult. After Emperor Constantine gave Christianity (of a kind) imperial sanction, the Roman Church acquired the power and might and muscle of the state of Rome. Thus, in AD 380 Emperor Theodosius I put his seal to the law *Cunctos populos*:

> It is our desire that all the various nations which are subject to our Clemency and Moderation, should continue in the profession of that religion which was delivered to the Romans by the divine Apostle Peter, as it hath been preserved by faithful tradition; and which is now professed by the Pontiff Damsus and by Peter, Bishop of Alexandria, a man of apostolic holiness. According to the apostolic teaching and the doctrine of the Gospel, let us believe the one deity of the Father, the Son and the Holy Spirit, in equal majesty and in a holy Trinity. We authorize the followers of this law to assume the title of Catholic Christians; but as for the others, since, in our judgement, they are foolish madmen, we decree that they should be branded with the ignominious name of heretics, and shall not presume to give to their conventicles the name of churches. They will suffer in the first place the chastisement of the divine condemnation, and in the second the punishment which our authority, in accordance with the will of Heaven, shall decide to inflict.

The punishment was indicated in the follow-up law, *Nullus haereticus*, in 381:

> Let them [the heretics] be entirely excluded even from the thresholds of churches, since we permit no heretics to hold their unlawful assemblies in the towns. If they attempt any disturbance, we decree that their

fury shall be suppressed and that they shall be expelled outside the walls of the cities, so that the Catholic churches throughout the world may be restored to the orthodox bishops who hold the faith of Nicaea.

The 'faith of Nicaea' argued over at the behest of Constantine in Nicaea in AD 325 was crowned in AD 451 by the *Definition* issued by the epoch-marking Council of Chalcedon. Had any of Jesus's family's descendants been attentive to the issue at the time they would probably have been distinctly surprised to find their ancestor described in the following terms by people who had never met him:

Therefore, following the holy Fathers, we all with one accord teach men to acknowledge one and the same Son, our Lord Jesus Christ, at once complete in Godhead and complete in manhood, truly God and truly man, consisting also of a reasonable soul and body; of one substance with the Father as regards his Godhead, and at the same time of one substance with us as regards his manhood; like us in all respects, apart from sin; as regards his Godhead, begotten of the Father before the ages, but yet as regards his manhood begotten, for us men and for our salvation, of Mary the Virgin, the God-bearer; one and the same Christ, Son, Lord, Only-begotten, recognized IN TWO NATURES, WITHOUT CONFUSION, WITHOUT CHANGE, WITHOUT DIVISION, WITHOUT SEPARATION; the distinction of natures being in no way annulled by the union, but rather the characteristics of each nature being preserved and coming together to form one person and subsistence, not as parted or separated into two persons, but one and the same Son and Only-begotten God the Word, Lord Jesus Christ; even as the prophets from earliest times spoke of him, and our Lord Jesus Christ himself taught us, and the creed of the Fathers has handed down to us.

This is not, you may see, a biographical approach. It is a definition with legal force. Go against any part of this and you are a heretic. The Family had gone missing.

Can we find them?

What do we have to go on? There is some historical evidence, disparate, sometimes obscure, nothing of strictly forensic value. What has come down to us may be sufficient to build a picture of reasonable probability, without recourse to excessive speculation, but any sensible picture derived from the evidence must still involve degrees of interpretation.

There is legendary material, of which much has been made for conspiracy-style narratives. This material will be examined rationally. There is also a good deal of what orthodox authorities have called 'apocryphal material', accounts not included in the official canon of the Churches, but which nonetheless offer the historical perspective something of value. For example, in several apocryphal gospels, the figures of James the Righteous and of a possible twin ('Didymos' or 'Thomas') brother, called Judas, are given special, indeed fascinating, prominence. James and Judas Thomas were important to some Christian Jews and others living in Syria in the 2nd and 3rd centuries. We cannot dismiss evidence simply because the Churches do not approve of it. The shortcomings of evidence will be highlighted.

We also have an abundance of historical and archaeological knowledge which helps us to establish real possibilities as regards social and political conditions relevant to the story.

———

It must be the case that behind both the historical and the legendary evidence, there exists a missing, truthful picture of the family of Jesus. The task of the book is to establish as much of that truth as is historically possible within the bounds of reasonable probability. We need to go back to the origins, cut through the Chinese whispers down the centuries. There is more to discover; important things have been missed. We are going back to the roots, back to the authentic seed of Christianity, back home to the missing family of Jesus Christ.

Lost in the New Testament

All that religious debate comes to is that A's idea is different from B's. Revelation does not help us because that materially consists in correcting the ideas of A&B by those of C. Hence in practice, in order to get a better idea of God, […] if you wish to make your idea of God nobler, the way to do it is to make your mind nobler, and in particular to cultivate that noblest part of it which you owe God. […] To anyone capable of pure thought it is simply disgusting to hear people squabble on the authenticity of manuscripts. It does not matter to me in the least whether the Gospel story is true in the police court sense of truth. If that story does not square with my highest ideas, so much worse for the story. Let God be true and every man a liar is intensely immoral. So long as by the truth of God is meant the truth of statements which are of unknown origin, which have certainly been tampered with both by ignorance and malice – statements which are in themselves revolting alike to good sense and good manners.

(Letter of Aleister Crowley to Aelfrida Tillyard, 1913, *Yorke Collection*; Warburg Institute)

The New Testament is exceptionally well-trodden territory. That is an under-statement. There are so many flags planted there declaring 'I was here first' that the explorer may find him- or herself bewildered, never mind depressed with the futility of any hope of finding anything in a 'fresh state of preservation'. Everything has been fingered, lifted, compared, sewn-in, resewn, interpreted, reinterpreted, overinterpreted, attacked, defended, denied, obscured, translated, transliterated, transmogrified or tranquilized. It seems you cannot say anything about any part of the New Testament without several armies of opinion-precedents turning up on the scene, bayonets fixed, to warn off the 'intruder' from the infinitely annotated, theologically violated 'sacred text'. The turf has long ago turned into mud; the original topography has been obliterated. Maps are available, but most disagree over the details. There are so many commentaries, concordances, conferences, councils, canonical constipations, footnotes, references, cross-references, indexes, cross-indexes, critical evalua-tions by liberals, conservatives, Catholics, Protestants, Jews, Muslims, Hindus, atheists, communists, fascists, philologists, evangelicals, prevangelicals, popes, bishops, priests, pundits, persons known, unknown, radicals, revisionists, rock'n'rollers, journalists, nuns, nobodies and numbskulls that any kind of 'fair assessment' has become an impossibility. You simply join one of the 'schools of thought' and get on with it, or not. The New Testament has been fought over for so very long that it has ceased to make any kind of coherent sense sensible in all its parts to everybody. As is common knowledge, anyone can find a quote to support their argument. And that is basically what the New Testament is, or has become: a bag of quotes, copyright-free. I certainly do not think I can make it prove anything that everybody will agree with. Still, the New Testament is with us. It is not going to go away, and if we are trying to find Jesus's family, common sense dictates its pages demand prior consultation.

Why the priority? The authority of the New Testament documents lies in their canonical status. This means that the Church authorities authorized their use in churches because they were deemed to have been so employed uni-versally since apostolic times, that is, sometime between the mid 1st century and the mid 2nd century. Works definitely in the 'word of God' category formed what was called a 'canon'. Outside of that were books that might be fairly inspired, inspirational or interesting, but you could not use them to produce doctrine, at least officially. Irenaeus, Bishop of Lyons in Gaul c.AD 180 said there were four gospels because God ordained a harmony in the world: four points of the compass, four winds and, well, four gospels. The rest were either 'the word of man' or heretical, inaccurate, fanciful or deceitful. The Catholic canon was more or less agreed and insisted upon by the middle to late 4th century, when a final clearing of 'apocryphal works' and outright banning of 'heretical' works was undertaken as bishops acquired and employed imperial legal support to weed out Christians who did not jump when the bishops spoke. By AD 400 'right doctrine' or orthodoxy had the full backing of the state.

And the bishops said this: what is to be found in the canon counts; anything else has no authority. It is a fairly circular argument, but effective. The authorities decide what is authoritative. The authoritative works condition the doctrine of the authorities. Nevertheless, in favour of the canon being seen as the primary source is the fact that the majority of the documents in the canon appear, in the main, to have been the oldest surviving records of the first century of the Christian experience. Catholic or orthodox teaching was largely in tune with the oldest Christian written sources. However, we have no original documents to compare our present canon with. Complete versions are not extant before the 4th century. Before that, we must suppose a more dynamic and creative period slowly running down, as all religious movements do, into convention and stolidity.

The fact that the Church has put the canonical documents under the seal 'the word of God' does not mean that their historical content is of the first order. They reflect their times; they would make a poor source for the history of the 1st century had we no other historical sources to go on. Then again, most of what they record appears only in these documents. In that sense, they are historical sources. The sources agree on many key points though not in all details, wording, emphases or interpretations. Common prior but unknown sources are discernible, while known sources include the Old Testament and Jewish apocryphal and historical works. While we cannot cross-check the details in most cases, it should be recognized that we should know nothing of the narratives without the texts we have inherited. We have little significant back-up or supportive documentation contemporary with many of the events described. The Sermon on the Mount, for example, or the 'feeding of the 5,000' are not mentioned anywhere else but in the gospels. This in itself makes the documents of the New Testament interesting, though not infallible.

The writers and users of the canonical gospels were satisfied that they contained the knowledge of the earliest Christian witnesses. We are not in a position to examine that assurance to any significant extent. Every New Testament work is the result of editorial choices made by writers, editors and compilers reliant on the memories or best guesses and prejudices of others. There may be eye-witness testimony here and there; there may be what is politely called 'oral tradition'; some statements may have been checked. But in order to grasp their value in establishing historical facts, rather than doctrine, it should be understood that there was no 'Golden Age' of the early Church, as so often portrayed in grand Hollywood movies, where every loving, patient Christian was as gentle, attractive and serene as Deborah Kerr in *Quo Vadis*, and good all-round honest American he-men like Victor Mature and John Wayne constituted the courageous faithful, led by kindly old Finlay Currie with his delightful Highland accent traversing the clouds of mystic vision between *Quo Vadis* and *Ben Hur* like a benign Moses, with never a bad word to say about anyone. Now *that's* religion!

The New Testament was not produced in the Dream Factory. The choices made by writers and editors about Jesus, his followers and enemies, reflect their political and doctrinal position. Sometimes, that is not easy to determine. But all the writers have one thing in common: the belief that Jesus was Son of God, Saviour, and would come again in judgement: bliss for the righteous, terrible for the wicked.

The New Testament is *Christocentric*. Everyone else gets a bit-part. In this scenario, Jesus's family are extras and can easily get lost in the crowd.

Such may not have been apparent to anyone coming upon the gospels of Luke and Matthew for the first time. Matthew 1:1–17 and Luke 3:23–28 provide genealogies for Jesus. They are not family trees as we know them; they are 'begatting' narratives familiar to readers of the Hebrew books of Chronicles and Genesis. The gospel genealogies are clearly modelled on more ancient traditional works. Jesus's family background is given space for a specific reason. The genealogies are not there as an aid to biographers. We might have learned a lot of great interest from the genealogical accounts, but for the fact that they are both very different, and neither tells us anything about the long lists of names, many of which are, sadly, just names, and, in the case of the post-Davidic identities, largely unknown to scripture.

Jesus's lineage is traced by Luke *via* King David and the patriarch Jacob through Seth to Seth's father Adam, 'the son of God', while Matthew traces Jesus's lineage down from Abraham. Abraham was father of Ishmael, progenitor of Arab peoples, and grandfather of Jacob or 'Israel' whose 12 sons constituted the inheritors of the promise Abraham received from God. Matthew is well known to be concerned with matters of interest to the circumcised, while Luke reflects the Pauline, pro-Gentile picture. This probably explains in the main why Luke's list goes back to the progenitor of the human race. These are by no means the least differences. While both genealogies make it absolutely clear that Jesus was descended from King David (usually dated *c.*1000–961 BC), the descendants from David down to Jesus's parents Mary and Joseph are almost completely different.

> And Eliud begat Eleazar; and Eleazar begat Matthan; and Mattan begat Jacob; And Jacob begat Joseph the husband of Mary of whom was born Jesus, who is called Christ.

The writer of 'Matthew' wrote this sometime between AD 80 and 100. The writer of 'Luke', writing sometime between AD 80 and 130, puts Jesus's recent ancestry another way:

> And Jesus himself began to be about thirty years of age, being [as was supposed] the son of Joseph, which was the son of Heli, Which was the son of Mathat, which was the son of Levi, which was the son of Melchi, which was the son of Janna, which was the son of Joseph ...

And so on. As one might expect, the thought that the word of God could be so at variance with itself over a matter so important as the Messiah's familial claim to that dignity has motivated theologians over the centuries to heights of ingenuity in attempting to explain why the two genealogies fail to match up either with each other or, in parts, with the genealogical information contained in the Hebrew scriptures. Suffice to say, they are different, though a fairly desperate case has been made that Luke followed the maternal line through Mary, and Matthew followed the paternal line through Joseph. But something is surely amiss where Luke traces the line through David's little-known son Nathan, while Matthew takes the line through the better-known Solomon. But the writer of Luke may not have been motivated by strict genealogical discipline. Nathan, according to I Chronicles 3:4 was Solomon's brother, born of Bath-shua, daughter of Ammiel. It is of course perfectly possible that both Mary and Joseph were relatives with common ancestry, but we cannot check this inference.

The House of Nathan appears mourning in Zechariah 12:12, directly after the House of David's family is also described as mourning. They mourn for a person who says: 'they shall look upon me whom they have pierced, and they shall mourn for him, as one mourneth for his only son, and shall be in bitterness for him, as one that is in bitterness for his firstborn.' This prophecy was clearly in the minds of those who constructed accounts of Jesus's crucifixion. It was probably in someone's mind when the decision was made to take Jesus's line back through Nathan rather than Solomon. Nathan's House was somehow involved with the ancient secret that the Messiah would suffer. Conversely, Nathan may have been Jesus's direct ancestor, if we set aside the question of whether one born without human paternal agency could claim paternal ancestors as their own.

Whatever the historicity may be of these genealogies, their function in the gospel narratives is primarily to identify Jesus as the fulfilment of prophecies that declare the Messiah shall come from the House of David. We can never know for sure whether the story was prompted by the prophecy, or the fulfilment discerned from the history. We can only say that many people in *Galilee* found the claim of Jesus to be the promised Messiah convincing. The case for Judea in Jesus's lifetime is not very clear, though, if Matthew is to be credited, Herod the Great took the threat of a Bethlehem-dwelling, House-of-David-descended, claimant to his throne very seriously indeed: seriously enough to slay the newborn sons of every family in the city. He had every reason to believe that Judeans would follow a person with such a claim.

And here we have another problem, or possibly, clue, in trying to locate the missing family. King David was of the tribe of Judah. Judah gave the region around Jerusalem and Bethlehem its name. The Greek word usually translated as 'Jews' means, strictly, 'Judeans', people of Judah. If you asked a Roman where the 'Jews' lived, he would say, Judea. We learn from the genealogies that Jesus was of the tribe of Judah, a Judean. Now this makes sense within the context of the prophecy of Micah 5:2 applied to the Messiah by Herod's advisors:

> But thou, Beth-lehem Ephratah, though thou be little among the thousands of Judah, yet out of thee shall he come forth unto me that is to be ruler in Israel; whose goings forth have been from of old, from everlasting. Therefore will he give them up, until the time that she which travaileth hath brought forth: then the remnant of his brethren shall return unto the children of Israel.

According to the prophecy, the Messiah, who would redeem the scattered remnant of his brothers, would come from the city of David, Bethlehem. David was of the tribe of Judah. The capital of Judea was Jerusalem. It would make sense for David's descendants to live in the land of their fathers, Judah.

But do we not think of Jesus as coming from Galilee, up north, the land of the ancient kingdom of Israel which fell to Assyrian conquest in 722 BC? The English poet Swinburne was not alone in referring to Jesus as the 'pale Galilean'. This is a little striking, and when we examine the accounts in Matthew and Luke regarding Jesus's homeland we find that the question of whether Jesus was Galilean or Judean has exercised the writers of these gospels too. Indeed, Luke and Matthew come to different conclusions on the issue.

According to Luke, Mary was living in Nazareth in Galilee, espoused to

'Joseph, of the House of David', when she received word of the angel Gabriel that 'the power of the highest' would overshadow her and she would conceive in her womb a son who would be given 'the throne of his father David' and would reign over the House of Jacob (Israel) forever. According to Luke, their visit to Bethlehem was a temporary coincidence with prophecy. Mary and Joseph went to Bethlehem in Judah to be taxed 'because he [Joseph] was of the house and lineage of David' and Bethlehem was where people of that lineage were ordered to go, apparently, as a result of a decree of Caesar Augustus. Luke's account of the tax-motive for the Bethlehem sojourn cannot be reconciled with Matthew's account without elaborate contortions.

Luke does not say Mary was of the House of David. Perhaps Joseph's role in the story was to provide the prophecy's required lineage. Anyhow, that is not Matthew's information.

According to Matthew, Joseph and Mary shared a house in Bethlehem, where Jesus was born, whither magi from the east journeyed to pay their respects to a king-to-be. Warned by an angel that King Herod would 'seek the young child to destroy him' Joseph took the child to Egypt with Mary by night, there to stay until Herod the Great's death in 4 BC.

Returning to 'Israel', Joseph learns that Herod's son Archelaus had succeeded to Herod's throne in Judea. For some reason, according to Matthew, Joseph was 'afraid to go thither', and received a warning from God in a dream that made him 'turn aside' from his *intended destination* (specifically stated as Judea) and head instead 'into the parts of Galilee' where 'he came and dwelt in a city called Nazareth'.

So, according to Matthew, Nazareth was fresh turf for Joseph, Galilee a place of refuge. He and Mary definitely came from Judea as far as we can tell from Matthew's text. Judea was where Jesus was intended to be raised, in the land of his fathers, the tribe of Judah. Galilee was apparently the place to go to avoid political trouble in Jerusalem. There was political trouble brewing in Galilee as well, but that is another story.

There is a well-known anomaly here. Matthew says that Joseph, Mary and Jesus went to Nazareth to fulfil a prophecy that 'He [the Messiah] shall be called a Nazarene'. This must be an error. First, because it is doubtful that

'Nazareth' as an established town existed at this time, but more importantly, the Greek word translated as 'Nazarene' almost certainly refers to religious practice, in particular the famous 'Nazarite' vow: a special vow of dedicated holy practices including fasting and visits to the Temple for prayer. Its performance would necessitate leaving Galilee for Jerusalem; the Nazarite must go to the 'door of the tabernacle of the congregation', as laid down clearly in Numbers 6:1–21.

Nazoraean, when spelt with a Hebrew 'tz' or letter *tzaddi*, means 'Keeper', as in a keeper of the Hebrew law. *Nazarite*, spelt with a Hebrew letter *zayin* or 'z' means 'consecrated' or 'separated', someone separated from the flock and dedicated to holiness to God. In practice, the meanings are close, being wedded to the whole concept of righteousness (*zedek*) and of great relevance to Jesus and his brothers. On a more banal level, there is also the possibility that 'Nazareth' has been confused with the Galilean seaside town of Gen*nesaret*. Such confusion of words abounded when writers and speakers whose first language was Greek had to work with Aramaic and Hebrew writing and oral tradition.

Contrary to Matthew, there is no prophecy extant about the Messiah coming from Nazareth. There is, however, a significant prophecy regarding the birth of the Israelite hero, Samson, that might lie within the root of the 'Nazareth' confusion:

> And there was a certain man of Zorah, of the family of the Danites, whose name was Manoah; and his wife was barren, and bare not. And the angel of the Lord appeared unto the woman, and said to her, Behold now, thou art barren, and bearest not: but thou shalt conceive, and bear a son. Now therefore beware, I pray thee, and drink not wine nor strong drink, and eat not any unclean thing: For lo, thou shalt conceive, and bear a son; and no razor shall come on his head: for the child shall be a Nazarite unto God from the womb: and he shall begin to deliver Israel out of the hand of the Philistines.
>
> (Judges 13:2–5)

Sounds familiar, does it not? And note how the child's mother must also be purified for the birth by taking on aspects of the Nazarite vow with regard to wine and meat: the deliverer is consecrated to God from the womb: 'the child shall be a Nazarite unto God.' Since a 1st-century Jew learned in messianic lore would undoubtedly see the reference to the 'Philistines' as symbolic of wickedness in general and the Roman army in particular, the destiny of the consecrated one who 'shall begin to deliver Israel out of the hand of the Philistines' fits comfortably into proto-messianic prophecy, suitable for a chosen son of the House of David.

So what can we take from the genealogies of Luke and Matthew?

Jesus was, according to both genealogies, a descendant of King David. If this were to be used as a claim to the throne, it would surely apply to Jesus's father and any brothers who might be born after Joseph was conjoined sexually to Mary following Jesus's birth. This is important. While Jesus is presented as the promised Messiah, or anointed king who would restore Israel as a whole to its right relation with God and the world, no specific claim is ever advanced on his behalf for the throne of Judea, a throne that would in due course cease to exist when Herod's successor failed his Roman overlords in keeping order.

But can we be sure of this?

Note the earlier statement in Luke that Jesus would inherit his father David's throne. It is fairly clear what such a promise would have meant to Judeans and Galileans at the time. Jesus would have been seen as a hot contender for the top spot. There is no record of Jesus encouraging this claim directly. To do so without an extraordinary level of public and priestly support would have been politically suicidal anyhow. The prevailing monarchical regime was backed and controlled by Rome, as well as by Herodian toadies in the dominant priestly party.

We also learn from the genealogies that there was believed to be some peculiarity about Joseph's role in Jesus's birth. Matthew says that Joseph was the 'husband of Mary of whom Jesus was born, who is called Christ'. Matthew does not call Joseph the father. This of course may simply be a legend designed to fit in with the ancient prophecy of Isaiah (7:14) that the Messiah would be born of a virgin (young girl) and later ideas about the divinity of the Son of God requiring unique biological circumstances. On the other hand, there may have been at some time a question mark over Jesus's precise paternity. What is difficult to understand is that if the Holy Spirit was the agent directly responsible for infusing Marian flesh with holy life, why would Joseph, or Mary, ever confide these sacred confidences to anyone else at all? Jesus makes no claim of this kind and Matthew does not belabour the point. It is possible that the virgin birth narrative provided the means to enable Jesus to lose his real family situation without losing the messianic claim background, possibly derived through Joseph, father or step-father.

The third thing we learn from the genealogies is that Jesus is of the tribe of Judah, but was apparently so familiar with Galilee from his upbringing that his recorded preaching and healing career takes place mostly in that northern territory associated with the 'lost tribes' of the ancient kingdom of Israel. Galilee in the 1st century was of mixed ethnicity and culture, separated from Judea by Samaria in the south-west and by Decapolis and Perea across the Jordan in the east. It is unlikely however, that Jesus was raised under the impression that he was a Galilean. Thus, he may have had the idea from an early age of a secret identity, or even a double identity. It is also just as likely that Jesus did not reach full maturity in Galilee anyhow. He may have grown up in Judea or even in another Jewish community abroad. However, we must take seriously Jesus's famous words about a prophet not being without honour 'except in his own country', a saying placed in Galilee among folk familiar with members of his family.

An important point here concerns the usage in the New Testament of a Greek word translated as the 'Jews'. The Gospel of John's authenticity, for example, is sometimes doubted on account of Jesus referring contemptuously to 'the Jews', as if he were not referring to his own, rather that he was critical of all the children of Israel in the manner of hostile Romans or Greeks. However, if, as seems likely, Jesus was referring strictly to 'Judeans', and more particularly to politico-religious factions of Judea, while himself preferring mind-sets he encountered in Galilee, this would account for the use of the phrase '*Hoi Ioudaioi*' (confusingly translated as 'the Jews') in original sources without imputing anti-Semitism either to Jesus himself, or to gospel writers putting words and alien concepts into his mouth.

By AD 140, 'Judea' as a political entity had ceased to exist and thence, if not before, the Gentile world simply interpreted the Greek for Judeans as meaning 'Jews' in general. Even now, it is difficult to make this point because of our inherited ideas of what a 'Jew' is. We do not think of a Jew as a Judean. The ancient distinction has been forgotten, but it was a distinction of signal political importance in Jesus's day, and should not be lost sight of, as commentators frequently do.

———

If we follow Matthew's account, Jesus was taken out of the reach of the Judean political milieu for his own protection. This does suggest at least some kind of political awareness on the part of his father or step-father. It might mean that a political role was intended for the boy, or indeed that the boy's family were already linked at a significant level to the religious and political problems of Judea. That Jesus's family were 'ordinary' is not a view with canonical support; it is a romanticism encouraged among Christian populations to help them identify with Jesus's background. The 'common touch' has always been a vital part of the armoury of aristocratic saviours; for those despairing of the ruling classes, a 'man of the people' might be preferred, until his new position so removes him from the people that he is quickly recast as a petty tyrant or would-be aristocrat and brought down 'a peg or two'.

If Matthew's account has any credible history behind its picture, it would make sense that if Herod had attempted to destroy Jesus or indeed his whole family for political reasons, he would have made efforts to locate them and sequestrate their possessions, had they chosen exile over his rule. It may have been a high-born family 'on hard times' and in need of some assistance that attempted to re-emerge from hiding. That Joseph could probably function as an architect may not only have been a symbolic reference to his role in establishing a new order, but the product of a civilized man's education. It is possible that he had to turn to his craft after being unable (forbidden?) to fulfil a traditional family role in Judean government, but this is pure conjecture. Judea and Galilee certainly afforded opportunities for technical skills in this period. The Temple was unfinished; masons were continually seeking new work. Galilee's rich Hellenized cities also required the vision of classically trained masons and architects. The gospels reveal a Jesus armed with symbol lore conceivably familiar to a pious mason of the time.

It is noteworthy that the gospels show no interest in, or perhaps deliberately skirt round, Jesus's political position as a viable claimant to the thrones of Judea or Galilee. The gospels do record people calling for him to adopt this status. Jesus is presented as unwilling to satisfy the clamour. How did people know he could furnish such a claim? Does the canonical record deny the centrality of such a claim because it was a claim that could have been shared by Jesus's family?

The emphasis in the canonical works is centred on what was claimed for Jesus alone.

Another possibility is that Jesus was only concerned with the throne of a *reunited* Israel as a beaming centre for a universal spiritual kingdom, on the Hermetic principle: 'As above, so below' or as the *paternoster* puts it: 'Thy will be done on earth, as it is in heaven.' *On earth, as in heaven.*

A messianic kingdom, as understood by a learned priest or pious 'Israelite', was very different to a mere political reign, however glorious. Found among the Dead Sea Scrolls is a text known as a *Messianic Apocalypse* (4Q521). It has been dated by Geza Vermes to the very early 1st century, the precise time we are dealing with. The Messianic Apocalypse lists the signs of the messianic kingdom to be perceived by the righteous. The signs are the recognition of the pious, the calling of the righteous by name, the renewal of the Lord's poor and faithful by His spirit, the glorification of the pious on 'the throne of the eternal kingdom', the liberation of captives, the restoration of sight to the blind, the straightening of the bent, the accomplishment of glorious things that have never been, the healing of the wounded, the leading of the uprooted, the feeding of the hungry, the giving of good news to the poor, and, notably, the revival of the dead when 'the Life-giver will raise the dead of his people'. The *signs* of the messianic kingdom were not merely the benefits of wise governance, but a complete transformation: very different indeed from the 'achievements' of the Herodian dynasty.

Jesus's career as told in the gospels ticks every box.

Nevertheless, we must ask the question of whether a political reality has been lost along with Jesus's familial reality, in the cause of claims made for Jesus's extraordinary messianic identity. While we have become accustomed to seeing the messianic kingdom as a spiritual 'kingdom of heaven', the traditional Jewish concept had a definite earthly dimension; indeed, it was seen as nothing less than a redemption of that dimension from the predations of evil. Certainly, any claim made by or on behalf of Jesus to the actual throne in the strictly political sense would have appeared, in retrospect, a crushing failure, as the ironic placing by Pilate of the placard 'King of the Jews' above the crucified Jesus in the canonical record grimly illustrates. If this be your king, mocks Pilate, mark his fate!

Jesus is reserved about his messianic role in Matthew, Mark and Luke. Christian theologians have spoken of a 'messianic secret', not to be revealed by his closest followers until the right time, when his 'hour' had 'come upon' him. Either the secret lay in the fact that he was the Messiah, or the secret lay in the nature of messiahship, that is, that Jesus held a secret understanding of the necessity of sacrificial crucifixion, a personal suffering that finally revealed the love of God's *complete* identification with the agonies of God's people: a sign of divine vulnerability and even, dare I say it, a sign of divine humanity.

According to the gospels, Jesus was interested to hear just who people thought he really was. Might we see behind these fragments an original scenario where Jesus was gauging the political temperature? Was there a dynastic plan that cleverly perceived that the people had to come by themselves to the conclusion that he was the One, so as to be carried willingly to the events that prophecy demanded must soon unfold? A mere political claim, with no real spiritual conviction, unsupported by significant numbers and dominant figures, would soon have soon brought the Roman legions in. The political realities were very well understood by the intelligentsia and all who had suffered so much for so long. When Peter blurts out at Caesarea Philippi that Jesus is the Messiah (*ho Christos*), he is told to guard his tongue (Mark 8:27–30).

It is possible that there was in Jesus's entourage an authentic conflict over how his royal role was to be understood. Such has been asserted many times. That is, that Jesus wanted his countrymen to see that God's promised redeemer was not the spiritual power behind, or chief of armed liberation in the mode favoured by coteries of 'Essenes', 'Zealots', 'Zadokites', Pharisees, 'Sicarii', 'Lestai' (the latter two names denoting 'robbers', 'bandits' and political assassins) and their followers, among whom appear to have been members of Jesus's team. On the other hand, reserve about the political implications might have been simply good political sense: keep the dynastic side quiet and concentrate on *getting the people themselves* to thrust the power upon him by establishing a political situation where the people could act decisively. This was playing with fire, since the messianic role *encompassed* the 'political' claim. For those faithful to the prophets, politics was an expression of religion, no more and no less. Jewish law was God's law and its application nearly always down-to-earth. But the flavour of righteousness changed when the tincture of enthusiastic messianism was added. The result was visionary, unstable and destabilizing; Judea's rulers had cause to fear it.

Political persuasion to get the people's support was a tricky business in Jesus's day, as we shall now see. For when we put Joseph's decision, as recorded briefly in Matthew, to take his son to Galilee instead of Judea, into its *political* context, the situation underlying the gospel narratives becomes not only more comprehensible, but startling and real.

Book XVII of the Jewish historian Josephus's *Antiquities of the Jews* gives a detailed picture of the political situation surrounding the assumption to power over Judea of Archelaus, son of Herod the Great in 4 BC.

Josephus was born in AD 37. He participated in the great Jewish Revolt against the Romans that took place AD 66–73 and penned his histories some time after the war. Writing for a mainly Roman audience, Josephus was not entirely unbiased. He tended to class messianic-inspired political activity as 'innovation'. He could barely bring himself even to discuss it. That judgement put him at odds with the views of a substantial number of his countrymen, and he knew it. In Josephus's judgement, from where he sat fairly safely in the imperial household in Rome, messianism had brought about the ruin of his country. He was not against mysticism; he was against challenging reality with dreams. The law, holy as it was, was down-to-earth; Jews needed to keep their feet on the ground. This insight is what makes Josephus such a good and readable historian.

Chapter Eight of Book XVII of the *Antiquities of the Jews* tells us that very shortly before Herod the Great's death, the old king changed his will. We might imagine at this time Jesus's family, still in Egypt, anxiously awaiting news of Herod's final demise after a hideous illness. But Herod had tricks in his dying tail. According to Josephus, he desired that his death be marked with the execution of a member of every family under his rule, so that the national mourning at his death would be the greatest in history, and not a mock mourning as was normal in such cases. He wanted an historic outburst of real grief. It is unclear whether this instruction was carried out. Herod also instructed that at his death a vast number of political prisoners held in the Jerusalem Hippodrome should also be shot to death with arrows, lest they imagine his death enabled escape from his rule. Again, he wanted widespread mourning, so he knew the prisoners had much popular support. There is also doubt over whether this 'final solution' was enacted. As it turned out, Herod's most politically disruptive move was the late change to his will.

While Herod's will still favoured his sons from his marriage to the Samaritan Malthace, Herod Antipas and Archelaus, Archelaus now replaced Antipas as heir to the kingdom of Judea. A disappointed Antipas was assigned the tetrarchy of Galilee and Perea, a less auspicious appointment. This change of inheritance was probably the news that made Jesus's father Joseph change his mind about returning to Judea. Joseph went on to Galilee, knowing that Herod Antipas would be its ruler. It is interesting that Joseph found the idea of Antipas's kingship tolerable. Is there a hint here of a relationship between Joseph's family and the household or supporters of Antipas? Could Joseph expect to remain unmolested living in Galilee? Matthew does not explain the reasons for Joseph's change of direction.

Now, it may be that the name 'Archelaus' alone was sufficient to alert readers of Matthew's gospel that Joseph's family would not have been safe under that brother's rule. Had Archelaus been party to the Bethlehem massacre that Matthew associates with Herod's attempt to be rid of the life of a royal claimant from the House of David? Or was it the association of Archelaus's name with subsequent horrors? In which case, why would Joseph have preferred Antipas to Archelaus *at the time*? Archelaus's bloody career had not yet begun, and Antipas was no angel. Did Joseph have inside knowledge?

Several possibilities, several fragments may illuminate the picture. According to the gospels, Herod Antipas was reluctant in years to come to follow the will of his wife Herodias in having the popular pious prophet John, known as the Baptist, executed, even though John was a critic of the Herodian dynasty's scandalous attitude to marriage laws. Herodias had been married to Antipas's half-brother, also called Herod ('Philip' in the gospels), the son of Mariamme, the daughter of Boethius, a high priest from Egypt. Herodias and Herod 'Philip' had had a daughter, Salome, who Antipas fancied: his half-brother's daughter. John left the ruler of Galilee in no doubt as to how God judged his actions. Antipas either had some personal respect for John and what he represented or was at least aware that having him removed permanently would be inflammatory. The Romans looked unfavourably on puppet rulers who could not keep their subjects from causing disturbances. Antipas entertained John for as long as he could stand Herodias's harangues on the subject. Josephus, however, entertains no such geniality between Antipas and John. According to Jospehus, Antipas anticipated social unrest due to John's preaching, and had him executed as a precaution.

Jesus, or his family, apparently had some kind of a connection with Antipas's household, which would not be surprising if Jesus's authentic family milieu was among the priestly class. Domestic politics in Judea was largely a matter of dealing with priests, a situation comparable to that in Iran today. Luke 8:3 refers to one of those who financed Jesus's operation in Galilee. She was Joanna, wife of Herod Antipas's steward, Chuza.

There is fragmentary evidence to suggest that Jesus's family milieu was of the priestly class. Indeed, the common notion of Jesus coming from humble stock is not borne out by the evidence at any level. While Jesus was of old aristocratic and regal lineage, the priestly background has barely registered at all. Luke 1:3–25 describes the birth of John, later called the 'Baptist', a holy man. John's father was Zechariah, a priest 'of the division of Abijah'. John's mother Elizabeth was 'of the daughters of Aaron'. Together they lived, according to Luke, in a city of Judea 'in the hill country'. Luke 1:36 says that Mary, Jesus's mother was a 'kinswoman' (Greek *syngenis*) of Elizabeth. Two verses later, Mary describes herself as a 'handmaid to the Lord'. The Greek word translated as 'handmaid' *doulē*, means a female slave, that is, one who has been rendered over wholly to Temple service, a possession of the priests. It was not unusual for pious virgin girls to be 'dedicated' to Temple service. Rabbinic sources note that the sons or daughters of the House of Rechab (the Rechabites) did service at the altar and married the sons and daughters of the high priests. Temple priests could find their wives from the ranks of the dedicated Temple slave girls. Once they had 'known' a man, their freedom from slavery to the Temple organization would be redeemed; they would then be rededicated to their husbands. According to Luke's telling, Mary's slavery would continue at least until a child was born. This must have been tough for Joseph, if not for Mary.

The detail about Mary's kinswoman Elizabeth being one of the daughters of Aaron almost certainly means that her father was a priest and had secured her marriage to another priest, named as Zechariah by Luke. Aaron's male descendants inherited priestly authority and could supervise Temple sacrifices.

There were lots of priests, 24 groups of them. Each group served twice a year for a week at a time, and their numbers necessitated the drawing of lots for morning and evening sacrifices. The most coveted lot was that drawn to officiate at the burning of incense in the Temple. The rising smoke signified the people's prayers rising to God. It was supposed to be performed only once in a priest's lifetime and many did not get the chance to officiate, so the story of Zechariah in Luke marks his number-one day as a priest. Unfortunately, when he emerged, instead of being able to crown his moment with a special blessing for the people, he found himself struck dumb after a vision of God's presence in the form of the angel Gabriel.

Luke was working from some authentic knowledge of Temple management. The reference to the 'division of Abijah' for example has an authentic ring about it. 'Abijah' means 'my father is Yahweh'. Fragmentary manuscripts from the Dead Sea Scrolls dated some time in the late 1st century BC include details of the six-yearly rotation of priestly courses, all of the divisions under the biblical names given in I Chronicles 24:10. The Qumran manuscripts (4Q323–324) refer to events and historic personages from the times of Herod the Great's father, Antipater, Roman governor of Judea.

However, there may be a kind of riddle involved in this textual detail. According to the account in Chronicles, composed about 300 BC, Abijah was a descendant of Eleazar, the son of Aaron, a chief of one of the 24 orders into which the priesthood was divided by David. Abijah received the eighth lot. The ninth lot went to Jeshuah. *Jeshuah* is of course the name we know better as Jesus, meaning 'God is salvation'. So, the choice of Abijah in Luke's text may have involved the idea that a new, spectacular course of priesthood would follow: that of Jesus, the next child born in Luke. That is to say, a new priestly order is on its way, one which will leave the old priesthood literally speechless. However, if such a line was contrived later, the authenticity of the source historically may be questioned, unless we suppose either coincidence or providence.

Interestingly, the order of Abijah apparently failed to return with Zerubbabel from the Captivity in Babylon (Ezra 2:36–9; Nehemiah 7:39–42; 12:1), so a restoration of exiles might also be implied who could say 'Yahweh is my father'. The Dead Sea Scrolls' priestly course fragments appear to demonstrate that the courses were recombined after the Exile under the traditional names, though, tantalizingly, the passages where one might expect to see the name Abijah have perished over time.

If this background to Jesus's family is authentic, we might suppose that Jesus was himself intended as a priest, not to say his father as well. Jesus's days of youth are absent from the New Testament, but for the well-known stories in Luke referring to Jesus being brought to the Temple first to offer sacrifices attendant on his mother's purification – arguably inconsistent with two immaculate conceptions – and secondly, another big family trip to the Temple on the occasion, apparently, of Jesus's being made a 'son of the covenant', a bar mitzvah boy on his 12th birthday.

Luke 2:21–9 preserves a story that at the time of Jesus's parents' purification following their child's circumcision, a man entered the Temple, led by the Holy Spirit, a man righteous and pious called Simeon, a variant of 'Simon'. He located the child, held him up, and, being a man looking for the Messiah to 'console' Israel, declared that now he could die in peace, as he had beheld Israel's salvation. At that very time, according to Luke 2:36–8, one Anna, 'daughter of Phanuel', a prophetess who dwelt day and night in the Temple, raised her voice in support of Simeon and gave thanks to God for the redemption of Israel.

It will be noted that Luke knows nothing of Herod's designs on the child, nor anything of any trip to Egypt, or of any return by the family towards Judea, then to Galilee. The dates between Luke and Matthew do not tally at all. Josephus appears to be on Matthew's side; the taxation of Syria and Judea by Cyrenius which Luke makes the basis of the sojourn in Bethlehem occurred, according to Josephus, in AD 6, *after* Archelaus was removed from office by the Romans. It therefore becomes impossible to harmonize these accounts satisfactorily, unless one is really desperate! If there is anything in the purification story with Simeon the righteous, the pious, a man led by the Holy Spirit, combining forces with Anna the prophetess to make dangerous declarations in the Temple that the Messiah had come, the dating must have been after Jesus's birth around 6 or 7 BC, before Archelaus assumed the throne (unless the Simeon and Anna incident properly belongs to the bar mitzvah story). Luke seems oblivious to the political implications of such declarations as Simeon and Anna voiced, as are most hearers of the story today. But prophecies of this kind counted greatly; they were the cause of wars.

Indeed, one cannot help observing that, according to Josephus, an Essene 'prophet' named Simon interpreted a dream of Archelaus in 4 BC that Archelaus would succeed his father in Judea and reign for ten years, which he did. Luke's description of Simeon/Simon making haste to the Temple by compulsion of the 'holy spirit' to greet the child redeemer would very well fit with that of the Herodian-employed Essene advisor who lived in Jerusalem, especially when we note those all-important qualifying adjectives, that Simeon was known for piety (*chesed*) and righteousness (*zedek*). He was probably a Zadokite priest of Essene or mystical persuasion.

As a dream interpreter, Archelaus's advisor Simon would almost certainly have been familiar with astrology, angelology and the Book of Enoch, a favourite work of Essenes according to Geza Vermes; several versions have emerged within the Qumran collection, and we shall see in the end how important this book is to understanding Jesus and his brothers' religious mission. But note also that Anna the prophetess, linked directly to Simeon the prophet, is identified as a daughter of *Phanuel*. Here we get to the nitty gritty, for Phanuel is no ordinary name.

Phanuel is the name given in the Book of Enoch to an archangel. His voice is heard next to Gabriel's. Phanuel is the enemy of Belial, arch-demon, cosmic 'Liar' and devil of the people whose disciplinary and prophetic works dominate the Dead Sea Scrolls. If Anna was a 'daughter' of Phanuel, then she was almost certainly an occult mistress, receiving messages from her archangel, dedicated to the path of light, out of the darkness brought upon Israel by the those servants of Belial, the Herodian dynasty.

According to I Enoch 40:9, archangel Phanuel was 'set over the repentance unto hope of those who inherit eternal life'. He could qualify then as both John the Baptist's and Jesus's holy guardian angel.

After such an outburst, it would have been wise for Jesus's family to up sticks and head for Egypt! But no, Luke has them all plodding back to 'their own city, Nazareth'. 'Nazareth' is obviously implicit to the tradition Luke is drawing on.

The problem is that Nazareth was unknown as a city before its appearance in the gospels. Josephus, who lived virtually next door and was charged with fortifying Galilean towns against the Romans, never mentioned it; nowhere is Nazareth mentioned in the Hebrew scriptures. Archaeology in Nazareth has uncovered no Roman-period remains from before the middle of the 2nd century. And yet even Matthew, who knows Joseph and Mary are Judeans, has Jesus's family finding haven in 'Nazareth'.

In Mark 6, when Jesus comes to his 'own country', to those who know his parents, brothers and sisters, Nazareth is not mentioned. Luke 4:16–30 on the other hand, supposed to have been based on the passage in Mark, adds Nazareth to the expanded story, saying this was 'where he had been brought up', while concluding his version with a bizarre attempt on Jesus's life. As punishment for announcing the dawn of the 'day of the Lord' in the synagogue, and relating it to himself, the villagers try to cast Jesus headlong from the brow of a hill on which 'their city was built'. But Jesus passes through the crowd, presumably by magic of invisibility. Not for nothing has Luke been called 'the romantic gospel'. The story, as it stands, does not ring true and the same doubt must be placed over the word 'Nazareth'. Arguably, Luke's account is an anti-Jewish polemic, blaming Jesus's 'own' for rejecting his message. But Jesus and his message were popular with the people; there was a lot in it for them.

Nazareth

Why did Jesus's father take the family to Galilee, far from home? The word 'Nazareth' holds the clue to understanding Joseph and his family's real business in Galilee. What did Joseph's family stand for? We hear of the prophecy of the 'Natsarim' – The Watchers – sent by God to declare against a spiritually rebellious Judah. The Dead Sea Scrolls help us to establish an historically credible family setting.

The spelling of the name 'Nazareth' is not consistent in the New Testament, and the etymology is obscure. In the 3rd century, we hear of a place with a similar name, spelt 'Nazara'. 'Nazara' is said to be in Judea, not Galilee. 'Nazara' is connected to Jesus's family, as we shall see.

The Greek transliterations 'Nazara' or 'Nazareth' might be related to the Hebrew word *netzer*, meaning 'branch' or 'shoot'. Did Joseph, as it were, 'plant' his family, that is, the 'tree of Jesse' in Galilee? According to the late John Fenton's commentary on Matthew, the only prophetic text that might have served as basis for Matthew declaring Jesus was called 'a Nazarene', on account of a link to 'Nazareth', was the messianic prophecy of Isaiah 11:1: 'There shall come forth a shoot from the stump of Jesse [King David's father], and a Branch [*netzer*] shall grow out of his roots.' Significantly, this famous prophecy was also linked to Jesus's birth, which of course took place not in 'Nazareth' in Galilee, but in Bethlehem of Judea.

The Hebrew 'nezer', on the other hand, means 'consecration', 'dedicated', 'separation', 'crown', and even 'hair'. The idea is of something that is set apart.

Naturally one thinks of ordination, and the setting apart of a priest for his devotion to God. In the context of a high priest's mitre, which was called a 'nezer', the 'setting apart' means that it is made holy, consecrated. We find the words 'nezer ha-kodesh' in Exodus 29:6 and Leviticus 8:9 in the context of the golden plate, the 'holy crown' upon the priestly mitre, where kodesh means 'sanctify', 'separate', 'set apart' and even 'transcendent'. On a high priest's mitre were inscribed the words 'Holy to God'. Taking the Nazarite vow made an individual 'Holy to God' for the duration of that vow.

Alternatively, 'Nazareth' might have once been connected to a pun on the Hebrew 'nasi' meaning 'leader' or 'prince', which might suggest a messianic implication.

Most intriguingly in my judgement, the word may stem from the Hebrew verb 'to watch' suggesting, prosaically, a hill look-out, or watchtower: prosaic in the first instance perhaps, but pregnant with possibilities. The Hebrew נצרים NATSARIM from natzar (or 'natsar') means 'watchers' and occurs, significantly, in Jeremiah 4:16–17:

> Make ye mention to the nations; behold, publish against Jerusalem, that watchers come from a far country, and give out their voice against the cities of Judah. As keepers of a field are they against her round about; because she has been rebellious against me, saith the LORD.

The theme of the 'watchers' and the 'watchtower' is familiar not only to Jehovah's Witnesses and fans of Bob Dylan's 'All along the Watchtower', but was also very important to those who established a 'New Covenant' in the 'land of Damascus' some time before Jesus's birth. A record of the New Covenanters' beliefs and organization has been left to us in the Dead Sea Scrolls. Their Damascus Document was found among the scrolls. In it, we hear of the End Times:

> But when the age is completed, according to the number of those years, there shall be no more joining the house of Judah, but each man shall stand on his watch-tower: The wall is built, the boundary far removed.

The source of the latter part of the passage is the prophet Micah (7:11): 'In the day that thy walls are to be built, in that day shall the decree be far removed.' The idea of 'watching' for the signs of the end of an age was important to the New Covenanters. 'Watching' kept you apart from the unrighteous. There appears to have been a pun played on the ideas of watching and being separated, made 'Holy to God'.

Natsar also means to 'keep' as in keeping the commandments of God. This also is a key word for the New Covenanters. Staying with the building theme, *natsar* occurs in Job 27:18 as 'keeper': 'He buildeth his house as a moth, and as a booth that the keeper maketh.'

In Acts 24:5 we find the Greek 'Nazōraiōn' which would be an adequate Greek transliteration of the Hebrew *Natsarim*. The name is given to the sect of the 'Nazarenes', that is, the early 'Christians'. Thus their name may originally have meant 'watchers', watching for the Lord, or 'keepers', keepers of the law.

If Joseph himself built 'the walls' of an enclosure for *Natsarim*, it would be the perfect name for a place for those who watched and waited for the Messiah, keeping faith with God and removed from the wickedness of the state. This is perhaps a radical interpretation of the meaning of a 'Nazareth' but it fits the material and the context seamlessly.

We may also consider an interpretation based on the idea of a place staked out, 'consecrated' or 'separated', removed from the sins of the world, so long as we note that the Hebrew 'Nazarite' is spelt with a 'zayin' ('z') not a 'tzaddi' ('tz') like *netzer* or *netser*. Again we see a kind of holy pun. The conditions of the 'Nazarite vow' are detailed in Numbers 6:1–8. They ordain that one who would become 'holy to God' should abstain from the grape, woman, barbers, the dead (including parents) and make offerings on the eighth day of the vow and at its completion in the Temple. Taking the Nazarite vow was a sign of personal dedication to the holiness of Yahweh; Jesus would almost certainly have taken it at least once.

I should just add that the Hebrew for *land* or *earth*, especially dry land, even desert or scrub, is 'aretz' or 'arets'. Coupled with the idea of the *Natsarim* or

Natzarim, we might in 'Nazareth' be looking at the remains of a compound word for 'consecrated land', 'keeper-land', 'watcher-land' or even 'earth-watch', corrupted over time to 'Nazareth', possibly being confused with Gennesaret, especially once its original meaning and purpose had been forgotten. Gennesaret was known in Hebrew as Chinnereth (meaning 'lyre'), and was a name given to the Sea of Galilee, not far away. It also appears in Joshua 12:3 in its plural form as 'Chinneroth'.

In fact, in Modern Hebrew, 'Nazareth' is called *Natseret*.

Were I to speculate further about the orbit of these words, I might suggest that behind the 'Nazareth' story was originally a kind of holy enclave, a separated and consecrated place, not a city or town but a Judean wilderness-style Zadokite 'camp' established in Galilee by Joseph the builder to further any familial or religious plans that he might have had at the time – unless of course such a place was already established for the purpose when he and his family returned from Egypt.

A 'natsret' could have been an ancient nickname for a pre-existing Zadokite, Essene or New Covenant group refuge for the devout. This would make sense of the confusion over the link in meaning between Jesus as a 'Nazarite', one who had taken the vow of holiness, and Jesus the so-called 'Nazarene', denoting background. Such a place may already have served as a refuge of Zechariah, Elizabeth and their son John. According to Luke, during Mary's pregnancy, her priestly relatives were apparently based at a 'city' (Greek *polin*) in a hilly place in Judea, possibly the Judean wilderness, where Josephus reports the presence of Essene holy men. Nor, in this context, may we forget the mighty symbolism of Sinai, where the Hebrews of the Exodus camped in expectation of the law and the Promised Land: the consecrated future for which the tribes had been set apart from Egypt by God's almighty hand.

On a less symbolic level, we may observe that after the destruction of Jerusalem in AD 70, priests appear to have retired to communities where they would have felt familiar. One might think in terms of priestly 'dachas' scattered about the country, perhaps long established. Such a place, possibly founded or resorted to by Joseph and his family, would have been as 'secret' as Geza Vermes and other scroll scholars suppose the sectarian 'Qumran settlement' to have been; that is, secret in its purposes, obscure in its location. Its original purpose having ceased by at least AD 140, if not long earlier, it could later have served as an ordinary settlement for the *hoi polloi*, a town growing up on or close to the site, the meaning of its name forgotten, its pronunciation garbled.

Is this misguided speculation or common sense?

It depends on your starting point. Clearly the canonical record is rather like a palimpsest: a manuscript with a hint or faint presence of an obscured, hidden history behind it. The texts as they stand are packed with anomalies and Jesus recommended that if we seek, we shall find: excellent scientific advice. So we keep looking. Is there any evidence for what I am suggesting?

In 1962, a 3rd- or 4th-century Hebrew inscription, found in Caesarea, mentions the residence of a priestly (*kohanim*) family, after Bar Kokhba's last-ditch Zealot revolt of AD 132–7. The priestly family supported the *Hapizzez*, that is, the 18th of the 24 priestly courses, as Zechariah's family supported the *Abijah* or 8th priestly division. The surviving inscription fragments indicate each town or village in Galilee where the family of the course settled. This was presumably after the priests, and indeed all living Jews, were expelled from Jerusalem for the last time by the Roman emperor Hadrian. (Hadrian favoured the partition principle, as is evident from the barrier wall he erected between what is now England and Scotland).

It is possible that the priestly residences predated the final ethnic clearance of Jerusalem ordered by the emperor. The place-name on the inscription is spelt with the Hebrew *tzaddi*: 'Natzareth'. That the 18th Kohen clan lived at a place of similar name is supported in the writings of Galilean poet Eleazar Kalir, who wrote some time between the 6th and 10th century AD about their presence at נצרת, pronounced 'Nitzrat' or 'Nitzrath'.

Searching for the Galilean base of Jesus's lost family gets even more peculiar when we look at the first reference to Nazareth outside of the canonical record. In about AD 200, Sextus Julius Africanus (*c.*170–245), wrote in Greek of 'Nazara', a village in *Judea*, not Galilee, close to 'Cochaba'. This passage was copied into Eusebius's *Church History* (1.7.14) around AD 300. One wonders if the origin of the name 'Nazara' then may have been a *noun* or even code-name used to designate a 'holy camp', a 'separated place' where the righteous Zadokite might find refuge. It is certain that the Essenes for example dwelt in communities in 'towns' but may have had a central control base in the 'desert'. The 'wilderness camp' was important to those who followed the Teacher of Righteousness in his rebellion against the Hasmonaean priest-kings, according to Geza Vermes, probably some time after 160 BC, and whose followers were apparently still active in Jesus's day. Such camps may remind us of 'al Qa'eda' training areas and hide-outs that we see on the News: *bases* for self-defined, super-righteous 'holy warriors' – but that is because we are living in the times we do. Superior righteousness or self-righteousness was the characteristic of those who revered the memory of the 'Teacher of Righteousness' and who waged ideological war against the dominant priestly faction in Jerusalem with the weapons of extreme purity and tacit support for violent conflict, so long as it was perceived to be in 'God's cause'.

The authority and inspiration for such 'wilderness camps' comes not only from the stories of Moses and the Children of Israel with their tents wandering the deserts of Sinai so as to purify the people before entry to the Promised Land, but from relatively more recent times. We read in 2 Maccabees 5:27 of the hero and liberator Judas Maccabaeus, progenitor of the Hasmonaean priest-kings. Having defeated the Syrian-Greek army of Antiochus in 167 BC, he removed the desecrated Temple altar from view and sought purification. In Jesus's time, Judas was the model of active holiness:

> But Judas Maccabeus with nine others, or thereabout, withdrew himself into the wilderness, and lived in the mountains after the manner of beasts, with his company, who fed on herbs [wild plants, vegetables] continually, lest they should be partakers of the pollution.

This Maccabean vegetarianism would become important to the observance of holiness in Jesus's family. Think of the famous wilderness diet of John the Baptist: locusts and wild honey (Mark 1:6), a diet omitted in the Pauline Luke's account. Meat sold in the marketplace had often been sacrificed to pagan idols. As meat might also contain blood, the pious Jew might choose to avoid meat altogether; the Nazarite certainly would. In Romans 14, Paul set himself against the vegetarian principle outright, casting aspersions on Jesus's followers in Jerusalem who were taking temporary Nazarite vows (Acts 21:18–23). Paul dismissed their scruples as matters of no serious importance: 'For one believeth that he may eat all things: another, who is weak, eateth herbs.' *Weak!* Thus Paul declared he knew better than Judas Maccabeus, John the Baptist and the holy men of Israel all together! No wonder some of Jesus's followers took oaths, vowing not to eat or drink (meat or wine), holding themselves self-cursed until they had killed Paul, the enemy of righteousness (Acts 23:12).

Obviously, Julius Africanus's reference to *Nazara* does not necessarily square with a Galilean Nazareth. There could have been several 'Nazaras', temporary enclosures. One thinks again of how when Jesus returns to his 'home town' in Mark 6:1–6 he encounters opposition from the religious assembly or synagogue. Conceivably, behind this story may have once been a situation where local peasants did not like Judean 'newcomers'. On the other hand, if we take the idea that 'Nazareth' was a self-defined sacred camp, with rules, we could imagine Jesus having formerly departed the place under a shadow, leaving his family behind him. The disciplinary codes of the so-called Qumran sect were adamant about the many failings that could lead to a person's being stoned to death or generally manhandled away from the holy camp, or simply kicked out and forbidden, or banned from returning for given periods of time, sometimes up to years. The possible coincidences here between attitudes in the Qumran Manual of Discipline and Luke's story about Jesus being physically forced out of 'Nazareth' by an outraged 'synagogue' are poignant and intriguing.

And lo and behold, we find that in the same passage in which Julius Africanus writes about 'Nazareth' in Judea, he also writes of *desposunoi*: the relatives of Jesus! He asserts that these heirs to Jesus's family line kept the records of their descent with great care:

A few of the careful, however, having obtained private records of their own [to avoid Herod the Great's wholesale destruction of the genealogical records of Judea's old high families], either by remembering the names or by getting them in some other way from the registers, pride themselves on preserving the memory of their noble extraction. Among these are those already mentioned, called Desposyni, on account of their connection with the family of the Saviour. Coming from Nazara and Cochaba, villages of Judea, into other parts of the world, they drew the aforesaid genealogy from memory and from the Book of Days [Chronicles] as faithfully as possible.

(*Ecclesiastical History*, Eusebius, Book I, 7:14).

Note that reference to *noble extraction*; Jesus was not an ordinary boy.

As for Cochaba, the other place mentioned by Julius Africanus, according to Taylor's *Christians and the Holy Places* (Oxford: 1993, pp. 36–8), possible Cochabas include one 15km (9m) north of modern Nazareth, on the other side of Sepphoris, two near Damascus and one to the east of Galilean Jordan in the Bashan area. There is a Kaukaba (that is, Cochaba) in south Lebanon today. Epiphanius (367–404) places a Cochaba in Syria, in the region of Damascus. A problem is that we do not know whether Julius Africanus in referring to these 'Judean' villages meant strictly that they were in Judea, which had ceased to exist politically by AD 200, or whether he meant they were Jewish or Palestinian generally; he was not himself a Jew. It would be fair to say that Julius's 'Judean' could mean either Judean or Galilean, or even Syrian, since the once separate kingdoms now came under the provincial title of *Syria Palaestina*.

The resonance of 'Cochaba' with the birthplace and pun of the last messianic pretender of Roman times, Simeon 'Bar Kokhba' (AD 130s), is, at first sight, striking. Nicknamed 'Son of the Star', from the important 'Star Prophecy' of Numbers 24:17, Simeon's birthplace was Choseba, thought to have been near Jericho in Judea. Choseba is not the same as Cochaba; Simeon might well have wished it was.

It looks most likely then that the Cochaba that was home to Jesus's family descendants recorded by Julius Africanus *c.*AD 200 was near Damascus. This may yet prove significant. The Qumran 'Damascus Document' speaks of a New Covenant having been made between the 'remnant' of Israel and the God of righteousness 'in the land of Damascus'. Geza Vermes dates this document sometime, but not long, before 70 BC, because it does not mention the Romans. It was, anyhow, a fairly new religious text in Jesus's time and was almost certainly being read and acted upon in Jesus's day:

> None of the men who enter the New Covenant in the land of Damascus, and who again betray it and depart from the fountain of living waters [possibly a reference to the biblical Dan or the 'Roman' Caesarea Philippi], shall be reckoned with the Council of the people or inscribed in its Book from the day of the gathering in of the Teacher of the Community until the coming of the Messiah out of Aaron and Israel.

Is it not possible that the community who first valued this and other 'Dead Sea Scrolls' might first have pitched their camp for their New Covenant 'in the land of Damascus', possibly at a place that came to be called Cochaba, if it was not already known by that name? Is it not also possible that some of the adherents to the holy New Covenant declared in the document were dwelling there at the time of Jesus, and beyond? I do not speculate for effect, but because these questions need asking.

Cochaba is based on the Hebrew for 'star' or 'constellation'. The famous messianic Star Prophecy of Numbers 24:17–19 was quoted three times in the manuscripts of the Dead Sea Scrolls, in the *Damascus Document*, in the *War Scroll* and in the *Messianic Testimonia* (1QM 11.6–17; CD 7.18–8.5, and 4QTest 9–13, preceded in 5–8 by Deuteronomy 18:18–19 on 'The True Prophet'). The prophecy about a 'Star out of Jacob', uttered by the Gentile Balaam, son of Beor, was very highly valued by the New Covenanters. Realizing that, it becomes even more vital to recognize that this prophecy was applied directly to Jesus, whose birth, Matthew tells us, was heralded by a star:

I shall see him, but not now: I shall behold him, but not nigh: there shall come a Star out of Jacob, and a Sceptre shall rise out of Israel, and shall smite the corners of Moab, and destroy all the children of Sheth. [...] Out of Jacob shall come he that shall have dominion, and shall destroy him that remaineth of the city.

(Numbers 24:17,19)

The coincidence of the words 'Nazara' and 'Cochaba' with the 'Branch' and 'Star' prophecies concerning the Messiah is as striking as it is, potentially, confusing. Simeon ben Choseba, the messianic pretender of the revolt of AD 132–7 could only manage a poor pun on his home town of Choseba to beef up his claim to be 'Bar Kokhba', 'Son of the Star'. So unimpressed were later rabbis with Shimon's crushing pretence to the messianic crown, they created a new pun on 'Bar Kokhba' just for him: 'Bar Choziba' – son of the Liar. The House of David, on the other hand, appears to have had the place-name coincidences, including Bethlehem (the Micah prophecy), wrapped up.

––––––––––

Sextus Julius Africanus accounted for the loss of genealogical information surrounding leading Jewish families in his Letter to Aristides, chapter 5:

But as up to that time the genealogies of the Hebrews had been registered in the public archives, and those, too, which were traced back to the proselytes as, for example, to Achior the Ammanite, and Ruth the Moabitess, and those who left Egypt along with the Israelites, and intermarried with them – Herod, knowing that the lineage of the Israelites contributed nothing to him, and goaded by the consciousness of his ignoble birth, burned the registers of their families. This he did, thinking that he would appear to be of noble birth, if no one else could trace back his descent by the public register to the patriarchs or proselytes, and to that mixed race called *georæ* [mixed race Egyptians or resident aliens who followed the Hebrew exodus]. A few, however, of

the studious, having private records of their own, either by remembering the names or by getting at them in some other way from the
archives, pride themselves in preserving the memory of their noble
descent; and among these happen to be those already mentioned,
called desposyni [= 'those who belong to a master' or possibly 'heirs'],
on account of their connection with the family of the Saviour. And these
coming from Nazara and Cochaba, Judean villages, to other parts of
the country, set forth the above-named genealogy as accurately as
possible from the Book of Days. Whether, then, the case stand thus or
not, no one could discover a more obvious explanation, according to
my own opinion and that of any sound judge. And let this suffice us
for the matter, although it is not supported by testimony, because we
have nothing more satisfactory or true to allege upon it. The Gospel,
however, in any case states the truth

We now have a reasonable picture that Jesus's family was an ancient Judean
family, very closely involved with the priesthood, with righteousness, with
piety, as well as with prophecy and messianic expectation, which in that
period makes them highly political. Family contacts provided Jesus with the
first shape or pattern of his earthly career. There is at least the suggestion that
Joseph's decision to dwell under the rule of Antipas may have been less
motivated by fear of Archelaus and more by a priestly and possibly domestic
connection with Antipas and his political supporters.

Was it obvious in 4 BC, when, according to Matthew, Jesus's family left
Egypt, that Archelaus would be bad news for the family? Not at all. On the
death of Herod his father, Archelaus did not bring out the knives. On the other
hand, he might have had a bad reputation already; he had been brought up in
pagan Rome with his brother. Rather than institute a national grief like no
other in history, Archelaus made soothing efforts to ingratiate himself with the
army, which included Thracians, Galatians and Germans, as well as the priests,
ruling class and people of Judea. He did this through a calculated stance of
magnanimity, acts of generosity, and an apparent willingness to consider
popular and priestly grievances, including the punishment of those who had

participated in the murders of their nearest and dearest by Herod's command. An insistent demand for the removal of the last high priest appointed by Herod was agreed, though Archelaus stopped short of acceding to a call for the high priest's death, at least until, Archelaus said, he had received approval of his succession from Caesar.

These facts alone should give one a clear picture of the political realities in which Jesus grew up, often only hinted at in the gospels, since we may suppose there would have been a severe propaganda problem for Christians if Jesus's name were too clearly linked to the violent politico-religious upheavals that tore the province apart in the 60s of the 1st century, after which tempests the canonical gospels were compiled and composed.

The tumult of the Jewish revolt was presaged right at the time Joseph and his family left Egypt. In spite of Archelaus's generous attempts to sweeten up Judea in readiness for his rule, there was, unfortunately for him, a sizeable group of Judean zealots closely associated with the Temple priesthood who had neither forgiven nor forgotten how Archelaus's father Herod had killed Matthias, a learned, pious Judean, zealous for the law and the Lord, a great teacher of righteousness. According to Josephus, Matthias, along with his fellow sage Judas, had galvanized a willing body of young Torah scholars into a militant band prepared to die for zeal of the Lord. Fired up by righteous enthusiasm, rendered fearless by constant preaching of the 'death is preferable to dishonour' kind, the young men had torn down a great golden eagle with which Herod had adorned the Temple entrance, holding it blasphemous. The law forbade the adornment of the Temple with the likenesses of living things. Herod, incensed, had condemned the resistance as blasphemy, since he had done more than anyone else to rebuild the Lord's Temple. Matthias was burnt to death and many were killed.

When Archelaus refused to recognize the 'martyrdom' of the late zealots for the Lord, a revived band occupied the Temple *in tents*. Were they making a 'wilderness camp' in the midst of the sanctuary, in conscious reference to the righteous who supported Moses about the holy tabernacle, the Ark of the Covenant at the time of the Exodus? Such was a dominant image of Zadokite, or priestly-righteous, utopianism.

So fired up were the demonstrators that they refused to listen to the king-designate's envoys, chanting over their voices of reason and preaching sedition in the Temple's precincts. We may be forgiven for identifying many of their sentiments with those of the previously unknown documents found in the Dead Sea Scrolls that date from this period and earlier and which called for the purification of the Israelite religion from foreign influences and lax observance. Indeed, the battle over the unnamed high priest, hated by his opponents for his failure to keep the law, resonates strongly with the famous Dead Sea Scrolls conflict between 'the wicked priest' and the 'Teacher of Righteousness' to be found in the Dead Sea Habakkuk and Nahum *pesherim* (that is, commentaries on the prophets). Were it not for Geza Vermes's sound identification of the 'wicked priest' with Jonathan Maccabeus (high priest and ethnarch 160–142 BC), we might consider a scenario wherein the Teacher of Righteousness equated to either Matthias or Judas.

While the 'Teacher of Righteousness' almost certainly resisted Jonathan Maccabaeus's corruption of the high-priestly office, Matthias and Judas, many generations later, also resisted Herodian rule and post-Maccabean corruption, becoming heroes of the anti-Herodian resistance. There is no evidence, however, that they were linked to a 'new covenant' community who went into the desert to apply themselves to perfect holiness and eschatological messianic conflict. When Josephus does have occasion to mention a group who followed a zealous man out into the desert, eschewing personal property, there is a note of contempt in his treatment; Josephus hated politico-religious 'innovators' and found it hard to convey their substance and meaning to Roman and Greek readers. There was nothing particularly philosophical about the New Covenanters, and Josephus tried to explain the factions of Judea and Samaria and Galilee in terms of philosophies, lest perhaps non-Jews come to the conclusion that his race was mad.

The 'wicked priest' despised by the Temple demonstrators at the beginning of Archelaus's reign would be the latest in a long line of wicked priests who had cut cards with the Hellenistic world to the detriment of Zadokite purity or priestly righteousness since Jonathan Maccabaeus (160–142 BC) had exercised high priestly and kingly functions a century and a half previously. Notably,

Josephus dubbed the demonstrators 'innovators', precisely the word he applied to all zealous activists with messianic programmes.

Since Archelaus was of an Idumaean Arab background on his father's side, he was, from the zealots' point of view, simply another abomination standing in the way of both the righteous community and the righteous one, the ideal '*Zaddik*' or True Prophet. Contemptuous of the messianic ferment, Archelaus was exasperated by the lack of any suggestion of compromise. Following his father's example of brutal reaction, Archelaus had his troops storm the Temple. Thousands of the rebellious demonstrators met with equanimity grisly deaths by fire, arrow, spear and sword. Suicidal tendencies would mark zealous resistance: death was embraced as the honourable path, demonstrating, as they saw it, ultimate loyalty to God.

Such was the destruction wrought in the Temple complex that Josephus records a figure of 18,000 workmen engaged on its reconstruction until Nero's reign half a century later. People must have got quite fed up with itinerant masons wanting to rebuild everything to stay in work.

In the wake of the harrowing massacre, Archelaus swiftly sought ratification of his kingship by heading from Jerusalem to Rome *via* Caesarea. Meanwhile, Caesar's steward for Syria, Sabinus, headed for Judea to 'secure' Archelaus's castles and possessions, but Varus, the Syrian governor, catching Sabinus up at Caesarea, persuaded Sabinus not to meddle, but to await Caesar's pleasure. Sabinus bided his time. His troops were unruly, wanted paying, and a rebellious Judea offered rich pickings. Pacification was profitable for officers and men alike. Poor soldiers needed a good war, or even better, civilian pacification.

Antipas, Salome and members of their family also hastened to Rome, feigning support for Archelaus's suit. Once there, however, Antipas unrolled a plan, fully backed by Salome, to persuade Caesar that Archelaus was unfit to rule. A significant mark against Archelaus was that he had stirred up sedition about the Temple, acting like a king on his own authority. Would Antipas have handled the situation differently? Did he have better relations with the priestly zealots and their followers? He seems to have thought so.

It should come as no surprise that Caesar could see nothing to dispraise in

Archelaus's ruthlessness, a quality Rome had come to expect and rely on during his father's remarkably long reign. After hearing the rival depositions, Caesar respected Herod the Great's will in the matter. Antipas, for his part, was confirmed as ruler in Galilee and Perea (Transjordan). Caesar offered Antipas 'assistance' should it be necessary. It was in fact not the will of Herod that was enacted, but that of Rome.

Archelaus would rule over a violent Judea for ten years. When Caesar's man Sabinus again attempted to seize Judean properties, Judeans revolted. Savagely suppressed by Varus with three Syrian legions, Judea was pacified; some 2,000 were crucified. Surely here was sufficient repression to account for the hiding of precious manuscripts as in the case of the Dead Sea Scrolls, secreted in caves in the Judean desert at what is now Wadi Qumran.

Joseph's decision to avoid his home country could have been easily justified on the basis of violence, brigandage and general disruption. That, however, is a retrospective view, unless, of course, Joseph knew in advance that Archelaus would be opposed by a militant priestly party desiring revenge for his father Herod's perceived attack on the law, customs and traditions of Judea. If Joseph knew anything about Antipas, he may have known that Antipas was less likely than his brother to make enemies of the pious, if he could possibly avoid it. Joseph's family move to Galilee strongly suggests a preference for government by Herod Antipas. It is worth noting that after his translation to Galilee, Antipas would have had even less reason to like Rome. Caesar had taken his kingdom from him.

While we know practically nothing of Jesus's upbringing, we do know that Archelaus's decade-long rule in Judea, during which Jesus approached his bar mitzvah, was a sore in Caesar's backside. It ended in AD 6. Archelaus was called to Rome and exiled with his entourage to Vienne in Gaul. The history of Judea entered a new, volatile phase, opened by a blunt statement of Roman intent: a new taxation regimen imposed on the province. The Romans had had enough of puppet kings in Judea. Coponius was appointed the first in a line of Roman prefects that would govern Judea and Samaria until AD 41, that is, for the duration of Jesus's life. Charged with keeping the lid on Judea, the prefects had troops at Caesarea on the coast, reinforcements in Syria, and a garrison right in the heart of Jerusalem, next to the Temple.

Judea was now without a king. From the strictly 'Israelite' point of view, it seemed that God had deposed the blasphemer Archelaus using the Romans as instruments of His will. Would God now use them to further it, or would He overcome them also through the agency of the true king, the righteous, the upright, the one expected. But surely, such a one would not come out of Galilee!

Brothers in the Wilderness

We explore the politics of Judea and Galilee in Jesus's form-
ative years. Jesus and John were political and religious
comrades. We establish that Jesus's family was at the centre of politi-
cal controversy. Jesus's rejection by a community familiar with his
family has been confused as a rejection by his family. What was
really meant by calling Jesus 'the builder' or 'son of the builder'? We
explore the '12 men and 3 priests' system in the Dead Sea Scrolls.
Jesus's family was at the core of his operation.

The canonical record gives us only one set of incidents involving Jesus's family from the period of Jesus's youth. Luke 2:40–52 describes a situation where 'his parents', having gone up to Jerusalem every year for the Passover feast, make a special return visit connected both with the feast and with their son's 12th birthday 'according to custom'.

At 12, Jesus was introduced to the privileges and responsibilities of being a 'son of the covenant', according to the law of Israel. If, as seems most likely, Jesus was born in 7 BC or 6 BC, his rite of passage would have roughly coincided with Archelaus's 'recall' to Rome and subsequent exile to Gaul in AD 6. Jerusalem and Judea would have been in a state of anxiety. Antipas doubtless anticipated his time to secure the throne of Judea had finally come. Desirous of Archelaus's wealth, however, Caesar Augustus sent Cyrenius, a Roman senator, along with Coponius, of the equestrian order, to Syria and Judea. Coponius would run the prefecture; Cyrenius would make a registry of Judea's wealth for tax purposes: a kind of Domesday Book. This was the tax innovation Luke identifies with Jesus's parents going to Bethlehem, his setting for Jesus's birth: an error if Matthew is to be credited.

Why should Luke make such an error? He may simply have been working on an alternative narrative wherein Jesus's birth was placed 'late'. Alternatively, he may simply have been confused about the common element of 'Bethlehem' as both tax venue and birthplace. The simplest explanation is that Luke hoped to reconcile his belief that Jesus was from Nazareth in Galilee with an established tradition of prophecy that the Messiah of the House of David was born in Bethlehem in Judea. Luke probably read of the tax history in Josephus's *Antiquities of the Jews* and put his own two and two together: sincere perhaps but almost certainly incorrect. Conversely, Luke may have given rein to a less innocent purpose in his account.

The issue of Jewish taxation was of the highest political sensitivity in the 1st and early 2nd centuries AD. Tax caused rebellion. Zealots declared that to hand over the fruit of Yahweh's Promised Land to a pagan 'god' was the height of culpable blasphemy. Paul, being as we should say today, 'relaxed' on the Roman tax issue, declared to the contrary that 'brothers in Christ' should pay their taxes to the Romans without complaint, even gladly. It would thus suit the Pauline purpose, advocated by Luke, to present Jesus's pious family obeying Roman law from the first, dutifully registering for taxation, even at great personal inconvenience. To really rub the salt in, Roman taxation and God's redemptive purposes for mankind are joined at the hip in Luke's unmistakably pro-Gentile, pro-Roman and to a Jew, collaborationist, narrative.

Given the political ferment that existed in reality at the time, Jesus's bar mitzvah may not have been the altogether happy occasion one might suppose. There may even have been some cause for unseemly rush in returning to Galilee, if, indeed, Galilee was the family's destination. With Archelaus gone, Mary and Joseph might rather have gone to see extended family and associates in Bethlehem or other places in Judea.

Luke's story of Jesus's parents realizing that they had left their son behind a day after leaving Jerusalem stretches credibility somewhat, unless, that is, their son had been entrusted to another family member or associate in their entourage, or had been generally doing his own thing, perhaps with his brothers, who, it must be said, are completely absent from the Lukan text.

Luke says that Mary and Joseph had travelled a day out of Jerusalem before the 'company' realized Jesus was not among them. Well, children can get lost in such circumstances, especially if there should be more than one of them; it has happened to me and perhaps to you too. The word translated as 'company' is *synodia*, a travelling company, or *caravan*. This may say something about the extent and possible wealth of Jesus's family at the time: a significant, sizeable clan. Alternatively, the caravan may have been a collective enterprise, like a pilgrim train made up of other families from the same area. In such a setting it might not be altogether difficult to imagine all were thought to be safely gathered in for a day. Joseph and Mary looked anxiously for Jesus among their relatives and '*tois gnōstois*', that is, people they knew. Again, we have quite a band. This is not the 'holy family' to which iconography has inured us.

Was the family concerned that Jesus might have been – God forbid! – *kidnapped*: a political move? Luke, oblivious to any such possibility, comes to his point. The family turns back to Jerusalem. They search the city for three days. *Three days*? What was Jesus up to? The family must have had other contacts in the city. Perhaps it was one of these who pointed them in the direction of the Temple. We are reminded of the Simeon story again (Luke 2:21–8), except this time it is not Simeon and Anna the daughter of Phanuel who astonish with rare teaching, but the new son of the covenant, Jesus.

Well in with a group of 'teachers' in the Temple, Jesus treats his family somewhat haughtily, curiously surprised that they should have been looking for him at all. Was this mere precocious sarcasm? Did they not *know*, asks Jesus, that he had to be about 'my Father's business'? The implication here, I think, is that they *should* have known. Jesus had been asking questions of the teachers in the Temple, hearing what they had to say and giving astonishing answers to the teachers' own questions. This was not a boy who was likely to follow any particular school or sect of established religious thought; this boy was on a quest.

The contrast the text makes between Mary's address to Jesus: '*Child*, why have you treated us like this?' and his reply about 'my *Father*' immediately reminds us of Zechariah's priestly course of *Abijah*, that is, 'Yahweh is my Father'. Yahweh's son seems to have practically disowned poor Joseph, his earthly dad in the sight of the world! Was Jesus considering a priestly career? Even more suggestive is the implication that his parents should have *understood* his new obligations. May we not conjecture then that Jesus had, in the flush of youthful pious enthusiasm, taken the Nazarite vow, requiring him to sacrifice in the Temple on the eighth day and at the conclusion of the vow period? One consecrated to the holiness of the Lord was separated also from family obligations. Even if his parents died, the vow forbade the Nazarite to come near their bodies (This explains several of Jesus's 'hard sayings' about filial obligations in relation to strictly religious ones). Was he now 'Jesus the Nazarite', separated, consecrated to the service of the Lord, zealous in His service?

We may surmise that Jesus's family was going to have to get used to the idea that the boy now trod his own spiritual road. But Jesus would also have known that it was his signal duty to the law to honour his father and mother, and when they called him back with them, according to Luke, Jesus obediently followed. Luke paints an interesting, if limited, picture. The reality behind it may have been very different.

———

If the family were heading back to Galilee in search of relative peace, they would soon find it disturbed. Cyrenius, the Roman senator out to serve his master, removed the popular Joazar as high priest and replaced him with Ananus, son of Seth – by no means the last high priest of that name. Another Ananus would, in time, have Jesus's brother clubbed to death. One may recall the Star Prophecy: the 'Star of Jacob' will 'destroy all the children of Seth': music to the ears of the prophetically-attuned righteous.

According to Josephus, a man called Judas, along with a Pharisee called Sadduc, immediately declared the Cyrenian taxation programme to be nothing more than the onset of slavery. Israel must be free! Judas preached revolt; God was surely on their side. The more the people rose in His name, Judas and Sadduc argued, the more God would help them. Slaughters and robberies followed. Judas came from Gamala in Philip's tetrarchy, 10 miles east of the Sea of Galilee, some 75 miles north-east of Jerusalem. The tremor was real, a foreshadowing of worse to come.

Josephus writes in his *Antiquities* that there were four philosophical sects followed by his countrymen at the time: the Pharisees, who brought the sacred law and prophets to the people; the Sadducees, who were the ruling priestly party; the 'Essens', who, according to Josephus, were Pythagorean-style, pious and mystical holy men, of whom some, intriguingly, were called *Polistae*, that is, 'of the city', and fourth, though he gives them no special name, that blight on Israel founded, Josephus says, by this Judas of Gamala, or 'Judas the Galilean'. He means what have come to be called 'the Zealots', though there is more to this designation than meets the eye.

Galilee acquired a reputation for unrest, most unwelcome to its ruler, Antipas. Josephus in his usual unexcitable, measured phrasing describes Judas's followers as being so much addicted to liberty, they could stand no rule but God's alone. This stance of righteousness and utterly immoveable conviction manifested in an *ésprit de corps* that was intolerant and intemperate. As indifferent to their own deaths as to those of others, including friends and family, it was they, the 'bandits' as Josephus calls them, who in time brought the country to outright ruin. God was not, in the end, on their side.

No doubt the sporadic outbreaks of violence and terror backed by Judas and his followers across the territories unnerved the Herodian rulers of Galilee and Gaulanitis, who ruled by grace of Rome. They wanted the peace that brought riches to their territories, not the one that passed all understanding. Philip rebuilt Bethsaida as *Bethsaida-Julias*, dedicated to Caesar's wife Julia, on *his* side of Galilee, while Antipas built the classically grand city of Tiberias after the new emperor Tiberius (AD 14–37), on *his* side of Galilee, 15 miles east of modern Nazareth. Galilee was not all murder and extremism, but the nation was walking on a knife's edge.

As Jesus and his relative John grew up, one prefect followed another, as one high priest after another was suddenly dismissed as politically inconvenient, while zealots of one party or another risked all, including their country's future, to spread revolt and assassinate perceived collaborators in God's name.

Luke tells us that it was in the 15th year of Tiberius, AD 29, that Jesus's relative, John, the son of Zechariah, began to cry out for national repentance in the Judean wilderness. John the Baptist quoted Isaiah: 'The voice of one crying in the wilderness: Prepare the way of the Lord... and all flesh shall see the salvation of God.' (Isaiah 40:3–5). Jesus's name means 'God is salvation' or 'the salvation of God' and Luke is in no doubt that anyone who saw Jesus in the flesh was seeing that salvation whose way John was preparing, in the wilderness. The Isaiah quote could be the inspiration behind the famous: 'The *logos* ['word'] was made flesh and dwelt among us' line that opens up the mystic gospel of John.

Jesus is now a man. He is strong, resourceful and resolute. He appears close to John, though not for long, for the man that Jesus respects above all others is soon cast into Herod Antipas's prison at his castle of Machaerus, less than five miles east of the Dead Sea, near the river Nahaliel. John had criticized the tetrarch's conduct, calling for his repentance and humility before almighty God who was bringing salvation to His people. According to Matthew, John also called the Sadducees and Pharisees to repentance, two of Josephus's 'sects' whom John's relative would also challenge. A battle was on for the soul of Israel.

How can we ignore how perfectly this battle is reflected in the Damascus Document, found at Qumran, just across the water from the castle where John was to be executed. The very thing John criticized Herod for: marrying his brother's wife Herodias and lusting after her daughter Salome, is related in that document as precisely that which defiles 'their holy spirit', opening their mouths 'with a blaspheming tongue against the laws of the Covenant of God, saying 'They are not sure.'' This phrase means the princes claimed to interpret the law as they found fit:

> And concerning the prince it is written, *He shall not multiply wives to himself* [Deut.17:17] [...] And each man marries the daughter of his

brother or sister, whereas Moses said, *You shall not approach your mother's sister; she is your mother's near kin* [Lev.18:13]. But although the laws against incest are written for men, they also apply to women. When therefore a brother's daughter uncovers the nakedness of her father's brother, she is [also his] near kin.

(Damascus Document 20, 10)

This could have been written for John. Come to think of it; this could have been written *by* John! In the same section, we read of the 'builders of the wall' (Ezekiel 13:10) who have followed a 'Spouter' who 'shall be caught in fornication twice by taking a second wife while the first is alive, whereas the principle of creation is, *Male and female created He them*' (Gen 1:27). This quotation was also the essence of Jesus's reply to those who asked him about the legality of divorce. As to the 'builders of the wall', the phrase would fit the Herodian builders of the Temple perfectly. The Temple organization was rejected by the righteous 'sons of Zadok' of the Dead Sea Scrolls, and it was condemned by Jesus who also foresaw woe to those who ignored the righteousness of God (Mark 13:3). Jesus apparently quoted a similar prophecy (Psalm 118:22): 'The stone the builders rejected has become the head of the corner.'

Jesus's family was right in the thick of the biggest political commotions of Judea and Galilee in the period. The bucolic image of Sunday School Jesus and his disciples does not stand up to the force of history. Jesus's relative John would be executed as a dangerous political activist. Josephus's record makes this absolutely clear. John was a holy man who lived like the Maccabeans in the wilderness. The Maccabeans took political power by power of holy living. John and Jesus would have been intimately familiar with the nature of this power; so would Herod Antipas, and he feared it.

Baptized by John, Jesus, relates Matthew, went into the Judean wilderness where, according to the canonical record, he faced the Tempter and won: a triumph over the snares of the lower self.

Qumran documents present a doctrine of 'two spirits' between which the righteous man must choose if he is to emerge upright and unbendable. Jesus emerges from the encounter with Satan upright: a True Prophet. Hearing of his cousin John's imprisonment across the Dead Sea, Jesus heads off in the opposite direction, north to Galilee (was he next on Herod's list?):

> And leaving Nazareth [this is not explained], he came and dwelt in Capernaum, which is upon the sea coast, in the borders of Zabulon and Nephthalim: That it might be fulfilled which was spoken by Esaias the prophet [Isaiah 9:1–2], saying, The land of Zabulon, and the land of Nephthalim, by the way of the sea [of Galilee], beyond Jordan, Galilee of the Gentiles: The people which sat in darkness saw great light: and to them which sat in the region and shadow of death light is sprung up.
>
> (Matthew 4:13–16)

It is interesting to find here references to the territories of the old long-lost tribes of the northern kingdom of Israel. The 'borders' Matthew refers to were no more. Seven hundred years had passed since they had any serious political meaning. Was Jesus – or his family – concerned with somehow reuniting the ancient kingdom of Solomon 'in all his glory'? Four verses after the prophecy in Isaiah that Matthew refers to, comes the famous messianic proclamation: 'For unto us a child is born, unto us a son is given: and the government shall be upon his shoulder...' It is not the right moment in Matthew's narrative for that particular quote, however. His Jesus is now in full manhood. Having faced the devil tempter, Yahweh's son begins his own operation, repeating or taking up the call that John had made from the wilderness. John might be chained up, but his message was still going to be heard. Jesus would show Antipas's gagging order was vain; perhaps this contributed to Herod's calling for the executioner – a warning to others who spoke in John's name. Risking much, Jesus carried the message to the towns: 'Repent: for the kingdom of heaven is at hand.' (Matthew 4:71) Jesus will give John's message his own twist. Not all of John's fans will thank him for it.

Plainly, Jesus and his cousin John had a lot more in common than genes. Their 'wilderness camps' were close, if not the same. Post-Jesus theology has obscured this; John is presented as the 'witness' to Jesus (John 1:6–8). This was because some of John's followers thought *he*, John, was the Messiah. While it may be that John himself may have seen or suspected his relative Jesus was the Messiah, demotion (from his own band's point of view) to witness-status also conveniently erased the two men's political and religious comradeship. I do not think Jesus would thank the Church for that.

But what had happened to the rest of Jesus's family? For just at this point in his career, Jesus appears completely alone.

———

The most important canonical record of Jesus's family at this time must surely be Mark 6:1–7. Mark's is generally acknowledged as the earliest canonical gospel (AD 65–80). According to Mark, Jesus enters 'his own country' (*patrida*) after having chosen 12 followers from elsewhere, allegedly the environs bounding the shores of the Sea of Galilee, some 20 miles north-east of modern-day Nazareth. He may have 'poached' some followers from John after John's arrest.

According to Mark, the 12 followers are Simon whom he renamed *Cephas* (stone in Aramaic), two brothers he nicknamed 'Boanerges' (interpreted by Mark as 'sons of thunder'): James (Jacob), son of Zebedee and John 'the brother of James'; Andrew, Philip, Bartholomew, Matthew, Thomas (which means 'the twin'), another James called 'the son of Alphaeus', Thaddaeus, Judas 'Iscariot' and another Simon called 'the Zealot'.

Is this a true record of 12 individuals? We may yet see. Anyhow, the 'twelve', called to train as preachers, holy men, exorcists and healers, witness Jesus expounding much parabolic teaching while working marvellous miracles across the Sea of Galilee near Gadara and back on the other side in Antipas's territory. From casting demons out of the insane to healing a leper, Jesus tops his record of never-before-seen marvels suitable for the Age of the Messiah, with the spectacular raising of Jairus's 12-year-old daughter from the dead. This miracle, however, was to be kept strictly secret.

The contrast between these events and the visit to 'paternal territory' is striking, and, one can hardly avoid thinking, deliberate. Indeed what follows may be regarded as a polemic in itself.

First there is wonder in the religious assembly ('synagogue') at Jesus's wisdom and his 'mighty works'; then come the doubts. Where did Jesus get all this incredible knowledge from?

> Is not this the craftsman ['builder' or 'architect'], the son of Maria, the brother of Jacob, and Joses [Joseph], and of Juda, and Simon? And are not his sisters here with us? And they were offended at him.
>
> But Jesus said unto them, A prophet is not without honour, but in his own country, and among his own relatives, and in his own house.

His own do not believe him. Lest there be any doubt about the fact that Mark means what it looks like – that these are the names of Jesus's real family – we notice that Jesus's word of wisdom about being treated dishonourably by those who know him from his home territory, refers specifically to relatives of his *own* household, not symbolic, spiritual or honorary 'brothers'. Indeed, the distinction of the brothers and sisters from the twelve could not be more marked. Only someone concerned about the effect of this passage upon the receivers of a doctrine of Mary's perpetual virginity would be moved to question the very plain sense of the Greek. Objection to what is obvious may be treated as 'special pleading', wilful blindness or plain ignorance.

Jesus had brothers in the ordinary sense of the term. Their mother was his mother.

Fortunately, we do not have to believe this plain sense because it is 'holy writ'. For all I know, the story could be a gross fabrication as it stands: a cut-and-paste job. What do we have? We have a saying about Jesus getting the bum's rush, or at least facing criticism, from his 'own' and then a story about an angry group in a synagogue. We get no telling detail. Where are Jesus's brothers and sisters when all this is allegedly said? Did Mary hear the rebuke of her son? Where is Joseph? Was he dead? Who are the 'they' who are offended by Jesus? How well did they really know his family anyway? Was this the original setting for the *logion* (saying) about a man being respected everywhere except in his own back yard? Many a person's gone back to their home town to find what they once thought was intimate affection was simply the result of long familiarity, which, when broken, is revealed to be hollow on reacquain-tance. Families are seldom able to judge the spiritual progress of a member, being concerned with the familiar sense of security gained from the blood-tie and the freedom in the brother-bond from outside social standards and alien judgements. We have all made a mess on our own doorstep.

In fact, the passage tells us little. We must even consider the possibility that the passage's function was as a rebuke of claims made by Jesus's family for primacy in the Church, that is, that it belongs to the political debate between the Roman, Gentile Christian Church and branches of the Jewish Palestinian Church who did not, to say the least, value Paul's contribution to the messianic kingdom. Paul's epistles and the much later Acts of the Apostles offer ample confirmation of this conflict.

Matthew (13:55–6) repeats Mark's account of Jesus's home territory rejection, though the reference to Jesus *being* the craftsman is changed to 'Is not this the craftsman's son [or 'son of the builder']?' Matthew does not like the idea of the son of David being 'in trade' any more than I do! Furthermore, Joseph may still be alive. 'Juda' is written plainly as 'Judas'. It was a common enough name; Matthew knows that and so do his readers. 'Judas', as in Judas of Gamala, or Judas the Maccabee: freedom-fighters.

There may be more to this 'craftsman's son' business. Several possibilities spring to mind. The 'Qumran' community or New Covenanters rejected Herod's impressive Temple system in Jerusalem. They saw it as being tainted by Herod's despised high priestly appointments as well as by his own conduct, politics and racial origin. The self-proclaimed perfect community had their own ideal temple and made elaborate plans for its future establishment. If such people constituted Jesus's former fraternity, or if kindred ideas were held by them, then Jesus's relationship to the Temple would have been an issue. If, for example, his father Joseph had contributed his technical and architectural knowledge to its reconstruction, Jesus's being that man's son could have been an authentic basis for criticism and rejection. However, the force of the statement, as it stands, centres around the accusers' *familiarity* with Jesus's family, and with that implication we must deal.

Robert Eisenman in his book *James the Brother of Jesus* has speculated that the whole 'son of Joseph' identity is a straight – well, almost straight – fabrication, based on a contemporaneous description of the Messiah as being 'messiah ben Yusef', that is, of the 'House', lineage or glamour of the great patriarch Joseph. Joseph had stood apart in God's favour from his wicked brothers, the fathers of the tribes. Joseph was by God's providential action reunited with his father Jacob (Israel) in the end. Thus, by symbolic implication, the 'craftsman' would be the architect of Israel's salvation, as Joseph was the overseer of Pharaoh's and his population's salvation, including the Hebrews.

Eisenman would have it that *all* the stories about 'Joseph' are either inventions based on a misunderstanding of the phrase 'son of Joseph' for the Messiah or, at the pre-textual stage, symbolic, coded stories for those 'in the know'. It's a theory, but it is not one that would jump out at you unless you were already committed to a kind of general demolition job on the Christian narrative, which, judging by his work, Eisenman is.

Nevertheless, I think Eisenman is quite right not to take many of the fragmentary stories that appear in the New Testament at face value, and he has done sterling work in demonstrating that the Dead Sea Scrolls, used diligently, can truly illuminate the complex situation in which Jesus and his brothers and sisters grew up. For example, if we liberate ourselves for a moment from the ordinary Christian bias with which Mark's text about Jesus's 'homecoming rejection' is almost always viewed, we might find not only a different story, but, conceivably, a more historical and meaningful one.

Let us suppose, hypothetically, that the truth behind Mark's story originally reflected a return visit made by him, possibly to the north, even to the 'Land of Damascus' (Cochaba?), to a 'New Covenant'-type camp or 'city'. Jesus's sisters still lived with the community; he may have come to get them out. Then, in this historically consistent context, Mark's reference to Jesus being dismissed as the 'craftsman' may not have been so much a comment on his parentage, as Luke obviously and possibly naïvely thought it was, but was in its original setting a *direct jibe*. Jesus was the 'builder' – and the builder was *bad*!

> But all these things the builders of the wall and those who daub it with plaster [Ezekiel 13:10] have not understood because a follower of the wind, one who raised storms and rained down lies, had preached to them [Mic.2:11], against all of whose assembly the anger of God was kindled. [...] But He [God] hated the builders of the wall and His anger was kindled against them and against all those who followed them; and so shall it be for all who reject the commandments of God and abandon them for the stubbornness of their hearts.
>
> (Damascus Document)

If Jesus declared or implied that he was himself the prophesied 'stone the builders rejected', his informed interlocutors declare, on the contrary, that Jesus was himself nothing less than the condemned 'builder' who spouts 'Peace' in Ezekiel 13:10–16:

> Because, even because they have seduced my people, saying, Peace; and there was no peace; and one built up a wall, and lo, others daubed it with untempered mortar: Say unto them which daub it with untempered mortar, that it shall fall: there shall be an overflowing shower; and ye, O great hailstones, shall fall; and a stormy wind shall rend it. [...] So will I break down the wall that ye have daubed with untempered mortar, and bring it down to the ground, so that the foundation thereof shall be discovered, and it shall fall, and ye shall be consumed in the midst thereof: and ye shall know that I am the LORD. [...] To wit, the prophets of Israel which prophesy concerning Jerusalem, and which see visions of peace for her, and there is no peace, saith the Lord GOD.

Calling Jesus the 'son of the builder', would have meant no less, as one might condemn a man by dubbing him a 'son of Belial'. Like Jesus, the New Covenanters could match prophecy for prophecy and target the visitor as a cause of offence, as Mark reports he was so regarded. Ezekiel was a beloved prophet of God; who dare contradict him? To this accusation Jesus might have replied: 'A prophet is respected everywhere except in his own country.' Could it be that his 'own' or former colleagues had heard him bless the 'peace-makers'?

While it is arguable that the 'authentic Jesus' and his family may rather have fully endorsed the uncompromising vision of the Damascus Document, it is also possible that an original teacher such as Jesus appears to have been, took issue with it at root, and suffered rejection for his beliefs from former comrades: a bitter pill. Thus a tradition of Jesus being rejected by his 'own', as well as by the powers of the world, could have been rooted not in a dispute over matters of substance *with his family*, which is nowhere supported directly in the synoptic gospels, but from a falling-out with New Covenanter people, former 'brethren' he perhaps grew up with and studied with. We shall see in due course that Jesus's brother James's position may have been more recognizable to those who read the Damascus Document and did not object to a word of it.

When in Mark 14:43, Jesus is captured by a 'great multitude' of chief priests, scribes, and elders, the band come armed with swords and staves. According to the Damascus Document's interpretation of Numbers 21:18: 'The *Stave* is the Interpreter of the law of whom Isaiah said, he makes a tool for His work' (Isaiah 54:16). Was the rejection of Jesus by 'his own' based on a bitter conflict over the interpretation of the law? This makes immediate sense of so much of the conflict with Pharisees and others reflected in the canonical gospels.

> None of the men who enter the New Covenant in the land of Damascus, and who again betray it and depart from the fountain of living waters, shall be reckoned with the Council of the people or inscribed in its Book from the day of its gathering in of the Teacher of the Community until the coming of the Messiah out of Aaron and Israel.
>
> (Damascus Document)

If such a one as Jesus had intimated for a second that *he* was that Messiah, then for the keepers of the New Covenant, the man they had known, whose family they had known, that man had signed his death warrant. The punishment for such blasphemy was death. If this context is correct, we must note another relevant consequence of a rejection of Jesus by the enthusiasts for the 'sons of Zadok', the true priesthood. Jesus's brothers and sisters – and perhaps mother and father as well – would have been thrown out also. For as the Damascus Document states: 'Neither they [the transgressors] nor their kin shall have any part in the house of the law.'

This would explain neatly why Jesus took up his own 'stave' as it were, and gathered his own following, his own camp, his own covenanters, his own 'new Israel'. Almost certainly this group would have included members of his own family.

Matthew's account of the *names* of the 'twelve' (10:2–4) is not a straight copy of Mark's: Simon 'who is called Peter' (Greek for 'stone'), here described as Andrew's brother (unlike Mark), James (Jacob) 'the son of Zebedee', and John 'his brother', Philip and Bartholomew, Thomas, Matthew the tax-collector, James 'the son of Alphaeus', Lebbaeus 'whose surname was Thaddaeus', (Mark only mentions a Thaddaeus), Simon the Zealot (called the 'Canaanite', a mistranslation of an Aramaic word for 'zealot' or 'holy warrior'), and 'Judas Iscariot'.

One can perfectly well understand the temptation of cornered Catholic dogmatists resorting to 'James the son of Alphaeus' to cover the embarrassing references of St Paul to 'James the brother of the Lord', or, alternatively, resorting to apocryphal and, by their own definition, non-authoritative sources to suggest Mary had a *relative*, maybe even a *sister* (!) or sister-in-law *also called Mary* who had sons, and who were thus in a general sense 'brethren' or 'kin', but not *so* close as to imperil the all-important dogma concerning Mary's virginity, without which Jesus would be tainted with original sin and the cosmic claims made for him dogmatically might collapse. But again, the canonical record makes a plain distinction between the twelve and the brethren of Jesus, and one of his brothers is called James and is not one of the twelve, at least, not in the canonical record.

Just as tempting is the more recent suspicion of seeing the coincidence of names between the twelve and the brothers of Jesus as leading to the not particularly brilliant conclusion that they must be the same people, or some of them at any rate, depending on what argument you are trying to prove. Thus Simon, either 'Cephas' or the 'Zealot' are either both or one of them, Jesus's brother Simon; Jesus's brother James has been misnamed as a 'son of Zebedee' ('Zebedee being derived from 'Zabda' a Jewish healer in a medicine book) or a 'son of Alphaeus', (or Alphaeus is another name for Jesus's 'real' father, one 'Cleophas' or 'Clopas'), 'Lebbaeus' is skewed from a nickname for James ('Oblias', perhaps a 'bulwark' or 'pillar' as St Paul calls James the brother of the Lord), so he must be a brother too; John (being James 'son of Zebedee's' brother) is also Jesus's brother; 'Thomas' meaning the twin (referred to as Thomas 'Didymus' – which also means 'twin' – in John 21:22) must be Jesus's or another disciple's twin brother; Judas Iscariot – well, he too may be the same as Judas, Jesus's brother, even his twin, since the apocryphal Gnostic Book of Thomas the Contender refers to *Didymos Judas Thomas* as Jesus's 'twin and true companion'. And only poor Joses or Joseph is left out – like the isolated brother in the famous story. (But perhaps *he* was Joseph of Arimathea!)

In this radical scenario, there were not strictly or necessarily 12 followers, but Jesus, his 3 brothers, then Andrew, Philip, Bartholomew and Matthew. John's gospel adds another disciple name, Nathaniel, which some have conveniently identified with 'Bartholomew', partly because the latter is not a proper name, being derived from 'Bar (son of) Tolmai' (Aramaic for a 'man of the furrows' or farmer) or Bar-Ptolemy, and partly to keep the 12-pack neat. *Yer pays yer money and yer takes yer choice.*

Does any of this really help us? It seems that in opposing the common Catholic ruse of denying fraternal reality to James by use of the coincidence of his name with a 'son of Alphaeus', radical opponents of Catholic dogma have jumped into the sea and swum to the opposite extreme. By God, they're nearly *ALL* brothers of Jesus! Hold on to your seats boys, it's a *DYNASTY*! Just wait until the Magdalenists get hold of his 'sisters'!

One thing is fairly clear to me: I do not have to trust the canonical writers' listing of the names of the twelve. This is partly because I can't see what the 'twelve' thing is really all about in the gospel accounts. Obviously, you have a parallel with the 12 tribes of Israel and perhaps even the signs of the zodiac. But other than in the case of Judas Iscariot, whose 'title' may well derive from the tribal name of Issachar, whose tribal land was by the Sea of Galilee and whose members were given financial and divinatory responsibilities under King Solomon (*ring any bells?* Judas was the 'purse-holder'), well, other than that, none of the other 'names' – and they are mostly just that – have special roles or symbolism attached to them. They are a pretty dumb chorus. The twelve-identity hangs loose, with no meaning to cover its nakedness. The implication must be that the canonical writers did not have much of a clue about what Jesus was doing when he formed a twelvesome. Then, of course, we get the 'inner cell': James, Peter and John, which is interesting for many reasons we cannot go into here. And then there are between 70 and 120 other disciples...

And then... Well, then there are the brothers of Jesus – and his dear mother Mary, given occasional but highly peculiar walk-on parts in the narrative. We shall come to these in a moment. But first, is there any reason to acknowledge the accuracy of Mark's record of Jesus's brothers and unnamed sisters, any more so than his account of the 'twelve'? Only this, that the record of Jesus's siblings is uniform in the few sources in which it appears, while there is variation in the names of all the twelve. This at any rate is the canonical record, of which one name at least is attested in contemporary record, the name of James. The name of Judas will also come to our attention. And we can hardly avoid noticing that if there was ever intended to be a meaningful connection between the 'twelve' and the patriarch Jacob and his 12 sons, Jesus's named brethren furnish us with a number of them: Jacob, Juda, Joseph. Jacob the patriarch led his family into Egypt during famine. And of course it was 'Joshua' ('Jesus') who led the tribes victoriously back into the Promised Land.

But before we leave the whining group who showed disrespect to Jesus simply because they were perhaps overfamiliar with his family (something we cannot claim for ourselves), we might consider one possibility that might bring the twelve and, possibly, the brothers together and which could thereby offer some account for these duplicated common names and identities.

It is widely thought that an ultra-strict New Covenant community was probably still operative at Khirbet Qumran by the Dead Sea, as well as in 'camps' and in 'towns', mixing, to a strict point, with non-members and Gentiles, in Jesus's time. Among the many community rules governing the New Covenant groups referred to in the Dead Sea Scrolls are rules for convening what they call a Council of the Community:

> In the Council of the Community there shall be twelve men and three Priests, perfectly versed in all that is revealed of the law, whose works shall be truth, righteousness, justice, loving-kindness and humility. They shall preserve the faith in the Land with steadfastness and meekness and shall atone for sin by the practice of justice and by suffering the sorrows of affliction. They shall walk with all men according to the standard of the truth and the rule of the time.
>
> (IQS VIII,1–4; *The Complete Dead Sea Scrolls in English*,
> Translated by Geza Vermes, Penguin Classics, 2004)

Twelve men and three priests. As far as may be known, something like this system was *still operative* at the time when John the Baptist was looking across the Dead Sea from his prison at Machaerus, if he had a window, while his relative Jesus was cooking things up in the north. Here, in this community rule, washed up onto the shores of the 20th century after some 2,000 years lost in a cave, we have a model for a leading council of 12 men, accompanied by 3 priests who shall 'walk with all men according to the standard of the truth'.

Uncanonical records make it plain, as we shall see, that James, the brother of the Lord, was a priest. Jesus, of course, will be described in the canonical Epistle to the Hebrews as a priest 'after the Order of Melchizedek'. You may recall Jesus being addressed on occasion as 'Master' (John 1:38). In other related 'Qumran' texts, the community's highest office was occupied by the 'Guardian', also called the Master (*maskil*). That is to say, the model for Jesus's operation may have been drawn from this or sources common both to 'Qumran' and to Jesus. Tempting though it has been to identify them, such a step might be seriously misleading. The teachings of the New Covenant community in the Qumran or Dead Sea texts, teachings of *zedek* and *hesed*, of righteousness and piety, enjoined to be kept secret from non-members, do not conform to the great bulk of canonical sayings attributed to Jesus, though they often deal with precisely the same issues and use common scriptural texts to make a point.

The theory that the 'gospel Jesus' was invented to contradict the legalistic approach of 'Qumran', as suggested by Professor Eisenman, for example, would require quite extraordinary creative inventiveness on the part of gospel fraudsters. And to what end? Was such an effort made simply to refute the convictions of a rival sect, opposition to whom would have required, unless I mistake, the invented convictions to exist already? The idea that the gospels are, fundamentally, little more than perorations on Paul's anti-'Qumran' or, better, anti-James the Righteous stance beggars belief. That Pauline thought has heavily influenced gospel theology, if considerably less so gospel narratives, is well established. Indeed, that influence might, as Eisenman has suggested, have been seriously underestimated as regards Luke's Acts of the Apostles. However, close critical attention to the gospels reveals their shortcomings as organized polemical tools. As history has shown, they can serve practically any religious interest – even, apparently, their own destruction as narratives of credibility and value!

It boils down to this. If 'Qumran' is a shoe, Jesus's foot, as seen in the gospels, does not fit into it. *Conclusion One*: it is not his shoe. *Conclusion Two*: the foot is an invention; the *real* foot was... his brother's! A brother, mark you, not of 'Jesus' as a person – 'he' did not really exist – but a doctrine of salvation, coded as 'Yeshua': God is salvation. This is one of the teasers offered in Eisenman's very clever, but arguably not clever-enough, analysis, *James the Brother of Jesus*: surely a gospel for all who believe that Christianity is inherently anti-Semitic.

If 'Jesus' was intended in the first instance as a polemical fabrication based on 'other' messianic figures, then the fabrication would have had more internal consistency about it than is evident from a reading of the sewn-together, uneven, sometimes astonishing, sometimes guileless, sometimes overimaginative, often confusing gospel narratives. As Eisenman's interpretative opponent Geza Vermes observes, it is the individuality, not to say profound humanity, of Jesus the Jew's approach that enables us to see the shortcomings of the 'Qumran' solution to Israel's problems, and why that solution is now a relic sought by the dead.

However, as we have seen, Jesus may well have had such an *organization* as the Dead Sea texts describe in mind, if not the full chest of doctrinal medicine that went with it. Since the canonical record allows that he spent time in the Judean wilderness, as well as the far north of the Decapolis – the 'land of Damascus', for spiritual purposes, and seems to have known his territory extremely well (he never needs a map!), could he have avoided coming into contact with persons familiar with the community rules such as we have indicated? He may have spent time with them before his 30th year, the age, incidentally, when community members were considered full members. Indeed, it is arguable, *pace* Eisenman, that Jesus framed his challenge to prevailing ideas of the application and spirit of God's law in conscious contradistinction to such as was to be found among the New Covenanters, rather than, as Professor Eisenman maintains, the teachings of Jesus being a retroactively placed product of Paul's opposition to the rules of the community.

However, it might be argued further, that having 'taken on' the Pharisees and the Sadducees, and even, if Luke is to be believed, the haughty Levite and Scribe, he, like the New Covenant community itself, had enemies enough! And if there is any substance in Mark and Matthew's accounts, he may also have had issues with his family. If they had, as has been suggested, been living in a town or camp setting among the community's righteous remnant, they may have picked up sufficient residual convictions to set them at odds with Jesus over a number of questions. Such a scenario could have elicited famous Jesus sayings such as, 'You cannot put new wine in old wineskins' and 'First clean the inside of the cup'. Jesus wanted a fresh, new organization; I do not think he would have been satisfied with anybody else's. This would also explain his disciples famously arguing over who was going to have what position in the supposed apocalyptic, messianic *dénouement*.

Eisenman has speculated that Jesus's brother James may have been the Qumran texts' 'Teacher of Righteousness', whose chief opponent, the 'wicked priest' or the 'Liar' or 'Spouter' he has identified with High Priest Ananus, the high priest who had Jesus's holy brother stoned to death. These experimental identifications are part of Eisenman's general suspicion that the first 'Christian' or messianic assembly in Palestine should be located within the Hebrew of the Qumran community texts, not in the Greek of the gospels and Paul's and Peter's and John's letters. Authentic 'Christianity' or proto-Christianity may apparently be found in the epistle of James, the Brother of the Lord. *Works* count for righteousness, and none of quisling-Jew Paul's 'justification by faith' for uncircumcised Gentiles rigmarole! This reminds me slightly of the 'Marcionite Canon' – you eject the works you don't like and venerate those you do. Eisenman's is a radical view, of use to many he would not himself personally agree with, but as Vermes points out, it bears the serious disadvantage of having been 'foisted onto' the Qumran material, rather than having emerged from it. That is, once you suspect the material is of such epoch-marking, sensational proportions that you can declare: *Qumran documents are authentic, un-perverted proto-Christian documents*, you then dig for your proof and then 'Connect, only connect'. The 'proof' comes as an endless string of speculations around the interpretation of key words and roots of words, on the basis that the Pauline position wherever it may be found in the gospels is spurious, anti-Jewish and cannot be trusted. Paul was an innovator who perverted a Jewish movement into something it was never intended to be: a replacement for the Holy law of Israel.

Is it not wiser to look at the Dead Sea Scrolls in their own terms?

I do not think 'James the brother of the Lord' was the Qumran community's 'Teacher of Righteousness', though he may have been *a* teacher of righteousness and true prophet, even if the canonical gospels know nothing of it. Paul's letters, however, do know something of it, and, as we shall see, it is Eisenman's understanding of Paul's conflict with the Jerusalem proto-Church that truly illuminates our search for the 'missing family'.

A Family Breach?

While he yet talked to the people, behold, his mother and his brothers stood without, desiring to speak with him and someone said to him, Behold, your mother and your brothers are standing without, seeking to speak with you. But he answered and said unto him that told him, Who is my mother? And who are my brothers? And he stretched forth his hand to his disciples and said, behold, my mother and my brothers! For whosoever will do the will of my father in heaven, the same is my brother, and sister, and mother.

(Matthew 12:46)

Was Jesus challenging his family?

While it seems reasonable to conclude from the canonical record that Jesus was attempting to establish his own dynamic new community, a new assembly, by challenging members of existing 'synagogues' to join him, the relation of his family to his efforts is, according to the canonical record, at best, ambiguous.

The speech recorded in Matthew 12 must have hurt his mother no end. She was put on the same level as anyone Jesus reckoned was on the right side of truth. Mark 3:31 has the same story but for the fact that the disciples are not directly mentioned as those who are Jesus's spiritual brothers, sisters and mother, just 'those who sat about him'. Matthew probably read this and presumed Mark meant the disciples in the exclusive sense. Luke's account (8:19) is much pithier:

> Then came to him his mother and his brothers, but could not get at him
> for the press [crowd, not reporters!]. And it was told him by certain
> which said, Your mother and your brothers stand without, desiring to
> see you. And he answered and said to them, My mother and my
> brothers are these which hear the word of God, and do it.

On the one hand, the blow is softened; on the other, there's a hint that his kin
may be lacking in their duties. Either way, he is not identifying his work with
them. There is no family dynasty here – at least when it comes to the spiritual
teaching, everyone is Jesus's subject: *Follow Me*. It is a case of the maverick son
'about his Father's business' again, somewhat impatient of interference or
the implication that family should take precedence over his on-going work. As
far as the spiritual operation is concerned, his kin might appear to be on the
outside. They can wait in line – and not at the front, either. Again, the very distinctions employed make it plain that he is practically indifferent to the wishes
of his blood relations.

Matthew allows for the possibility that Jesus's brothers are the result of
Joseph and Mary's sexual union:

> Then Joseph being raised from sleep did as the angel of the Lord had
> bidden him, and took unto him his wife: And knew her not till she had
> brought forth her firstborn son: and he called his name JESUS.

> (Matthew 1:23–5)

It's all there. He did not 'know' her, that is, enjoy conjugal marital relations,
until after Jesus's birth. Jesus was her firstborn; there would be others. Matthew
might support the agency of the Holy Spirit in Jesus's conception, but he does
not support the idea that Jesus had no brothers with whom he shared a blood
mother. But what Matthew also gets, presumably from Mark, is a picture that
Jesus did not necessarily see eye to eye with his family. Jesus was set aside, consecrated. He seems to have claimed the right to choose his own family.
However, records show that at least one of his brothers, James, was 'holy from

his mother's womb' as well. Consecrated to God, they must have had a great deal in common.

Family relations, however, can be very complex. Some have ignored their family for most of their professional life, only to leave all their possessions to family members they may never even have met while alive, leaving their close friends and lovers with memories and not much else. It does not have to be an either/or situation. However, the gospels do not show us much love lost between Jesus and the family. It is clear that the authors of the gospels are simply not privy to family secrets.

Matthew 27:56 does include what at first sight appears to be Mary his mother, watching the Crucifixion from afar: 'And many women were there beholding afar off, which followed Jesus from Galilee, ministering unto him: Among which was Mary Magdalene, and Mary the mother of James and Joseph, and the mother of Zebedee's children.' It seems an odd way to speak of Jesus's mother: 'the mother of James and Joseph'; brother Judas has dropped out of the picture altogether. Perhaps the text has been messed with. Some early versions of Matthew have 'Joses' rather than 'Joseph', so variants have existed. Still seems odd, though.

Luke does not mention 'Mary' at all, just the women of Galilee in general. Mark, probably the oldest version in this regard, has 'Mary Magdalene, and Mary the mother of James the less and of Joses, and Salome; (Who also, when he was in Galilee, followed him, and ministered unto him;)' Some ambiguity here, surely: what's this 'James the less'? The Greek word is *mikrou*, as in 'microscopic'. It means he was either 'the small' or 'the little' or even 'junior'. None of which helps much. Small in relation to whom? *Odd.* And we hear of 'Salome', though the text is ambiguous, it appears that the Mary concerned might have been her mother. Father of the Church, Epiphanius, thought so around AD 400. Salome was named by him as one of Jesus's sisters. But again, this Mary is not specifically named as Jesus's mother. This of course has offered a mild get-out clause for Catholic perpetual virgin apologists and could be used by a determined opponent to throw doubt on the whole Jesus family scenario. And then, just when you thought you might be able to come to terms with the confusion, John (19:25–7) throws the spanner completely in the works, giving us the following:

> Now there stood by the cross of Jesus his mother, and his mother's sister, Mary the wife of Cleophas, and Mary Magdalene. When therefore Jesus saw his mother, and the disciple standing by, whom he loved, he saith unto his mother, Woman, behold thy son! Then saith he to the disciple, Behold thy mother! And from that hour that disciple took her unto his own home.

Though admittedly the last gospel to gain broad acceptance in the canon, this does not mean the Gospel of John is necessarily devoid of credible history, though one should recognize that history was not the writer or compiler's purpose. Wherever it came from, this is a very powerful scene, almost a tragic riddle. Unlike the synoptic gospels, these women are not far off the Crucifixion site. They are close enough for a final, intimate conversation. However, the precise identities of the participants are not clear from the Greek, if clarity was the intention of the writer.

There are several possible readings. You may have four women, consecutively, Jesus's mother, Jesus's mother's sister, then Mary 'of Cleophas' (Greek: *Maria hē tou Klōpa*), and Mary Magdalene. Or, if you take the phrase *Mary of Cleophas* as an explanation of the identity of 'the sister of his mother', you would have three women: Mary the mother of Jesus, her sister 'Mary of Klopa', and Mary *Magdalēnē*. On that basis, Mary the mother of Jesus would have a sister of the *same name* which rather destroys the point of giving children names in the first place: 'Mary, come here please! Not *you*, the *other* Mary!' And while we mention 'the other Mary', look at Matthew 28:1, when the women go to the crucified Jesus's sepulchre: 'In the end of the Sabbath, as it began to dawn toward the first day of the week, came Mary Magdalene and the other Mary to see the sepulchre.' Matthew has picked up something about 'the other Mary' as well, though he does not appear at all sure who she is. Did John get his 'other Mary' from Matthew, or is there a common tradition about another Mary behind both?

An explanation may lie in Mark. Mark 16:1's version of the 'Easter Sunday' scenario has 'Mary Magdalene, and Mary the mother of James [Jesus's brother or possibly, 'James, son of Alphaeus' of the twelve], and

Salome [identified as Jesus's sister by Epiphanius 400 years later] who bought sweet spices, that they might come and anoint him.' If John was aware that the name 'Cleophas' was equivalent to 'Alphaeus', as a highly suspect fragment of the works of Church Father Papias (*c*.60–135) asserts, then this could explain John's 'Maria of Klopa'. John's Mary 'of Klopa' could be the mother of James (possibly a half-brother of Jesus, possibly not!) To add further to the mystery, Mark's previous verse indicates that Jesus's first lying in the sepulchre on the Friday night was witnessed by 'Mary Magdalene and Mary the mother of Joses [Joseph]'.

Again, why is this Mary mother figure not identified as *Jesus's* mother? In one verse it's Mary the mother of Joseph, in the next, Mary the mother of James. If James and Joseph were Jesus's brothers as indicated by Mark 6, then why call Jesus's mother, and the mother of Joseph and James, by separate designations? *How many Marys were involved here?* The confusion over just who was there seems to be the result of variant testimony or conflicting traditions, or deliberate tampering or obfuscation. John's ambiguity of phrasing may simply come from a similar bewilderment with Mark's record. Thus, according to John you have a 'sister of Jesus's mother' who *might be* Maria 'of Klopa'. Klopa or Klopas is nowhere else identified in the canonical record. Matthew seems to have read Mark's account and, similarly confused, come up with a composite identity: '*the other Mary*'. He chickens out of the whole problem; perhaps he was short of time that day.

And who is this 'other Mary'? She may be Jesus's mother's 'sister' – half-sister from another marriage of Mary the mother of Jesus's husband Joseph, or, if the 'sister' is distinct from 'Mary of Klopa', the daughter of Mary the mother of Jesus from a subsequent marriage to one 'Clopas' or 'Cleophas', or the daughter of another marriage of Mary the mother of Jesus's apocryphal mother, 'St Anne' or Hannah, though why a mother would call another daughter, even from another marriage, the same name is anyone's guess. Alternatively, the 'other Mary' could be the daughter of a previous marriage of another of St Anne's husbands. All of these spectacularly conflicting views have found their apologists among 'patristic' writers – early Christian apologists or 'Church Fathers'. The variants also find their way into apocryphal gospels, which build a lot on these anomalies or discrepancies in the canonical records and create nice little stories about them, attractive to Christian romantics by their suggestive novelty and strangeness.

All of these speculative identities depend on variant readings of the Greek. For example, does *Maria hē tou Klōpa* mean 'Mary of Klopa', that is Mary, wife of Klopa or 'Clopas', or does it mean 'Mary, *daughter* of Klopa'? The latter interpretation gives an excuse for having Mary, formerly married to Joseph, being subsequently married to a Klopa or Clopas. That allows nervous Catholic dogma to reassert itself in that Jesus's so-called brothers may come from second husband Clopas's previous marriage to someone else who then became Mary, Jesus's mother's step-children. It's tempting to give up the search at this point! Other commentators would simply say Jesus's brothers and sisters came from a second marriage of Mary, and were therefore Jesus's step-brothers and step-sisters. But in John, Mary the mother is distinguished from the sister and from 'Mary of Klopa'. Most commentators take John's phrase to mean Mary, wife of Klopa or Clopas or Cleophas, rather than Mary, daughter of Klopa.

Equally valid, and in accordance with the Greek, is the simple explanation that 'Mary of Klopa' was Mary the mother of Jesus's *sister-in-law*, that is, the wife of her brother. Then, Klopa would be Mary's brother and the problem is solved, unless you want to throw the doctrine of the immaculate conception in and insist, on no evidence whatsoever, that Mary was the 'only begotten' daughter of her mother. That Mary had a brother or uncle or other kinsman called Klopa would seem to be the most straightforward conclusion, if John was intending to be straightforward, naturalistic and rational in the ordinary sense. It would also neatly allow for two Jameses: one the son of Mary, and one the son or step-son of Mary's sister-in-law of the same name.

The fact is, the families of working messiahs can do embarrassing things, like living ordinary lives in tune with their times, unaware that their private lives clash with future religious dogmas. Did these women *want* to be canonized; can the dead refuse posthumous decorations? Does anyone ever listen to the family in such matters?

Personally, I see no reason to close the ambiguities down. The Greek allows for Mary 'of Klopa' being the sister of Mary the mother of Jesus or another person. A sister of Mary the mother of Jesus is definitely mentioned, though, as we have seen, this could well be Mary's sister-in-law. If it is confusing for us, it must have been confusing for them too: two or three Marys at the foot of the cross, plus the beloved disciple! And in case anyone thinks the 'beloved disciple' was Mary Magdalene because they have read the Gnostic Gospel of Philip or the fragmentary Gospel of Mary, or because Mary Magdalene was there, John is quite clear that the beloved disciple may be referred to by Jesus's mother as 'thy son'. Jesus gives his beloved disciple to his mother and his mother to her son.

Jesus's relation to his mother here seems a trifle peculiar; are we in the presence of a riddle? Jesus calls her 'Woman' where we might expect at this extreme moment (he is dying on the cross), 'Mother'. The right to call Mary 'Mother' he gives to his beloved disciple, suggesting the beloved disciple take her into his affections, and, we are told, his home as well.

I should have thought sound principles of logic would not permit anyone to build a safe structure of speculation on this significant passage. That has never stopped the curious, and many's a rickety old thing passed for a 'tower of strength' to those who prefer not to check the foundations. Papias's alleged titbit for example allows Robert Eisenman to identify James the brother of the Lord as James the son of Alphaeus (or Cleophas), allowing for the patronym 'Joseph' to return to its alleged general messianic reference for a Messiah of the northern tribes, on the basis that the northern kingdom of Israel (which ceased to exist politically in 722 BC) was also known as 'Joseph'. Thus, James *gains* historical identity as 'Jesus' *loses* it. This does rather leave open the question of just who 'Mary the mother' was mother of! But I suppose one could always argue that Mary the mother of Jesus was in fact the *true* 'other Mary' and this *other Mary* was nothing less than an invention to provide an imaginary salvation-principle ('Yeshua') a gateway to earth.

I prefer to apply Occam's trusty razor to this merciless mass of tangled nazaritic hair.

Perhaps we should ask ourselves what the author of the 'spiritual gospel' of John was trying to say here. Well, for a start, why has no one asked the question: 'Why should Jesus consign his mother to his 'beloved disciple' as if she were a lonely old widow in need of social security? This would suggest that *he* had been looking after her before his untimely arrest, and that she needed a surrogate carer. Every scrap of evidence suggests the contrary; his mother and her friends had been looking after *him*. Besides, Mary surely had other relatives to rely on – and perhaps a second husband – and numerous connections.

The story as we know it does not make sense.

But it has made sense to one peculiar class of commentators. Second-century 'Gnostic' interpreters seized on the passage and interpreted it as a revelation that Jesus was referring to the secret of the *Great Mother* whom they called 'Barbelo' which name, in my book dealing with the Sethian Gnostic Gospel of Judas, *Kiss of Death*, I suggested may be derived from the Greek for 'a wild peach tree', (*barbelos*) whose roots are in heaven, yet suspended above the material realm, heavy with spiritual fruit.

'Barbelo' is the secret of divine Wisdom, the feminine *Sophia*. The point is that a Gnostic *must know who his or her true Mother is*, because the spirit of the Gnostic has come through the activity of the Mother, Barbelo, Mother of all spirits. Thus, if John were indeed conveying an esoteric secret, the passage is well composed, the ambiguities are deliberate, intended to point the discerning to a hidden truth. Thus 'the beloved disciple' or the 'disciple whom Jesus loved' is the one who sees himself or herself in *him*, that is, has become Jesus's 'twin' or reflection on earth. *You* could be the 'beloved disciple' if you put yourself into the story and stick close to its meaning. Thus John's story is an allegory. Jesus introduces his 'Mother', incarnate as 'Woman', to her new 'son', the beloved disciple or spiritual Church, and the new 'son' must recognize his true Mother and take her to his 'house', or heart or temple. This union will constitute the new seed of the spiritual life on earth after Jesus leaves the sight of flesh. Knowing his true Mother – and Father – he or she may ultimately ascend to the divine tree from which the spirit first fell.

As the old story associated with Isaac Newton suggests, the fruit falls, enlightenment occurs, and enlightenment allows the fruit to rise again, knowing its law.

Now, it may be argued that this interpretation is a Gnostic gloss, back-dated onto an 'innocent' gospel of John. But John is an ocean of allegory, and it is just as likely in my view that it is the writer of John who has read the blunt passages in the synoptic gospels where Jesus asks rudely 'who is my mother?' and has seen that Jesus was not merely being insulting to his parents but was trying to open a window to a deeper truth, and that truth is not simply the Catholic idea that Jesus's followers will constitute his new divine family 'in Christ' as Paul would put it, but was most specifically referring to a secret, esoteric relationship to be understood by those who were truly his 'beloved' disciples. Yes, Jesus was thinking of an élite body in touch with high spiritual realities. Jesus in John is available to a new, mystic family, a kingdom of heaven in which he reigns eternally among those who *Know Him*. He lifts his beloved out of time, transfigured.

John's awareness of spiritual depth does not mean that he is indifferent to historical sense. There is a close weaving of historical remnants with his arch-story of the Word made flesh and dwelling on the lineal historical plane for a season. Thus we cannot say that behind his account there is not the reflection of events that took place, though apparently recollected in considerably more earth-free conditions of mind.

———

John's record of Jesus's ministry is remarkable for many reasons, not least of which is the fact that Jesus at several points links his family to his activities with his followers.

———

Cana is a little less than 15 miles west of the westernmost point of the Sea of Galilee. According to John 2:1 Jesus went to Cana 'on the third day' after two of John the Baptist's disciples took note of John's hailing of Jesus as the Messiah. Duly inspired, they followed Jesus from 'Bethabara [some texts have 'Bethany'] beyond Jordan' to where Jesus dwelt, the location of which is not indicated, whither the two, of which only Andrew is named, joined by Simon Peter, are taken into Galilee.

The day before the Cana wedding, Philip and Nathaniel are called by Jesus, and they, along with the other three, presumably, are called to the marriage.

The call appears to stem from the presence of Jesus's mother at the wedding. But this is no ordinary occasion. When his mother points out to her son that 'they' have no wine, Jesus says, 'What do I have to do with you, woman?' adding: 'My hour is not yet come.' Then, unabashed, Jesus's mother orders the servants: 'Whatsoever he says to you, do it.'

This phrase, this direct order, is a straight lift from the Greek Bible version of Genesis 41:55. The setting in Genesis is the famine of Egypt, when all the Egyptians cry to Pharaoh for bread: 'and Pharaoh said unto all the Egyptians, Go to Joseph; what he says to you, do it.' This Genesis passage is followed by an account of how 'Joseph was the governor over the land, and he it was who sold to all the people of the land: and Joseph's brothers came, and bowed down themselves before him with their faces to the earth.'

Now, note verse 8 of Genesis 42: 'And Joseph knew his brothers, but they knew not him.' Now look at John 1:11: 'He [the Word] came unto his own, and his own received him not.' And look at the section immediately preceding the wedding at Cana, John 1:45, where Philip declares to Nathaniel: 'We have found him, of whom Moses in the law, and the prophets, did write, Jesus son of Joseph the one from Nazareth.' Jesus: 'son of Joseph'.

Jesus's mother is treating her son as the 'new' Joseph, or 'son of Joseph' as Philip says, that is, a *saviour of the people* – from famine: 'they have no wine'. Spiritual famine. *They have no wine.* This was the claim for the Nazarite, by the way: *they have no wine.* According to Ezekiel 44:17–31, the 'Sons of Zadok', when entering the inner court of the temple, must wear only linen; they must neither shave their heads, nor allow the hair to grow too long, neither 'shall any priest drink wine'.

A Son of Joseph: *A saviour of the people.* Who are the people? The people are they who have no 'wine', the spirit, or life of God. Jesus will declare in John that *he* is the true vine, the true saviour, the genuine elixir of life: the reflection of God in man. Where once there was famine; now there is wine. Where once there was only law; now there is Holy Spirit. We see the spiritual critique of legal righteousness so central to the Pauline Church. A saviour who offers the fruit of the grape would be well understood by pagan converts to the faith (Bacchus/Dionysios): unholy anathema to the sons of Zadok.

The author of John has obviously looked into the more prosaic scenes in Matthew, Luke and Mark wherein Jesus's 'brothers' are identified as those who heed God's will. Here in John, taking this idea an unpleasant stage further, the brothers of Jesus are linked *directly* to Joseph's unperceiving brothers, and Jesus is a 'son of Joseph'.

In the section previous to Cana, when Nathaniel learns that Jesus is the son of Joseph, the one from Nazareth, Nathaniel asks if anything good could ever come from Nazareth. For this remark Nathaniel wins high praise from Jesus, who quotes from Psalm 32:2, hailing Nathaniel as the 'true Israelite in whom is no guile'. Nathaniel's rejection of Jesus's apparent or *visible* home wins him praise (and would make even more stunning sense if Nathaniel knew a 'Nazareth' was a New Covenant-style camp!). The scene ties in perfectly with that shortly before where Andrew and another disciple of John the Baptist ask Jesus where he dwells, and Jesus says: 'Come and see.' Come. And *see*. There's more to this invitation than meets the eye, and Jesus's true dwelling place is also somewhere that does not meet the unenlightened eye. Nathaniel guesses this.

'Nazareth' in John has become a kind of allegorical symbol for 'the world' from which the beloved is called. The 'world' or *kosmos* in John is always wicked. Perhaps the root conception of this 'world' was the 'house of the law' feared by the New Covenanter.

While all this is another indication, at the least, of a now established tradition that Jesus was in some fundamental breach with his family, it would be unwise to use passages so heavily laden with allegory and symbol as bases for historical judgements. The wedding at Cana story is saturated with allegory; it is perhaps *all* allegory and, like Freemasonry, 'a peculiar system of morality veiled in allegory and illustrated by symbols'.

John even implies that Jesus is God, because the 'governor of the feast' calls the 'bridegroom' and remarks that whereas normally people receive the best wine first at a wedding, in this case 'thou hast kept the good wine until now'. Now, I do not think this is an argument for Jesus being the one getting married at Cana, even though his 'mother' seems to have charge of the occasion; it is a plain recognition that the messianic end time is on the horizon and the true Israel is to be reconciled to his creator. The messianic banquet has begun with a call to guests, a call to outsiders. A redeemed Israel and Yahweh are the bridegroom and bride. The bridegroom image is picked up again in the mouth of John the Baptist in 3:29: 'He that hath the bride is the bridegroom', where the bride is apparently Israel. Christian theology has taken it that the Church is the divine bride to be wed to God. Thus, in John, we see the 'Missing Family' motif given a wholly spiritual colouring that may well have been galling for Jesus's actual relatives and their descendants.

The concluding verse of the Cana 'sign' narrative informs us that Jesus's *disciples* believed in him (John 2:1). This line acts as a *preludium* to what follows. The next verse tells us that after Cana 'he [Jesus] descended to Capernaum, he and his mother and the brothers and his disciples, and they continued there not many days'. Note *the* brothers and *his* disciples. This little verse tells us that at least for a while Jesus operated in the company of both brothers and disciples, but the passage is a *non sequitur*. Capernaum, which is not explained as a destination, is north-west of Cana but since Cana is in hilly territory and Capernaum is by Galilee's shores, we may allow for a 'descent', though the term may be figurative, as in 'coming down to earth'. Cana's transformation of water into wine, a sign of the kingdom coming, occurred at a higher level than linear life below.

From Capernaum, Jesus truly 'goes down' or heads south to Jerusalem, to Judea, the occasion given for his scandalous scourging of the money-changers in the Temple. Jesus, alone, encounters suspicious Judean pundits. In particular, Jesus meets a Pharisee and 'ruler of the Judeans' named Nikodemos at night. This Judean sympathizer becomes the blessed recipient of an extraordinary lecture on the need to be born again. Apart from the spiritual message, this highly influential exchange with the Judean ruler may be taken as implying a certain slight on the spiritual value of one's parentage or family. That is to say, our earthly birth is insufficient to acquire either heaven or divine recognition: 'That which is born of the flesh is flesh: and that which is born of the Spirit is spirit.' Claims for family membership or dynastic primacy do not, in this perspective, add up to a 'hill of beans'.

In chapter seven of John we find Jesus accompanied by his family again. The encounter adds diabolical venom to the sorry picture we have already witnessed:

After these things Jesus walked in Galilee: for he would not walk in Judea, because the Judeans sought to kill him. Now the Judeans' feast of tabernacles was at hand. His brothers therefore said to him, Depart hence, and go into Judea, that your disciples also may see the works you are doing. For there is no man that does any thing in secret, and he seeks to be known openly. If you do these things, show yourself to the world. For neither did his brothers believe in him.

Then Jesus said to them, my time is not yet come: but your time is always ready. The world cannot hate you; but me it hates, because I testify of it, that its works are wicked. You go to this feast; for my time is not yet full come. When he had said these words to them he abode still in Galilee. But when his brothers were gone up, then he also went up to the feast, not openly, but as though in secret.

(John 7:1–10)

This is not a well known sequence of events. It is hardly surprising. The 'brothers' seem to be in a competition to outdo the sheer nastiness of Joseph's brothers in the famous many-coloured coat story. It is almost a case of history – or legend – repeating itself. And this is I think exactly what the author wishes to convey by secret or mystical means. In the salvation-history of Israel, which the author of the gospel believes is about to find its final act with the manifestation of the Word to flesh, what was prefigured in Genesis, in the beginning, is to be repeated once more with the full meaning or glamour of glory attached. Yes, Jesus is a 'son of Joseph'. He *is* a Joseph. And who are his brothers? Why, they are the unnamed Children of Israel: the fathers of the tribes, the jealous young men who cannot bear the divine gift made of a father's love to one of their own. The author of John has looked right through the synoptic gospel story and seen, not history, but a divine process that transcends history, of which mere history is but the husk of a meta-history in which divine dramas such as Joseph and his wicked brothers may be played out again and again in the dimension of time. When eternity touches time, the drama is played out again. This is an eternal story.

We see Jesus's brothers, always called 'the brothers', with loads of allegorical pitch attached to *them* who have strayed from the father's love; we see them virtually plotting Jesus's downfall, practically conspirators in his crucifixion, hiding behind 'wise words' dipped in poison. Their questions are reminiscent of the cruel goading of Jesus on the Cross, 'can not he who saved others save himself?' Here the brothers suggest Jesus should walk 'openly' into the trap set for him by his enemies. This, they argue, would exemplify the kind of openness expected of one who wishes to be recognized openly. They want him to surrender his 'messianic secret' before 'the hour' is come. This is the work of Satan, as John understands it; such would definitively thwart salvation. On the earthly plane, the brothers' sly temptation is nothing short of an invitation to assassination, precisely on a par with the pit into which Joseph's brothers cast him, leaving him for dead. The brothers try to ensare him through an appeal to vanity and, even, righteousness.

John's treatment of Jesus's family is awe-inspiringly vicious. If, as it appears to be, a kind of 'midrash' or 'pesher' on Mark or Matthew, then one can only say that its author, in order to thrust forward a spiritual message of enormous power, has simply taken 'history' and used it for his own purposes, massively exaggerating alleged differences between Jesus and his kin, giving an operatic contrast between the world, the flesh, and eternity. John's defence would be, I suppose, that the seed of the story was well known, that is, that 'Jesus's own received him not' in every sense, and that since everything Jesus did was prefigured in the prophets (that included Genesis, attributed to Moses), then he was inspired by God to see the obvious, startling truth that Jesus's brothers did not believe in him, a prophetic replay of Joseph and his brothers.

If John's convictions on this issue were ever widespread, we have ample reason to understand how Jesus's real family got lost.

It should be added that from this perspective, any Gnostic interpretation of the Mother/Woman passages in John set at the Crucifixion may have been a straight misreading of John's intention. Where Jesus calls his mother from the cross: 'Woman', he meant only to distinguish between his divine parentage and the mere 'woman' who brought him into the world.

And lest anyone think Jesus was afraid of his enemies, John has Jesus going to Jerusalem, but not because his brothers told him to, or with their 'protection', but because he has a somewhat secret plan; he will operate at night, shrouded from the eyes of the wicked world. Again, we see the 'Joseph and his brothers' motif, for they, the brothers, also go up to the feast first, an act prefigured by the *feeding* in Egypt, where Joseph's brothers fail to recognize the one who has mastered the whole situation and is, as it were, secretly drawing it to the conclusion where, at its divine *dénouement*, the brothers will bow down and worship him, the one they rejected, the one they conspired against. And who are the 'brothers'? They are the fathers of the Jews who were, according to John, too blind to see the salvation being prepared for them; they are not the ones whom Jesus loved. The stone the builders *rejected* became the cornerstone of the new Temple.

If you are inclined to any level of sympathy with the family of Jesus, then you must agree that John is a most hateful gospel in their regard, drenched with a spiritual triumphalism that has kicked history and the characters of the Missing – or lost – Family into another cosmos.

But *did* Jesus's brothers reject him, as the gospel of John wants us to believe?

It is certainly the case that the canonical gospels do not come out strongly in favour of the brothers' tolerance, encouragement or complicity of Jesus. That statement is of course the kind of understatement that obscures the issues! It seems, anyway, that the gospels, insofar as they are interested in Jesus's family at all, are working with a persistent tradition that his family had some kind of differences with him, which John takes to the most dramatic, painful, and one must suspect, unhistorical extremes.

On the other hand, if one looks at the synoptic passages again, it is not so much the case that the brothers have differences with Jesus, but that Jesus appears practically indifferent to *them*. They treat him without honour or respect in his own house, he says. Their territory, deficient in faith and belief, offers poor pickings for his operation. Jesus denies that their blood relation has any spiritual implications. He, Jesus, will decide who is his brother or sister. He keeps them waiting. He prefers the company of his chosen disciples. How much of this attitude, we may ask, is a retroactive projection from a future time when Jesus's family and the religion they represent had become a sceptical nuisance for a new, *arriviste* Gentile Christian experience?

According to Gentile-friendly Dr Luke, these tendencies of family indifference began when Jesus was about 12, when he tells his mother she ought to know better than to try to distract him from the things of his 'father', Yahweh. He was 'separated', consecrated for divine service. John the Baptist seems to have been the only relative who understood him.

Admittedly, this underlying family-rejection polemic belongs most to the *later* canonical works. Luke is usually dated about AD 80–130, while John is dated later still: AD 90–130. Mark and Matthew do not press the idea of a breach or rift with the family, and they are probably earlier; Mark having appeared around AD 65–80, and Matthew AD 80–100. There appears to have been a hardening of the arteries where Jesus's family was concerned, especially as the Christian churches absorbed the impact of the Jewish revolt against the Romans that began in AD 66 and which culminated in the destruction of the Temple in AD 70 and the suicidal defence of Masada in AD 73. The conclusion cannot be avoided that the denigration of Jesus's family seems to coincide with the increasing rejection of Judean identity by the Roman Empire, and the increasingly Gentile constitution of the Christian Church, raised on the slur that Judeans had failed to recognize either the Messiah of their own prophecies, or the universal Christ of the new age. God was punishing 'them' indiscriminately. Not to mention Judas Iscariot...

Paul's letters did not encourage respect for Judean followers of Jesus; Paul regarded his doctrines as superior to those held by either James, Jesus's brother, or of his disciple Cephas (Peter). Paul believed he had privileged intercourse with 'the mind of Christ' which he felt compelled to share with anyone who would listen. The Judean followers of Jesus who criticized, or were horrified by his stance on the Hebrew law, Paul taunted as being 'weak', old-fashioned revisionists determined to keep the Gentiles in bondage to an 'alien law'. Since Peter and James knew Jesus personally, while Paul emphatically did not, his upfront claim staggered those on the Judean side of the argument, living in a tough Judea on the verge of cataclysmic revolt.

The denigration of the Judean messianic experience was not only aimed at

Jesus's immediate family, but at the followers of his relative, John the Baptist as well; John's legacy was increasingly marginalized. By the time of John's gospel, its writer sees fit to make it absolutely clear that John was not 'that light' but was only called to bear witness to it. The fact that Jesus's 'Repent!' message and water-baptisms were a straight borrowing or continuation of the John message was practically forgotten. Everyone in the gospel narrative, save Jesus, becomes a supporting actor. In Paul's letters, it is arguable that the human, historical Jesus has become a supporting act as well.

The case of the women of Jesus's family is not so clear. While there is apparently nothing against them, they are simply presented as lamenting hangers-on, like professional mourners and tidy-up home helps 'ministering' to Jesus. As has been often remarked, one victim of this treatment was Mary Magdalene, mentioned in all of the canonical gospels, but whose character or significance is nonexistent. As stated before, the gospels just aren't interested in Jesus's dynastic position in relation to the Judean House of David, except insofar as it supports his universal messiahship, which the Gentile world could *never* accept as being political, although the *imperium* correctly perceived the long-term threat that even a heavenly Messiah would one day be used to dictate political action. According to the canonical gospels, those who crucified Jesus had 'no king but Caesar'. We cannot claim with certainty that Jesus saw matters this way at all. If Jesus's family had become awkward for Church leaders, it is because they were still standing there. And if they were standing there, it must have been because Jesus accepted them in some way, and, in some way, they must have accepted him; *how*, is another matter.

The earliest coherent Christian documents, if we discount the allegedly proto-Christian elements of the Dead Sea Scrolls, are some of the letters attributed to St Paul: I Thessalonians, Philippians, Galatians, I–II Corinthians, Romans, Philemon and Colossians are all dated some time between AD 50 and 60. Do any of them give any clues as to the position held by Jesus's family in the formation period of Christianity?

Yes, they do.

But before we look at them, we should first recall that the common idea of 'Paul' is largely based on Luke's 'Acts of the Apostles' (*c.*AD 80–130) which is largely devoted to Paul's adventures and is highly influenced by Paul's point of view. Thus it is interesting that even here in Pauline territory we find the active presence of Jesus's family in the Jerusalem community of Jesus's followers. Two of his brothers may even be represented among the remaining 'eleven' disciples, Judas Iscariot having, according to Luke, died a curious death. Regardless of the fact that much of the chapter seems to be a garbled and distorted account based on a primary source concerning how *James* came to be bishop of the Jerusalem assembly (*see* v.23), it is interesting that Jesus's family are neither rejecting of Jesus nor are themselves rejected by the disciples:

> And when they were come in, they went up into an upper room, where abode both Peter, and James, and John, and Andrew, Philip, and Thomas, Bartholomew, and Matthew, James the son of Alphaeus, and Simon the Zealot, and Judas the brother of James [literally 'Judas of Jacob']. These all continued with one accord in prayer and supplication, with the women, and Mary the mother of Jesus, and with his brothers.

> (Acts 1:13–14)

The list of disciples (the 'eleven') is peculiar. Where is the 'Thaddaeus' of Matthew 3:18? And we have an extra Judas: '*Ioudas Iakōbou*': Judas of James. This could be Judas, son of James or simply, Judas, James's brother, the preferred translation. *Which* 'James' is not indicated, nor do we know which 'Judas' we might be meeting here. One thing though is that according to Matthew and Mark, 'Judas' and 'James' were indeed brothers … *of Jesus*. Do we see here a full habilitation or even rehabilitation of the brothers?

Anyhow, the brothers of Jesus are also mentioned – perhaps twice then – along with Jesus's mother, and they, the assembled believers, are all in one accord. As far as we can tell, they stayed that way until Saul of Tarsus appeared on the scene, first persecuting unto death the Jerusalem messianic movement with self-righteous mania, then, following dramatic conversion and sojourn in the desert and in Damascus, returning to Jerusalem and falling out with the established leadership. Just who constituted that leadership is open to question.

According to Acts, the assembly appointed two to take the place of Judas Iscariot. This after Peter has quoted from Psalm 69:25 and Psalm 109:8. The second quote is adapted: 'and his bishopric let another take'. The original Psalm 109 refers to the 'wicked man' having his '*office*' removed. The word 'bishopric' is used deliberately, but confusingly. Since when was *Judas Iscariot* the 'bishop' of the Jerusalem assembly? When did Jesus appoint a 'bishop' to succeed him, or Judas? It is arguable that Judas's role of 'purse-bearer' for the operation was what was intended by the Greek word '*episkopos*' (=bishop) in the first instance. 'Episkopos' means overseer, or ruler, not treasurer. A corresponding New Covenant role, according to the Dead Sea Scrolls, is the Hebrew *mebakker*. The 'bishop' role may stem in some way from that.

Has Judas become confused with another figure altogether? Robert Eisenman has drawn attention to the death-story of Judas Iscariot in Acts, comparing it with the murder of James the Brother of the Lord in AD 62, who also, like Judas, fell headlong, before, in James's case, having his brains smashed out with a fuller's club. Judas's guts were spilled out in fulfilment of a psalm and a prophecy of Zechariah. He was not forgiven.

Be that as it may, the Acts narrative refers to one taking the place of Judas Iscariot, to complete the 'twelve' – *but on whose authority?* What authority does the twelve – or eleven – now have? From the context of Acts, there are some 120 disciples. Were the twelve a governing council, along with Jesus's family? That appears to be the Acts picture. Were the disciples then appointing a 'bishop' for the first time? Not according to the main text. They were appointing a replacement for Judas. But the word 'bishopric' is there, deliberately inserted into Peter's quote from Psalm 108.

Now, according to Jewish historian Hegesippus (*c.*AD 165–75), quoted by Eusebius (b.*c.*260), the first *bishop* of Jerusalem was James, the Brother of the Lord.

According to Luke's Acts, two names are put forward to replace Judas. Eisenman sees them as historically suspect and I suspect Eisenman is right.

'Joseph called Barsabbas, who was surnamed *Ioustos*' (*Justus*=the Righteous; the *Ziddik*) appears as one name; Matthias as another. The disciples then cast lots to decide who will plug up the twelve; Matthias wins and we hear next to nothing about this Matthias ever again.

But who was Joseph called Barsabbas, surnamed *Justus* (Latin form of *Ioustos*). Well, 'Justus', the 'Just', the 'Righteous', the *Ziddik*, is the title given by sundry patristic writers to James, the Brother of the Lord, also known as James the Just. The English 'Just' hides the Zadokite identity of James; Zadokites were priests, 'sons of Zadok' whose emphasis on *zedek*, righteousness, would find itself in direct opposition to Paul's Gentile-friendly and Judea-*lite* Christianity. Zadokite interpretations of the law dominated the sectarian ordinances of the non-canonical Qumran manuscripts. From this coincidence, if that is what it is, Eisenman deduces that proto-Christianity was identical with the doctrines of the Qumran 'Teacher of Righteousness'. This radical view we must explore in due course. For the time being though, we may note that Joseph Barsabbas is equally intriguing as a name, not only because Mark 6 tells us that Jesus had a brother called Joseph, and because 'Joseph' was the patriarchal name associated with Galilean Messiahship, but 'Barsabbas' suggests a link with an Aramaic word for 'washing' or purification, *subba*, (the 'Bar' means 'son of'), and sounds suspiciously like the otherwise meaningless 'Barabbas' ('son of father') between whom and Jesus, Judeans were ordered to choose by Roman authority. Were the Judeans asked to choose between *brothers*? That would be a particularly vicious Roman stroke, consistent with Pontius Pilate's bloodthirsty, thorough, reputation.

According to the late medieval, apocryphal *Golden Legend*, Mary's mother St Anne's sister was called 'Sobe'. 'Sobe' was St Elizabeth's mother and thus, John the Baptist's grandmother, which, if 'Sobe' was a corrupted form of 'Subba', 'Joseph called Barsabbas' could have been John the Baptist's uncle – and has been confused with James the Just, or used deliberately to obscure James's true position in the Church in Acts.

Alternatively, James could have been dominant *alongside* brother Joseph, since Acts sees Jesus's brothers as a collective: 'the brothers'. Then we could include Luke's 'Judas of James' – and all of them working hand in hand with

Cephas and John. Clearly there was confusion by the end of the 1st century as to who had run the proto-Church in Jerusalem in the 30s, 40s and 50s. We are not compelled to accept Hegesippus's account as 'gospel', nor are we compelled to accept the gospels as 'gospel' either!

Whatever Luke may have thought, Paul's letters leave us in no doubt as to who was running the show in Jerusalem after Paul gave up persecuting and 'wasting' it (Galatians 1:13). Indeed, Paul's letter to the Galatians also leaves us in no doubt as to his contempt for that leadership when it crossed him.

> Neither went I up to Jerusalem to them which were apostles before me;
> but I went into Arabia, and returned again to Damascus. Then after
> three years I went up to Jerusalem to see Cephas [Peter], and abode with
> him fifteen days. But other of the apostles saw I none, save James the
> brother of the Lord.

> (Galatians 1:17–18)

Nothing here about Matthias or 'Joseph called Barsabbas surnamed Justus'. It is of course possible that by the time Paul fully embraced his peculiar conversion and went to Jerusalem, 'Matthias' had passed on the crozier – or *nezer* – to Jesus's brother, if indeed Matthias ever existed. The question would revolve about when it was decided that the assembly of disciples needed an 'overseer', (*episkopos*) a word, by the way, that Paul does not use, not that he would have respected it, in any case. Paul received his 'gospel' not 'after man'. He was not *taught* it; it came 'by the revelation of Jesus Christ'. God's Son was revealed, says Paul, *in himself*. Christ was in him. Effectively, that made Paul a law unto himself, a point which he urges upon the Gentiles. Only through communion with an inner Christ can man come to know truth.

According to mystic Paul, the Jewish law simply made man a persistent failure, a condemned man, and therefore closed the spiritual realm to his sight. Paul's Judean opponents, amongst whom we must count Jesus's family, believed that only through adherence to the law could man be purified and made open to grace and loving mercy and prophecy. Righteous acts, not thoughts, made the difference. Jesus's concern, they argued, was not with what men said, but with what they *did*. Faith was powerful, but works of righteousness were essential.

In Galatians, Paul describes going up to Jerusalem again in AD 53, 14 years after his last visit. We know practically nothing of what had happened in Jerusalem between Jesus's exit from this world and this time, except that the assembly of Jesus's followers existed and exercised authority over the preaching activities of the apostles among Jews and Gentiles, but predominantly Jews outside of Palestine, in Syria and eastwards towards Edessa and Mesopotamia.

According to Galatians, Paul had established a 'working principle' or relationship with the Jerusalem leadership. He, Paul, would concentrate on the 'uncircumcised' and they would concentrate on preaching the coming of the Messiah to the 'circumcised'. We do not know if James accepted the resurrection; we do not know precisely what the doctrine was that was being preached, other than that there was an acceptance that the messianic kingdom was upon the world and Jesus demanded righteousness and mercy and love before the final judgement of mankind when he would appear again. The literature of interest was the Hebrew Bible which was regarded as a virtually non-stop testimony about Jesus. 'Search the scriptures,' said Jesus, 'for they testify of me.' And they did.

Returning to Jerusalem, Paul met 'James, Cephas, and John, who seemed to be pillars'. Paul regards them almost as outsiders to his conception of Christ's service: '*seemed to be pillars*'. This means they *appeared* to be the pillars, but the caustic note of scepticism is there: Paul was not impressed. Paul was the true 'architect' working on the foundation of Christ; if Cephas and James were Jachin and Boaz, as it were, the pillars of the Temple, then he, Paul, had capped them. Nevertheless, the pillars shook Paul's right hand in fellowship, suggested he carry on, but asked him to remember 'the poor'. This referred to the poverty of the Jerusalem assembly and their followers who had apparently embraced Jesus's teaching on property either by choice or by circumstance. Paul, we know, collected money for a famine that was ravaging the country. Judean Christians would come to be known as 'the Poor', if the name was not already in existence for those who strove for righteousness.

Things did not go smoothly. Paul went to Antioch. Cephas (Peter) turned up to what Paul regarded as his patch. This 'Antioch' may well have been, as Eisenman has argued, Edessa, renamed after the Seleucid King Antiochus IV, in the kingdom of Osroene. Edessa's Queen Helen had converted to the faith of the Bible and wished to send gifts of food to the sufferers of Judea. The likelihood is that Paul had tried to convince her that her sons need not be, or have been, circumcised, as the Jerusalem assembly demanded of Gentiles who joined the righteous community. According to Galatians: 'But when Cephas was come to Antioch, I withstood him to the face, because he was to be blamed. For before that certain people came from James, he did eat with the Gentiles: but when they were come, he [Cephas] withdrew and separated himself, fearing them which were of the circumcision.'

This is plain – and very dramatic. Paul told Peter where he could 'get off'. Cephas respected, if not feared the authority of James; he did not wish to upset James's envoys. James's men had come to put the converts right on the issue. The issue was circumcision. James believed that it was an essential prerequisite both of purity and of spiritual identity with Israel, for whose salvation as a beacon to the world, Jesus had come.

Now, was James following the teaching of his brother? Since Paul claims pride in the fact that *his* doctrine was not taught, did not come from man, then we may conclude that James's doctrine *was* taught, and did come from man, and that man was Jesus, his brother. Paul claims that 'Jesus Christ' revealed the doctrine to *him*. Gentiles should be treated very differently to Jews. Paul's authority came from the fact that he, Paul, was now 'dead': 'I am crucified with Christ: nevertheless I live; yet not I, but Christ liveth in me: and the life which I now live in the flesh I live by the faith of the Son of God, who loved me, and gave himself for me.' Paul believed he was incarnating Jesus Christ's *will*; those who followed Jesus 'after the flesh' could not be compared in authority. He had the *gnosis*! Paul did not give a damn about Jesus's family as such. That contempt may well have informed the canonical gospels that began to appear after this tumultuous doctrinal conflict of the 50s, possibly during, and certainly in the twilight, of the Jewish Revolt. The classic Platonic 'flesh and spirit' dichotomy has been used by Paul, as it would be by the author of

John's gospel, to distinguish the relative authority of Jesus's fleshly brothers and his spiritual brothers. The awful conclusion seems to be that if one is Jesus's fleshly brother, one is *ipso facto* inferior! Jesus's family must have found Paul's position outrageous and intolerable; Paul was taking over in the name of their own.

If we wish to know what James thought of Paul's 'justification by faith doctrine', or of Paul's attitude in general, we may consider looking closely at the Epistle of James. If it was not written by Jesus's brother James himself, it certainly coincides with the kind of view Paul opposed at Jerusalem, Edessa/Antioch and elsewhere:

> What doth it profit, my brothers, though a man say he has faith, and has not works? Can faith save him? If a brother or sister be naked, and destitute of daily food, And one of you say to them, Depart in peace, be ye warmed and filled; notwithstanding ye give them not those things which are needful to the body; what doth it profit? Even so faith, if it has not works, is dead, being alone.
>
> (James 2:14–17)

Compare this to Paul's tirade in Galatians 2:16:

> Knowing that a man is not justified by the works of the law, but by the faith of Jesus Christ, even we have believed in Jesus Christ, that we might be justified by the faith of Christ, and not by the works of the law: for by the works of the law shall no flesh be justified.

'Justified' refers to that which will be held in credit in your favour in the face of final judgement by God. Paul's doctrine of salvation hinges around the failure of the law to justify man in the end, for none can abide by it perfectly.

The author of James sees no incompatibility between the life of faith and the doing of good works according to the law. He would simply be astonished by Paul's contention that 'if righteousness come by the law, then Christ is dead in vain'. If righteousness did not come by the law, where did it come from? Was not the law the essence of God's covenant with His people?

It may well be the case that the letter of James is the sole authentic writing which we can attribute to a member of Jesus's family, James, first bishop or overseer of the first Church of Jerusalem:

> Hear my beloved brothers, Has not God chosen the poor of this world rich in faith, and heirs of the kingdom which he has promised to them that love him? But you have despised the poor. Do not rich men oppress you, and draw you before the judgement seats? Do they not blaspheme that worthy name by the which you are called? If you fulfil the royal law according to the scripture, Thou shalt love thy neighbour as thyself, you do well: But if you have respect to persons, you commit sin, and are convinced of the law as transgressors. For whosoever shall keep the whole law, and yet offend in one point, he is guilty of all. For he that said, Do not commit adultery, said also, Do not kill. Now if you commit no adultery, yet if you kill, you have become a transgressor of the law. So as you speak, so do, as they that shall be judged by the law of liberty. For he shall have judgement without mercy, that has showed no mercy; and mercy rejoices against judgement.
>
> (James 2:5–13)

This understanding of the law seems to this author both austere and humane. It fulfils the known teaching of Jesus that men should see the goodness of the basic law of God and not be false or hypocritical or think that an act without heart is acceptable to God; that it is the condition and intention of the heart which fulfils the meaning of the law, not mere speech or externally visible observance. Note too that James intends to bring his reader to *God*, not to a Christocentric experience of the kind that Paul pounds into his readers. We might imagine James as saying, when opposed by Paul: 'This man believes he knows Jesus better than Jesus knew himself.'

Paul had lost touch with the family of Jesus and created his own. But then, Paul argued – he was always arguing – he *had* seen Jesus Christ, where it mattered, *in himself*:

> Am I not an apostle? Am I not free? Have I not seen Jesus Christ our Lord? Are not you [the Corinthians] my work in the Lord? If I am not an apostle to others, yet doubtless I am to you: for the seal of my apostleship is that you are in the Lord. My answer to them that are examining me is this, Have we not power to eat and drink? Have we not power to lead about a sister, a wife, as well as other apostles, and as the brothers of the Lord, and Cephas?
>
> (I Corinthians 9:5)

If both Paul and Cephas and the brothers of the Lord had all seen the same Jesus Christ, how is it that they could find themselves opposed? Who could speak for Jesus now Jesus had gone?

The Apocryphal Lost Family

H*aving examined the official gospel records, we now search*
for the Missing Family in lesser-known 'apocryphal' gospels
and writings. We find that Jesus's family members were identified
with Jews suspected of rebelliousness against Rome – more reasons
for the Church to erase Jesus's family from history. We reveal the
identity of the famous 'Beloved Disciple'.

The priestly background to Jesus's family is attested in apoc-
ryphal sources; accounts of Jesus's family become obscure after the
destruction of the Temple system in AD 70. James the brother of Jesus
is highly significant in apocryphal writings. We find that Paul was
hostile to Jesus's brother, James. James was murdered. Did Paul
encourage James's murder after cursing him?

Paul established a precedent. If he could speak in Christ's name because the
'risen Jesus' had appeared to him, then anyone who likewise laid claim to what
he called 'the mind of Christ' could produce works whose authority rested
solely on personal revelation. For the old guard this was an ominous development, and it would intensify.

The assemblies that received copies of Paul's letters read them as authoritative apostolic instruction, and in this way they became canonical works.
Testimonies that could be linked to Paul also gained authority: the gospel of

Luke and the Acts of the Apostles are prime examples. Some letters in the canon attributed to Paul were not written by him, but his name gave them authority. 'Paul' became a kind of rubber stamp of legitimacy. However, once a Pauline canon had been recognized, there was a limit to the use of the Pauline badge of authority.

As the men and women of Jesus's generation died out, and the last of those with memories of the first disciples and their activities faded from the stage of life, who could judge the veracity or usefulness of a new work, the correctness of a doctrine? Who was in charge?

The Church in Jerusalem was in trouble. According to Eusebius's *Ecclesiastical History*, the leaders of the Jerusalem assembly were warned before the Jewish Revolt broke out in AD 66 to get out of the city and head for Pella across the Jordan 60 miles to the north and form a kind of Church government 'in exile'. The move cannot have been unconnected to the fact that the chief leader of the Jerusalem assembly, James the brother of the Lord, had been brutally killed by order of the high priest Ananus in AD 62, and while another relative of Jesus succeeded James as bishop, the ensuing breakdown of normal life in Judea, culminating in the mass carnage surrounding the destruction of the Temple in AD 70, doubtless dislocated the established order of Christian organization in the east. Jerusalem lost authority as the Pauline churches of Asia Minor and the Western Roman Empire acquired it.

New Christians were cut off from the original order of things in a way analogous to that by which the late Victorian and Edwardian eras suddenly seemed remote or incomprehensible to the generation that matured after World War One. The past must have seemed like a lost dream. After the military and economic collapse of Judea in the late 60s and 70s, 'Christianity' looked very different. The power base of the family of Jesus had been smashed. The more *Judean* they appeared, the more suspicious they would look. In his commentary on Matthew, the patristic writer Origen (*c.*AD 230) recorded a tradition that it was the murder of *James the Righteous* that had sent God's judgement upon Judea and Jerusalem in the form of the Roman Emperor-to-be, Vespasian and his son, Titus. Eusebius, some 80 years after Origen maintained Judea's toppling into the abyss was rather a result of the Judeans' rejection of Jesus and subsequent embrace of indiscriminate violence. Eusebius's was a view without nuance, an inherited bigotry. Many Judeans had accepted Jesus.

After AD 70, being a Judean Christian was going to be even more difficult than it had been before. The 'Poor' would become poorer still, their priest-led structure of life obliterated as Titus despoiled the Temple of its treasures and violated its sacredness with human gore. Deprived of the Temple, the family of Jesus, along with the Judean people, lost their focus, a large swathe of their identity, and their authoritative footing. The loss was traumatic. Paul's cause looked victorious and the family of Jesus looked old-hat. Rome was *it*, while pre-war Judea and Galilee would become the stuff of romance, the factual edges smoothed off to provide chiaroscuro background to the 'life of the saviour'. Had not his 'own' rejected him, and did they not suffer oblivion for it?

The family of Jesus was invisible, missing, lost.

Still, new Christians needed information. The question was: 'whose information could you trust?' In the main, for a work to be accepted, it had to show a link with an original apostle, and receive approval from a new generation of Church leaders who collected what they could. Approved writings were read in assemblies where psalms and simple hymns were sung by those baptized into 'Christ's body', the new 'family of Jesus'.

Inadvertently, Paul established a principle that personal revelation furnished authority. If vision was the path to revelation and the new age of the saviour promised visionaries, visionaries duly appeared. Visionary writers astral-travelled or meditated their way into the 'eternal past' and found themselves in the presence of mighty signs, divine words, apostles, angels, heavens, Jesus, Paul, Peter and Mary Magdalene. If Paul could enter 'the mind of Christ', such protection of the Christian vouchsafed entering the mind of Judas Thomas as well, or even the Divine Mother. Who needed Jesus's family, when the whole of heaven and history was opened to the 'living Jesus' within the baptized and raised Christian? What profit flesh, over spirit?

The canonical gospels that appeared after the cataclysm of the Jewish Revolt of AD 66–73 did not satisfy everyone. Later generations were interested in what appeared to be missing details. What was Jesus's *secret* teaching to the 'spirituals' of the new age? What happened to Jesus when he was a boy? What did Jesus see when he was transfigured? Who were his parents and grandparents? What happened to the other disciples? To satisfy the need, *apocryphal* gospels began to appear in Christian communities. The authority of the family and the authentic apostle gone, often it was a choice between the bishop and the book, the secret book.

The word 'apocryphal' derives from the Greek for a 'secret work' (*apocryphon*) or esoteric commentary or discourse. However, while 'Gnostic Gospels' often fit this category of secret or esoteric transmission, most surviving Christian apocrypha do not. St Augustine thought about this disparity in his *City of God* (Book XV, 23) and concluded that 'They are called Apocryphal books, because their origin was not evident to the Fathers', or because there was some secret concerning them, or because the evidence for their authority was not made manifest, or because the claim for authority rested upon conjecture. Another idea to explain the 'apocryphal' tag was that the works were studied in secret, apart from the church assemblies: private study might lead to private heresy, for heretics met in secret to dispense secrets. In practice, this all meant that apocryphal works were books that Church authorities refused to accept into the canon, often with good reason, since they were at a chronological or personal distance from the sources they claimed as primary inspiration.

If apocryphal works were not contrary to Hebrew scripture or the apostolically attested gospels, they might be interesting, contain things of value or novelty, but they were not the 'word of God' as the Psalms, the Hebrew prophets, or the earliest gospels and Pauline epistles were. William Ralph Churton's *Uncanonical and Apocryphal Scriptures* (London, 1884, p.10) informs us:

> Perhaps the definition of an Apocryphal writer which would include the largest portion of the writings so designated, is that of an author who uses some kind of disguise, either to conceal his own name or position, or in the case of narratives, the persons and events which form the subject of his history.

Apocryphal works do not have a foot in the 1st century. However, it is impossible to assess their reliability historically, except to say that it was questioned when they were new, and we should be wise to be cautious when seeking in them authentic knowledge about the lost family of Jesus.

———

Given the prominence of James in proto-Christianity it makes sense to look first at a series of variant editions of a work that has appeared under different titles but which is generally known as the 'Infancy Gospel of James' or the *protoevangelium* of James. It is presumed that the name of James, the brother of Lord, has been used to lend the tales authority, since they concern themselves with the generation of Jesus's family prior to Jesus's birth, and appear as lore derived from his family, though the work contains no such endorsement. The core of the work is thought to have been written AD 140–70, a full century and a half at least after the matters described. James is assumed to be a son of Joseph from a previous marriage. This detail was remarked upon by Church Father Origen (AD 185–254), himself the first to refer to the text and doubtless relieved to find a text supporting Mary's perpetual virginity.

The Syriac version is presumed older than the Greek and has marked differences of content to Greek versions. It has been observed that while the work is imitative of the Old Testament (especially the account of Samuel's birth) the author's knowledge of Jewish life and customs is apparently limited. It is therefore unlikely to have come directly from its apocryphal source. Still, it is not without interest.

Drawing on the birth of Samuel from a barren mother, and Luke's similar account of the birth of John to Elizabeth and Zechariah, even the name given to Mary's mother, Anna, is similar to that of Hannah, Samuel's mother. The work is a hymn to virginity; its provenance may be the circle about Polycrates, Bishop of Ephesus in the late 2nd century. Polycrates recalled that the beloved disciple to whom, according to John, Jesus entrusted his mother, had worn a priestly *petalon* (a 'petal', that is: gold leaf). The Jewish Talmud reveals much about this *petalon* or *ziz*, described in Exodus 28:36–8. The *petalon* was a gold-leaf plate worn on the mitre or turban of the high priest. When Mary's father Joachim has his gifts accepted at the altar, the *petalon* glitters: a sign of the Lord's favour; Joachim is not childless for want of virtue. The *petalon* has propitiatory virtue. This detail chimes in with the significance we have already given to the high priest's mitre or *nezer*, the 'holy crown' on which was written 'Holy to God'. This would mean that the 'beloved disciple' could well have been James, the brother of the Lord, at once making sense of John's account of Jesus's exhortation to his mother from the cross: 'Woman, behold thy son!' (John 19:26). In that case, Jesus's words were simply a statement of fact.

Mary's mother is a slave of the Temple, as her daughter will be. But Joachim, not having children, is reproached for it by other priests. He and his wife lack the Lord's favour. It is to find out if his childlessness is a sign of lack of divine favour that he seeks a sign from the priestly *petalon*. He had done all that a priest of the Temple should. Note in this context the ordinances for priests in Ezekiel 44:22:

> Neither shall they [priests in the Temple] take for their wives a widow,
> nor her that is put away: but they shall take virgins of the seed of the
> House of Israel, or a widow that had a priest before.

After singing a lament for her childless, socially inferior condition, an angel appears to tell Anna the good news that she will conceive. Anna says that if such a thing were possible, she would offer the child to the Lord's perpetual service as a Temple slave. Joachim hears the story and seeks a sign of its truth. Hence:

> If the Lord God be reconciled unto me, the plate that is upon the
> forehead of the priest will make it manifest unto me. And Joachim
> offered his gifts and looked earnestly upon the plate of the priest
> when he went up unto the altar of the Lord, and he saw no sin in
> himself. And Joachim said: Now know I that the Lord is become pro-
> pitious unto me and hath forgiven all my sins. And he went down from
> the temple of the Lord justified, and went unto his house.

The scene could derive from someone taking communion from a priest wearing a *petalon*, indicating the persistence of the Temple priesthood among Syrian Christians.

Mary is duly born to Anna and enjoys an idyllic childhood around the Temple, dancing on the third step of the Temple to all Israel's delight. At 12, Mary's future becomes a problem for the priests. The Syriac version of the text becomes more realistic than the Greek at this point; it may hold genuine historical information. Sometimes Mary's mother is called Dina, sometimes Hanna. Her father is named as Zadok Yonakhir.

These variant names for Mary's parents also appear in another Syriac work *The Cave of Treasures*, attributed to Ephrem Syrus from Nisibis, 100 miles east of Edessa, Mesopotamia (c.AD 306–73). This attribution may also be apocryphal since *The Cave of Treasures* did not acquire its present form until at least the 6th century. The author's title was *The Book of the order of the succession of Generations (or Families)* – of the patriarchs and kings of Israel and Judah. Perhaps he should have put 'the *correct* order' since he believed the ancient genealogies of the Jews had been lost to fire when Nebuchadnezzar captured Jerusalem in 587 BC. Subsequent reconstructions were held by Arabs and Jews to be unreliable. Arabs shared the interest since they assumed descent from Abraham *via* Hagar and Ishmael. Arabic translations of *The Cave of the Treasures* derive from this interest; Christian portions of the text were not translated.

The author complains that 'the Jews', holding Mary to be an adulteress, had pressed the sons of the Church for her true genealogy:

> And here the mouth of the Jews is stopped, and they believe that Mary
> was of the seed of the House of David and of Abraham. Now the Jews
> have no table of succession which showeth them the true order of the
> families of their fathers, because their books have been burned thrice
> – once in the days of Antiochus [IV, *Epiphanes*], who raised up a
> persecution against them, and polluted the Temple of the Lord, and
> forced them to offer up sacrifices unto idols; the second time in the days
> of...; and the third time in the days of Herod, when Jerusalem was

destroyed. Because of this the Jews were greatly grieved, for they had no trustworthy table of the succession of the generations of their fathers. And they toiled eagerly that they might obtain the truth, but they were unable to do so.

'I, however,' says the author, 'possess the knowledge of the correct genealogy, and will show the truth to everyman.' When the children of Israel went up from Babylon:

Zerubbabel begot Abiud by Malkath, the daughter of Ezra the scribe. Abiud took to wife Zakhyath, the daughter of Joshua, the son of Yozadak, the priest, and begot by her Eliakim. Eliakim took to wife Halabh, the daughter of Dornîbh, and begot by her Azor. Azor took to wife Yalpath, the daughter of Hazor, and begot by her Zadok. Zadok took to wife Kaltin, the daughter of Dornîbh, and begot by her Akhin. Akhin took to wife Heskath, the daughter of Ta`il, and begot by her Eliud. Eliud took to wife Beshtin, the daughter of Hasal, and begot by her Eleazar. Eleazar took to wife Dibath, the daughter of Tolah, and begot by her Matthan. Matthan took to wife Sebhrath, the daughter of Phinehas, and begot by her two sons at one conception, Jacob and Yonakhir.

Jacob took to wife Hadbhith, the daughter of Eleazur, and begot by her Joseph, the betrothed of Mary. Yonakhir took Dina, the daughter of Pakodh, and begot by her Mary, of whom was born the Christ.

Returning to the considerably earlier *protoevangelium*, it is fascinating that this apocryphal text illuminates the key word in Luke, when Mary calls herself a 'handmaid' (female slave) to the Temple of the Lord. Has the author picked up on this word and simply elaborated, or is there a source of real history common to both? Either way, there is a sense of authenticity that comes over in the priestly setting of Mary's family. The loss of that setting with the fall of Jerusalem in AD 70 must substantially account for the obscurity of Jesus's family in the next century.

The Syriac version has Mary still at home aged ten, when she acquires a baby sister called Paroghitha. Aged 12, Mary joins 7 other virgins to be entrusted to the care of an elderly priest called Zadok and his wife Sham'i. Mary was called the daughter of Zadok 'according to the law of the Lord, but she was rightly and strictly the daughter of Yonakhir by promise'. Presumably, Mary was adopted by a Zadokite priest and lived with him and his wife, for we are told that Yonakhir and Hanna died when Mary was 12. Sham'i, Mary's stepmother, died when she was 14.

The high priest, named as Zacharias, father of John the Baptist, is advised to enquire of the Lord as to her getting married now her step-mother has died and she is an adolescent. Zacharias enters the Holy of Holies where an angel tells him to assemble 'the widowers of the people' whereupon the Lord would give a sign of the man to marry her. The sign is a dove that comes out of Joseph's staff and lands upon his head. The Syriac version reduces such miraculous elements. The match-making meeting is ordered by the angel, but it is a meeting of men belonging to the royal House of David. The dove is a Temple dove. It alights on Joseph's rod, then his head. Joseph is considered right in any case, for he and Mary were 'each the child of the other's uncle'. Joseph objects because he is old and his wife is alsready the mother of sons and daughters. His wife's name is given as Mary; her sons were Jacob (James) and Jose (Joseph). In the Syriac, this other Mary seems to be alive, but in the Greek he is a widower, while his second son is Samuel, sometimes corrected to Joses or to Simon. Surely we see here an apocryphal writer trying to get round the 'other Marys' we have seen associated with Jesus's brothers in the synoptic gospels and in John. Mary's virginity is important to the work.

Both Greek and Syriac texts see Joseph's objections overcome. He accepts charge of his little cousin and takes her to his home in Jerusalem or Bethlehem: Judea anyway. In the Syriac, he was building a house in Bethlehem. This version implies that Mary becomes a ward of Joseph's wife Mary, and is given status of a wife to protect her name when a child is conceived. Such a picture may be historically valid. In this picture, James took the lead in the Jerusalem assembly because he was older than Jesus, more conservative too. Perhaps his mother was Mary, Joseph's first wife, the *other Mary*, mother of James and Joses who sees the Crucifixion from afar in Matthew's gospel, is present at Jesus's burial in Mark, and is among the resurrection witnesses in Mark and Luke. Alternatively, this is all tortuous myth-making to preserve the virgin birth story, and is little more than wishful thinking. If so, belief in Jesus's mother's unique maternal status seems ingrained in very early strata of Christian mythology and lore. However, Mark chapter six's basic account of Jesus's brothers contains no caveat of their being half-brothers or coming from 'another Mary' or being anything other than straight brothers of Jesus. On the other hand, if Jesus's mother was related closely to their father Joseph, other than by marriage, perhaps Mark may have thought his audience already understood that Jesus's brothers were so in a special sense, or, Mark simply knew no better – and had no cause to know any different – and accepted that Jesus's brothers and sisters were as he presented them since that is how he received his information.

This is one of those thorny problems that arises when we are asked to compare the credibility of an apocryphal with a canonical source. As a rule of thumb, we should favour the earliest source, but in truth, we cannot be certain on the issue, since the earliest sources also contain anomalies and ambiguities. One thing is certain, both this infancy gospel and the canonical gospels accept that Jesus belonged to the same family as his brothers! It should be added that Matthew's gospel does not favour Mary's *perpetual* virginity, and it is arguable that it is *this* doctrine that the complex picture of the infancy gospel is designed to support. It is nonetheless possible that some of Jesus's brothers came from a previous marriage of Joseph, and some or one arrived *after* Jesus's birth. Perhaps the family kept the precise fatherhood of Mary and Joseph's children a general secret, a family affair. Matthew already maintains that Joseph had to protect Mary from the possible scandal of being an unmarried pregnant girl (the *protoevangelium* says the Temple virgin was 16). In this regard we must look again at the ordinances for priests laid down in Ezekiel 44:22:

> Neither shall they take for their wives a widow, *nor her that is put away* [my italics]: but they shall take maidens of the seed of the house of Israel, or a widow that had a priest before.

If Joseph was a priest, which would fit the *protoevangelium* picture perfectly, he knew it was forbidden to take for wife a girl who was already pregnant. *Something* scandalous had occurred. Whatever it was, the 'virgin' Mary accepted the facts as God's will and pleased the system to which she was enslaved.

We might be disposed to accept the simple picture that Mary told Joseph that her child had no earthly father, was a gift of God and that he could either accept the fact or not. One may presume that relations between temple priests and temple slave girls were not always straightforward; marriages among such families would already carry a great deal of religious and mythological baggage. If barrenness was a curse of God, pregnancy was surely a blessing. If readers of gospels could believe in Mary's unique blessing, then we must allow that Joseph could have accepted the possibility of such a miracle also. As a man subject to divine dreams, he must have been a *believer* in the sincerest sense. Only Jesus's mother, we might say, knew the absolute truth, and, if we dare to allow in this leaden age the possibility of a miracle, Mary may not have been entirely sure of what happened herself. She was a slave to the Lord and did as she was told. How much sex education did 16-year-old girls get in those days?

We can be certain of this: there was confusion on the issue in the 1st century. Possibly, James, called by Paul and the Church Fathers 'the brother of the Lord' knew the full story, and may have told someone at some time. The lack of evidence for such disclosure suggests something has been lost, or become garbled in the losing, or deliberately suppressed at some time, or remained a secret of the missing family.

In the infancy narrative, Joseph is not presented as a holy fool; he knows the facts of life:

> Now it was the sixth month with her, and behold Joseph came from his building, and he entered into his house and found her great with child. And he smote his face, and cast himself down upon the ground on sackcloth and wept bitterly, saying: With what countenance shall I look unto the Lord my God? and what prayer shall I make concerning

this maiden? for I received her out of the temple of the Lord my God a virgin, and have not kept her safe. Who is he that hath ensnared me? Who hath done this evil in mine house and hath defiled the virgin? Is not the story of Adam repeated in me? for as at the hour of his giving thanks the serpent came and found Eve alone and deceived her, so hath it befallen me also. And Joseph arose from off the sackcloth and called Mary and said unto her O thou that wast cared for by God, why hast thou done this? thou hast forgotten the Lord thy God. Why hast thou humbled thy soul, thou that wast nourished up in the Holy of Holies and didst receive food at the hand of an angel? But she wept bitterly, saying: I am pure and I know not a man. And Joseph said unto her: Whence then is that which is in thy womb? and she said: As the Lord my God liveth, I know not whence it is come unto me.

And Joseph was sore afraid and ceased from speaking unto her [or left her alone], and pondered what he should do with her. And Joseph said: If I hide her sin, I shall be found fighting against the law of the Lord: and if I manifest her unto the children of Israel, I fear lest that which is in her be the seed of an angel, and I shall be found delivering up innocent blood to the judgement of death. What then shall I do? I will let her go from me privily. And the night came upon him. And behold an angel of the Lord appeared unto him in a dream, saying: Fear not this child, for that which is in her is of the Holy Ghost, and she shall bear a son and thou shalt call his name Jesus, for he shall save his people from their sins. And Joseph arose from sleep and glorified the God of Israel which had shown this favour unto her: and he watched over her.

Mary's condition soon becomes obvious to the circle of the high priest. 'Annas the scribe' presumes Joseph has consummated the marriage without the proper formalities. Mary and Joseph are made to drink the bitter water prescribed for a suspected adulteress in Numbers 5:26. They go for a walk in the hill country and return in good heart: *prima facie* evidence for their innocence: 'And the priest said: If the Lord God hath not made your sin manifest, neither do I condemn you. And he let them go. And Joseph took

Mary and departed unto his house rejoicing, and glorifying the God of Israel.'

That virginity is a key issue for the author of the infancy gospel is plain. When Mary's time to be delivered comes, Joseph finds a cave outside Bethlehem. In the Greek version, Joseph experiences time stopping still; eternity has entered the world, the laws of nature momentarily suspended:

> Now I Joseph was walking, and I walked not. And I looked up to the air and saw the air in amazement. And I looked up unto the pole of the heaven and saw it standing still, and the fowls of the heaven without motion. And I looked upon the earth and saw a dish set, and workmen lying by it, and their hands were in the dish: and they that were chewing chewed not, and they that were lifting the food lifted it not, and they that put it to their mouth put it not thereto, but the faces of all of them were looking upward. And behold there were sheep being driven, and they went not forward but stood still; and the shepherd lifted his hand to smite them with his staff, and his hand remained up. And I looked upon the stream of the river and saw the mouths of the kids upon the water and they drank not. And of a sudden all things moved onward in their course.

A midwife appears:

> And I said to her: It is Mary that was nurtured up in the temple of the Lord: and I received her to wife by lot: and she is not my wife, but she hath conception by the Holy Ghost. And the midwife said unto him: Is this the truth? And Joseph said unto her: Come hither and see. And the midwife went with him.

The midwife examines Mary after the birth; she is still a virgin. That covers the forensic angle.

The concluding lines of the *protoevangelium* mark it out as classic apocrypha:

> Now I, James, which wrote this history in Jerusalem, when there arose
> a tumult when Herod died, withdrew myself into the wilderness until
> the tumult ceased in Jerusalem. Glorifying the Lord God which gave
> me the gift, and the wisdom to write this history. And grace shall be
> with those that fear our Lord Jesus Christ: to whom be glory for ever
> and ever. Amen.

No, it can hardly have been written by James, long dead, and yet is there not
something in this last echo of the tumult around Archelaus's succession we
explored in chapter two? This James, like the New Covenanters of the Dead Sea
Scrolls, 'withdrew into the wilderness'. Is this what happened to the family of
Jesus after the destruction of Jerusalem?

The infancy gospel's close weaving of apparent history with romance made a
great impact. It was especially dear to people who rightly felt the need to give
consideration to the reality of a family about Jesus, with feelings and attach-
ments and griefs and deep hopes. Although apocryphal, it was read at the feasts
of Mary by the Copts, Syrians, Greeks and Arabians. It was largely shunned in
the Roman Church until Jacobus de Voragine's *Golden Legend* appeared in
Europe in the 13th century, whereafter St Anne became a much loved saint,
integral to religious iconography across the Catholic continent. Without the
protoevangelium we should never have seen Leonardo da Vinci's great paintings
and drawings depicting Anne with the Holy Family.

The *Golden Legend* account of St Anne was built on apocryphal material
and the anomalies of the canonical gospels. It asserted that St Anne was not
married once, as was held in the patristic period by such as St John
Damascene, but that Anne was married three times, first to Joachim, then to
Clopas, and finally to a man named Solomas. Each marriage produced one
daughter: Mary, mother of Jesus, Mary of Clopas, and Mary Salomae, respectively. The sister of Saint Anne was named as Sobe who was the mother of St
Elizabeth. The *Golden Legend* was extremely popular, attesting to people's
need for Jesus to be fully humanized, someone to be involved with through the

common affections, needs and profound realities of family.

Medieval speculation concerning the 'other Marys' fuelled legends, each attempting to solve the riddles of the Marys in the canonical record, featuring these obscure personalities in relation to venerated sites. Since practically nothing was known about them, mythology abounded as many a 'mystery' is born in a void of knowledge. There is no doubt that it was the women's humanity and their mystery combined which attracted interest. Thus we find in the lore of Occitania a medieval legend of three Marys cut adrift in a boat from their homeland in Palestine, arriving miraculously off the Provençal coast. The village of what is now Saintes-Maries-de-la-Mer, the 'Saint Marys of the Sea', has benefited from this legendary association with Mary, 'wife of Alphaeus', mother of James and Jose, Mary Salome, and Mary of Clopas. The mother of James has an Egyptian servant, Sarah, venerated by gypsies. It is odd how folklore and grassroots mystical legends have instinctively gone for the rare, apocryphal and semi-apocryphal characters. I think it is their combination of humanity and mystery-magic: some intuition perhaps that truth is always at a distance from the official presentation which so often lacks the imagination and the wonder proper to a child of God.

Apocryphal relationships between the Marys fuelled what is perhaps best called an apocryphal patristic history, attributed to the Church Father Papias (c.AD 60–135). Eusebius, Bishop of Caesarea identified Papias, whom he thought lacking in intellectual skills, as Bishop of Hierapolis, now Pamukkale, in Turkey. Papias is best known for having memorized the testimony of a 'presbyter John' who had himself heard at least one authentic apostle among ancient elders. Papias also mentioned in his 'five books' a miracle relating to Justus, surnamed Barsabbas. Eisenman would have Luke's 'Joseph Barsabbas, surnamed Justus' as a garbling of the name of James the Just.

Papias reported a curious story from 1st-century elders that Justus swallowed a deadly poison, and received no harm, on account of the grace of the Lord. It is to Papias we also owe the information that Mark's gospel relied on the memory of Simon Peter for its content. Either Papias is trustworthy or he is not. Besides, these stories have better provenance than what is to follow, an apocryphal 'Papian' source that is particularly relevant to our story because it has been used by Robert Eisenman for the contention that the name Cleophas is interchangeable as a name with Alphaeus. This titbit allows Eisenman to identify the canonical disciple 'James the son of Alphaeus', with Jesus's kin (the 'Cleophas' 'Clopas' or 'Klopa' Mary-connection).

This is the alleged fragment of Papias's work containing the identification:

> (1.) Mary the mother of the Lord; (2.) Mary the wife of Cleophas or Alphæus, who was the mother of James the bishop and apostle, and of Simon and Thaddeus, and of one Joseph; (3.) Mary Salome, wife of Zebedee, mother of John the evangelist and James; (4.) Mary Magdalene. These four are found in the Gospel. James and Judas and Joseph were sons of an aunt (2) of the Lord's. James also and John were sons of another aunt (3) of the Lord's. Mary (2), mother of James the Less and Joseph, wife of Alphæus was the sister of Mary the mother of the Lord, whom John names of Cleophas, either from her father or from the family of the clan, or for some other reason. Mary Salome (3) is called Salome either from her husband or her village. Some affirm that she is the same as Mary of Cleophas, because she had two husbands.

This 'Fragment Ten' of Papias's testimonies, was found by a scholar called Grabe in a Bodleian Library manuscript (a copy is also to be found at Cambridge). On the margin was inscribed 'Papia'. Westcott believed it formed part of a dictionary by a medieval 'Papias'. Its medieval provenance is supported by the fact that the words 'Maria is called Illuminatrix, or Star of the Sea' have been added to the text. This symbolism used with respect to Mary is medieval; it appears in the *Golden Legend* in the story of Mary Magdalene. Mary is the morning star, Venus, Love, herald of the dawn, reflected in nature, whose number is eight. The Papian fragment seems to me more fitted to explain the plethora of different Marys appearing in medieval apocryphal romance than an authentic text. If Eisenman wants it to prove Alphaeus and Cleophas are interchangeable, then by that token he must accept that the same patristic authority regarded Barsabbas Justus as the name of a real personality.

It is difficult to know whether we should call The Gospel according to the Hebrews an apocryphal gospel since so very little of it remains. It is quoted by a number of Church Fathers with Egyptian, and in particular, Alexandrian associations: Clement of Alexandria, his co-student Didymus the Blind, Origen and Jerome all had recourse to a work that seems to have appeared in the first half of the 2nd century, intended for Jewish Christians active in the city. As far as can be known, the gospel contained an independent oral tradition of the key events of Jesus's life.

Most notable in the surviving extracts is the obvious respect accorded James, the brother of the Lord. The seven gospel fragments reflect openness to the Gnostic philosophy of religion that would flourish in Alexandria, Syria and Rome in the mid 2nd century and beyond. In a gospel fragment employed by Origen in his commentary on John (2:12), we learn that the Holy Spirit is regarded by Jesus as his 'mother'. Didymus the Blind drew from the gospel of the Hebrews the idea that Levi is not Matthew as in Luke's gospel, but was instead Matthias 'the one who replaced Judas, who is the same as Levi, known by two names'. This is a rare testimony to the reality of Matthias within a gospel that understood and respected the first bishop of Jerusalem. Indeed, a unique story about James, the brother of the Lord, was recorded in fragment 5 from the gospel 'which the Nazareans are accustomed to read' by Jerome in his *Illustrious Men*, (2):

> The Gospel that is called 'according to the Hebrews', which I have recently translated into both Greek and Latin, a Gospel that Origen frequently used, records the following after the Saviour's resurrection: 'But when the Lord had given the linen cloth to the servant of the priest, he went and appeared to James. For James had taken a vow not to eat bread from the time he drank the cup of the Lord until he should see him raised from among those who sleep.' And soon after this it says, 'The Lord said, 'Bring a table and bread.'' And immediately it continues, 'He took the bread and blessed it, broke it, gave it to James the Just,

and said to him, 'My brother, eat your bread. For the Son of Man is risen from among those who sleep.'"

James, Bishop of Jerusalem, brother of the Lord, features as a star in another work prized by Jewish Christians. Heresy-hunter Epiphanius writes in his *Panarion* (*c*.AD 400) that this work was cherished by a 'sect' of 'Ebionites', 'the Poor' Jewish Christians of Syria in his time. The work is an apocryphal narrative, a romance or novel, attributed to Clement. 'Clement' is taken to be either the bishop of Rome at the beginning of the 2nd century, or Domitian's cousin Titus Flavius Clemens, a member of the imperial household.

The novel has come down to us in two main forms, *The Clementine Homilies*, consisting of 20 books in Greek, and the *Clementine Recognitions*, a Latin translation made by Rufinus before his death in 410. The versions often coincide word for word and are probably based on a lost primary text. Such a text may be that which first appears to history in the following writing of Eusebius, Bishop of Caesarea in AD 325: 'And now some only the other day have brought forward other wordy and lengthy compositions as being Clement's, containing dialogues of Peter and Appion, of which there is absolutely no mention in the ancients.' (*Ecclesiastical History*, Book III:38) Right at the composition's genesis, sharp-eyed Eusebius was on the case. The *Homilies* and *Recognitions* were fiction.

The narrative, nonetheless, is fascinating. It purports to contain Clement's reminiscences from a youth spent questing for spiritual truth. Thus, in Alexandria, Clement comes upon Paul's co-missionary Barnabas, and witnesses the discourse of Peter, one of the two heroes of the work. The other hero of the work, arguably the more important, is James, the brother of the Lord, who is presented as one exercising primacy over the whole Church. This we should perhaps expect from a text emanating from the 4th-century Syro-Phoenician coast, in the midst of the Arian Controversy (*Was Jesus divine?*). Arius and the Jewish Christian churches were content with Jesus being the Son of God, the human Messiah, divine only insofar as all creatures of the Father may be called so who heed His will perfectly and live in the grace of His Holy Spirit. As far as the flesh went, Jesus was 100 per cent human. James's position on this issue was their defence. James, the 'bulwark' of the Church did not preach that Jesus was 'of the same substance of the Father' as regards his divinity, as Athanasius and Rome now pronounced. Thus the *Clementine Homilies* begin with a letter from Peter to Jesus's brother, Peter's superior in Jerusalem:

> Peter to James, the lord and bishop of the holy Church, under the Father of all, through Jesus Christ, wishes peace always.
>
> Knowing, my brother, your eager desire after that which is for the advantage of us all, I beg and beseech you not to communicate to any one of the Gentiles the books of my preachings which I sent to you, nor to any one of our own tribe before trial; but if any one has been proved and found worthy, then to commit them to him, after the manner in which Moses delivered his books to the Seventy who succeeded to his chair. Wherefore also the fruit of that caution appears even till now. For his countrymen keep the same rule of monarchy and polity everywhere, being unable in any way to think otherwise, or to be led out of the way of the much-indicating Scriptures. For, according to the rule delivered to them, they endeavour to correct the discordances of the Scriptures, if any one, haply not knowing the traditions, is confounded at the various utterances of the prophets. Wherefore they charge no one to teach, unless he has first learned how the Scriptures must be used. And thus they have amongst them one God, one law, one hope.

The author is here accounting for why the *Homilies* have taken a long time to appear; James was asked to reserve the true doctrine from the inadequate and the unworthy. We then get to the nub of the argument: a powerful insinuation of how *Paul* perverted Peter's – and James's – original doctrines. It is a devastating attack on the alleged perverting-power of Paul's writings, whence, it is inferred, the latest definitions of Jesus as God have found their ammunition:

> In order, therefore, that the like may also happen to those among us as to these Seventy, give the books of my preachings to our brethren,

with the like mystery of initiation, that they may indoctrinate those who wish to take part in teaching; for if it be not so done, our word of truth will be rent into many opinions. And this I know, not as being a prophet, but as already seeing the beginning of this very evil. For some from among the Gentiles have rejected my legal preaching, attaching themselves to certain lawless and trifling preaching of the man who is my enemy. And these things some have attempted while I am still alive, to transform my words by certain various interpretations, in order to the dissolution of the law; as though I also myself were of such a mind, but did not freely proclaim it, which God forbid! For such a thing were to act in opposition to the law of God which was spoken by Moses, and was borne witness to by our Lord in respect of its eternal continuance; for thus he spoke: 'The heavens and the earth shall pass away, but one jot or one tittle shall in no wise pass from the law.' [Matthew 5:18; loose quotation] And this He has said, that all things might come to pass. But these men, professing, I know not how, to know my mind, undertake to explain my words, which they have heard of me, more intelligently than I who spoke them, telling their catechumens that this is my meaning, which indeed I never thought of. But if, while I am still alive, they dare thus to misrepresent me, how much more will those who shall come after me dare to do so!

(Chapter Two, *Homilies*)

Paul is undoubtedly the villain of the piece. Whether the *named* villain, the magician and arguably proto-Gnostic Simon Magus, is intended as a stand-in for the unnamed Paul in all cases is uncertain. Certainly, Simon Magus with his magic and bedevilments and cunning is used to represent at times the Neoplatonic, pagan-miraculous backlash against imperial Christianity backed by Constantine's successor Julian the Apostate, but Simon also seems to stand for the earlier effect of Paul on the Lord's teaching. So strong is this identification in fact that F C Baur, the founder of the early 19th-century 'Tübingen school' of theology, became convinced that the Clementine literature preserved authentic facts of Christian origins: Paul was an apostate from an original Jewish, Torah-loving gospel. Baur dated the work in the early 2nd century. Demolished by 1850, Baur's view has recently been revived on a fresh basis through the works of Robert Eisenman, for whom the Clementine material is a key element in his hypotheses concerning Christian origins. Eisenman pays particular attention to a passage where James the brother of the Lord is physically attacked, relating it to James's eventual death in AD 62 at the hands of the Herodian High Priest Ananus.

Eisenman draws attention to a strong expression in the *Recognitions*: 'the true Prophet'. He relates the expression to analogous words from the sectarian texts of the Dead Sea Scrolls. The true Prophet is the righteous one, the 'Zaddik', the 'standing one'; Jesus is presented as the true Prophet by Peter in the *Recognitions* and in the *Homilies*; Eisenman considers the soubriquet most appropriate for James the Righteous, the Zadokite. In the *Recognitions* (1.22–74), Peter shows how the Old Testament was fulfilled in the coming of the 'true Prophet'. He gives an account of the true Prophet's rejection, passion and resurrection, and how this was to be preached to the Gentiles. The preaching is consistent with the skills and divine knowledge of the 'true Prophet', consistent in Peter, consistent in Jesus, and consistent in James.

According to the *Recognitions*, the Church at Jerusalem had been governed by James for a week of years before the apostles returned from their mission-travels to give James an account of themselves. High Priest Caiphas then asks the apostles if Jesus was the Christ. The apostles show how the views of the Sadducees, Samaritans, Scribes, Pharisees, disciples of John, and Caiphas himself, have been successively quashed by them. Peter then foretells the destruction of the Temple. This prophecy enrages the priests, who are only subdued by a speech from Rabbi Gamaliel. James then preaches for seven days. At the very point when the people are persuaded and about to be baptized, an unnamed *enemy* excites them against James. James is thrown down the steps of the Temple and left for dead. This dramatic scene may be an allegorical account of Paul interfering with the preaching of the proto-Church, of how Paul cast aspersions on James, calling his ideas 'weak', provoking riots in the Temple, as Acts relates, or rather, not *entirely* as Acts relates; Paul was not the *victim*, but the trouble-maker, relying on Roman and Herodian forces to protect him.

Eisenman suggests that the *Recognitions* account of the man-handling and shameful attack on James has been transformed by Luke into his account in Acts where 'Stephanos' (meaning 'crown') is stoned to death for declaring the Temple will be destroyed. Luke describes Saul (Paul), the well-known and self-confessed *persecutor* of Jesus's followers, standing by holding the clothes of the stoners: 'And the witnesses put down their clothes at the feet of a young man called Saul. And they stoned Stephen as he was praying [...] and Saul consented to putting him to death.' (Acts 7:58–8:1).

The picture is further enriched when we realize that in patristic tradition, the issue of who witnessed the murder of James the brother of the Lord, who also prayed as he was stoned for condemning the Temple to ruin, varies in an intriguing manner. Epiphanius (*c*.400) sees the witness to James's stoning as Jesus's cousin, Simon bar Cleophas. In the much earlier writing of Church historian Hegesippus (fl. AD 165–175), the witness is a 'Rechabite' priest, though, as we shall see, the 'Rechabite' and the cousin could have been identical. If, as Eisenman maintains then, that Luke in Acts has 'replaced' an 'extremely embarrassing, actual physical assault by Paul on James' (Eisenman, p.444), as reflected in the considerably later *Clementine Recognitions*, with an *inverted*, substitute account of Stephen winning the martyr's 'crown', then he has also replaced the presence of Jesus's cousin, Simon bar Cleophas, with the pseudo-Clementine 'enemy', that is, Saul. This is a powerful charge, a singular instance of how Jesus's real family has gone 'missing' as a deliberate result of conflicts in the early Church.

Eisenman only reflects a well-established principle in treating Acts as a heavily biased, pro-Pauline production, but in seeing its content as reflecting a concealed anti-Jamesian position, it goes a step further than most theologians would permit or like. But Eisenman's argument is a very good one. Even the name 'Stephen' could easily have been introduced from Paul's first letter to the Corinthians (I Cor.1:16; 16:15). Paul writes: 'I beseech you, brethren, (ye know the house of Stephanas, that it is the firstfruits of Achaia, and that they have addicted themselves to the ministry of the saints).' In Acts 7:51, 'Stephen' even uses a distinctly Pauline phrase to condemn the high priest and his supporters: 'Ye stiffnecked and uncircumcised in heart and ears'. This jibe is tantamount to comparing, or lumping-in, Jesus's saintly brother with his own high-priestly murderer! When Paul rejects James's call for the circumcision of the Gentile if they would join the Church (for example, Galatians 2:12), Paul argues that the 'circumcision of the heart' is what counts. In Acts, 'Stephen', probably a Gentile, gives the Pauline position to the high priest, arguably replacing a more factual Jamesian sermon to the high priest that eventually got him killed in AD 62. It was, after all, Paul who insisted on bringing uncircumcised Gentile followers into the Temple precincts, outraging James and the Jerusalem Church (Acts 21:18;28), and causing a riot which was quelled only through the assistance of Roman soldiers and centurions.

Eisenman sees Paul's role in this victimization of James as precisely consistent with the ravings of the 'Spouter' or 'Liar', the enemy of the 'Teacher of Righteousness', in the remarkably apposite Dead Sea Scrolls *pesherim* (commentaries), on the prophets Nahum and Habbakuk. However, it may simply be a case of spiritual history repeating itself, since the issues dividing the righteous from the worldly compromisers remain fundamentally the same throughout the period: law or corruption. All you need is a wicked priest and a teacher of righteousness and all the prophetic quotations work again; there were numerous representatives of both types of figure throughout the post-Maccabean era. Geza Vermes's dating analysis of the 'Qumran' material seems to fit the documents' scattered internal historical references better than hazarding a date chiefly on ideological grounds.

Anyhow, according to the *Recognitions*, James survives this particular attack, as the 'Poor' outlived their 1st-century opponents. In the apocryphal *Recognitions*, James is carried to Jericho, with 5,000 disciples. Recovering, he sends Peter to Caesarea to refute 'Simon' (Magus). He is welcomed by Zacchaeus, who relates Simon's doings to him. Perhaps thinking the story inconsistent with Acts, the author of the pseudo-Clementine *Homilies* omitted it. The *Recognitions* were probably written by a clever person who perceived an inside story going on in Acts that had been twisted by its biased author. Whether the Clementine novelist had better history to go on is unknown. The independence of the author's point of view may preclude any dependence on Luke's Acts of the Apostles. James's direct persecution by Saul may be a tradition rooted in fact; it is anyhow canonically established that before his conversion, Saul persecuted unto death Jesus's followers. The issue Eisenman raises is whether his opposition to Jesus's brother was so intense as to provoke James's death, *after* his conversion.

The idea that Paul is the figure intended by the pseudo-Clementine 'Simon Magus' has much to commend it. However, passages relating Simon's peculiar doctrines, for example that God did not create the heavens and the earth, seem to be genuinely Simonian. They are certainly not Pauline, but it may be that the author was being super-subtle, leaving the underlying identification to the sense of the reader. Simon Magus was an early perverter of the Lord's teaching; so was Paul, according to the writer. Furthermore, a staple of Simonian and related heresies was that the God of the *law*, was an inferior being to the remote 'Father' of Jesus. A Jewish Christian would see anti-legal, radical 'Gnosticism' as being the misbegotten child of a fundamental attack on the law first given literary form by Paul. Paul himself is not mentioned in the Clementine novel. This probably means the author wished he had never lived.

The basic situation in the pseudo-Clementine novel is that Peter and James possess the words of the 'true Prophet' and the sense to understand them; someone, 'Simon', has perverted the truth. Anti-Pauline stress is clear from a passage in the *Homilies* (Book II, 17) where the doctrine of double-opposites or *syzygy* is enunciated: first darkness, then light; first Ishmael, then Isaac, the inheritor; first foolish Esau then godly Jacob; first Aaron, priest, then Moses, Law-giver; first Antichrist, then the actual Christ. In this scheme, the better follows the shadowy forerunner:

> Following up this disposition it would be possible to recognise where Simon belongs, who at first and before me went to the Gentiles [as Paul did], and where I belong, I who came after him and followed him as the light follows darkness, knowledge ignorance, and healing sickness. Thus then, as the true prophet has said, a false gospel must first come from an imposter and only then, after the destruction of the holy place,

can a true gospel be sent forth for the correction of the sects that are to come.

First Paul went to the Gentiles, then Peter, backed by James. Now that Jerusalem is destroyed, the true doctrine can at last be brought to the world: after the chaos, the revelation.

If the Jewish Christians, and, possibly, the descendants of Jesus's family, believed that the strife of the 4th century in the Church would lead to the glorious revelation of their true doctrine, they were mistaken. The very reticence in the Clementine novel in referring directly to Paul suggests the sheer power his name had accrued by this time. His name had become an authority. Very soon, the Ebionites would be branded as heretics. They rejected a true apostle!

How much history underlies these very late Clementine writings is an issue that is all too influenced by the preconceptions of the enquirer. They are good ammunition if you want to assert the anti-Pauline polemic, but as evidence, it must be stated that they belong to a world far-off from the original period, that their stories are fictional, that they have been constructed within the setting of doctrinal controversies unheard of in the 1st century, and that the Clementine works were understood to be propaganda at their inception. What we have left is a sense of grievance among Jewish Christians that their point of view was being bulldozed by the political weight of Rome, and that their traditions – which included the primacy of Jesus's brother, James – should have been accorded primary respect. Furthermore, one must face the fact that the Clementine material makes a case of no essential polemical interest to Eisenman, and yet is clearly essential to the text. Peter is *theirs*; he is with the *Poor* and does not belong to Rome: Roman primacy is a fallacy, a poor replica of the true holy temple in the Promised Land. Peter and James were one in doctrine, but Peter heeded James. If you want authority, you go to the believing family of Jesus, his own, who did not reject him, as the western Church was in fact doing, by allowing the perversion of the spiritual fountain of truth and holiness.

The Brother in Secret

We have seen that the pseudo-Clementine literature defends Jewish Christianity against the institutional and doctrinal incursions of the western Church in the 3rd and 4th centuries by claiming the special favour of James, the brother of the Lord, and of Peter. They – the Jewish Christians – not Paul, held the true doctrine. Curiously, the claim to Peter and James's special favour was also used to assert the truth of so-called 'heretical' Gnostic principles, in several important Gnostic manuscripts. What are these Gnostic manuscripts and what do they have to tell us about Jesus's family?

In 1945, an Arab peasant called Muhammad Ali al-Samman from the village of al Qasr, near Nag Hammadi in Upper Egypt chanced, with his brothers, upon a cache of 52 previously unknown texts, bound into books called codices. Unpublished in their entirety until 1977, this collection is now known as the Nag Hammadi Library, sometimes 'The Gnostic Gospels'. While written down *c*.AD 300–67, some of the compositions derive from the 2nd century and some parts, such as the Gospel of Thomas, may be even earlier. Not all of the works 'sing from the same hymn-sheet', but the theme held in common by the majority of the books is that the ultimate gift of Jesus is *gnosis*. Gnosis, or spiritual *knowledge*, comes to those who through grace, faith, wisdom and spiritual insight have looked beyond the 'corrupt' material world for the source of law, of love, and of life. Gnosis is salvation from the world, its sign: a new mind. Receiving 'knowledge' means awakening to the relative, transitory nature of the world, awakening to its imprisoning capacity, awakening to the meaning of the fatality of the body and of nature, and awakening to the true parents of that prize secreted within the person, the living spirit of God. Note that word 'parents' or 'true parents'. The Gnostic is one who has found, and who has *been found*.

The Gnostic is one who has come to know the Father, reflected as the Christ *in himself*. This knowledge is the hidden pearl for those lost in the world, a pearl hidden from the 'dead' of the world that, once found, reawakens the memory of the home of the spirit, whence the 'one who knows himself' originally came. This process involves imitation of the mercurial guide of souls who, according to John, said: 'No one comes to the Father except through me' and 'I and my Father are one'. Reunion with divinity is the aim; *knowledge* the means. Coming into the world is coming into unconsciousness. Ultimate salvation is super-consciousness, knowing God the Father in oneself, ascending to the Father through knowledge and selfless love of the Father; Jesus charted the path.

Gnosis was called by Clement of Alexandria (*c*.AD 150–215) the *fulfilment* of faith, realizing that in the the secret, unknown *Self*, the Gnostic is one with the Father; the fruit of that union: love. This knowledge Jesus brought to the world from a higher level of existence: this, according to those nicknamed 'Gnostics' was the ultimate and essential purpose of Jesus's being in the world, the reason why he consciously suffered this world, this 'prison of the soul'. He came to shake the drunk and wake the dreamer. In practice, he was a kind of supreme '*gnana* (knowledge) yogi', teaching union or reunion with God through spiritual knowledge. Man was originally made not on earth according to time and space, but in eternity, in the image of God. However, the primal reflection had been obscured and distorted by attachment to the flux of the cosmos, the life of the senses without enlightenment. Man had fallen into the world, in love with his material reflection, his ego, not his authentic spiritual being.

Man's ordinary self or ego is bound to the world, a false identity. His True Self comes to him from above as an angel. When the false self surrenders to the Light from above, the Gnostic experiences super-consciousness, obliteration of the ego bound by time and space, and union with the previously unknown

'Father'. This interior situation or psychic and spiritual drama is projected in Gnostic parables or myths onto the cosmos beyond. Thus, the 'Lord of this World', the Demiurge or angel of time and space, the self-proclaiming Pantocrator of the cosmos, functions as false self, a 'jealous god' or ego, above whom, *although the false god knows it not*, is the unknowable Father of incalculable and utterly unlimited spiritual depth. The 'God' of the unenlightened is basically nothing more than the Ego of the Cosmos, the 'Big I AM', always angry and thundering on about himself and how there's nothing bigger than himself: a mighty being for sure whose very 'size' has reduced Man to earthbound obeisance and fear and self-loathing. The big Demiurge has an almighty 'I, ME' complex. Gnostics were encouraged to laugh at this image, to see it as the duplicitous Demon or chief archon, whose rule is reflected on earth in the behaviour of the power-hungry: the politicos, the emperors and the rich, the materialist merchants who eat men and spit out their families as slaves, bond-servants, unfit.

The Gnostics' stance, parodied and grossly misrepresented, simply horrified their enemies. *How could they? How dare they?* They must be mad! Heretics in the grip of the Devil! Outraged, Bishop Irenaeus in c.AD 180 called Gnostics people dwelling in an abyss of madness and blasphemy. Of course, it is possible that some 'Gnostics' took their teachers' myths of false gods and true angels too literally, who can say? But those myths were based on a systematic, in many respects revealing, analysis of certain biblical passages. Their conclusions might appear outrageous, but made pristine sense to those with the gnosis.

Thus, the Gnostic looked at certain passages in the Bible and perceived what we should now call 'neurosis' – if not full-blown *psychosis* – in the alleged 'almighty'. They looked, for example, at the Genesis story of Adam and Eve and saw that the god of Eden was selfish and vindictive, keeping Man to himself on a level with the unconscious animals. The fruit of the tree of knowledge of good and evil was the gnosis, full consciousness, symbolized by the eternal-life-giving serpent, which stands for knowledge. The Gnostics recognized that the offering of knowledge to the first man and woman had been perverted in the Genesis text as a crime, so that through partaking of the knowledge they come not to light, but to the darkness of the material world.

Taking what was properly his, man is sentenced to death for disobedience and woman will know the pain of childbirth. *What kind of God is this?*, asked the Gnostics. This behaviour, quite astonishingly for the period, they perceived as the egoistic 'jealousy' of the neurotic, if I may use the term, God of Eden, in the Gnostics' view a false paradise. The neurotic 'jealous' god took revenge on Man for taking something that the false god himself was ignorant of: higher spiritual knowledge. This was the basis of the Gnostic claim to be 'above the world'. Jesus came from that 'mother' or tree called Barbelo whose roots are not in this world (the material garden), but in the higher world; Jesus came with gnosis, awakening and healing knowledge. Jesus is thus a kind of angel that the lord of this world mistook for something he could destroy on a cross, as the Romans did. Perhaps you can now see why Jung called the Gnostics the first psychologists. Everything he discovered, Jung said, the Gnostics knew already.

Some Gnostics speculated on the question of how, being wholly concerned with pure spirit, the Father in Heaven could also have been responsible for the spiritual ignorance, harshness and fatality of Nature. This ignorance and fatality Gnostics saw revealed in the cosmos's spirit-stifling, soul-blinding hurricanes of whirling matter, ceaseless, imperfect cycles of reproduction and fallen-angelic chorus of vanity and pain. Radical Gnostics assumed the *ignorance* of the natural order was shared by its creator. Thus they came not only to baleful conclusions about the 'Elohim' or 'Gods' of the Hebrew Genesis, but also about the 'jealous God' who had given Moses the negative law: 'Thou shalt not'. Taking a tip from Paul's critique of the law, the radical Gnostics saw the law merely as infant training for the ignorant, inadequate for 'higher education' and, when adhered to slavishly and as an end in itself, a positive evil, preventing the spirit from coming to awareness within the being of the Gnostic, cutting off full consciousness of miraculous, divine identity.

The Gnostic must come through the bonds of law, pierce the shells of the cosmos, to an illimitable freedom of the spirit beyond. In short, the 'God' who kicked Adam and Eve out of Paradise was a *lesser being*, masquerading as the Heavenly Father. This being's law was *derived* from knowledge of something higher, but it lacked the essential spiritual summation, the 'truth of our freedom' as the Gospel of Truth, found at Nag Hammadi, puts it. The Gnostic is advised not to get attached to his roots in the earth; his true family is above.

Gnostic Christians in Egypt and in Syria after the mid to late 2nd century began to identify the episcopacy's growing monopoly of doctrine as nothing less than the manifest work of the ignorant, the blind, those devoted to the limited perceptions of the lesser god, a false god. On the other hand, 'orthodox' bishops, such as Irenaeus of Lyon were themselves scandalized by the notion that the creator of the earth was not the Father God of Jesus. To the orthodox, the creation was a manifestation of divine Wisdom; the heavenly being in Jesus was party to that creation. Seeing their opponents' emphasis on the word *gnosis*, orthodox leaders condemned Gnostic views as heresy and referred contemptuously to the 'gnosis falsely so-called'. The 'Gnostics'' knowledge, declared the orthodox, was *false* knowledge, true knowledge consisting in humble faith in the Lord Jesus Christ, knowledge of his crucifixion, resurrection and ascension to the Father prophesied in the scriptures, followed by and in obedience to His apostles and their successors, the bishops of the Church.

The answer of the Gnostic movement to this was simple: 'On the contrary, bishop. The apostles spoke of gnosis; they (the true apostles) speak for *us*.' Gnosis was a *reserved* insight for those closest to the saviour, revealed directly *after* the Resurrection, and available to persons who had experienced spiritual resurrection in this life. The bishops, they said, were 'dry canals', they did not have the water of life: nourished solely on their inadequate food, the flower of potential gnosis would wither and perish. The Church knew not the secret of spiritual rebirth; in their hands, the seed remained sterile. The orthodox message was mere morality, legality: spiritual incarceration.

It is remarkable that an aspect of this polemic is also to be found in the equally apocryphal Clementine *Homilies* and *Recognitions*. The 'western' Church had, these latter writings implied, suffered under the deficiency of a false and inadequate doctrine, a doctrine alien to that held by Peter and by James, the brother of the Lord. The queer thing though is that while the Nag Hammadi Library was copied down around the same time as the appearance of the Clementine material, their fundamental viewpoints could not, superficially speaking anyway, be more different. The Jewish Christians insisted on keeping the law and on a humane picture of Jesus. Gnostics, by and large, held to a supernatural image of Jesus and a disdain for the law. Could these points of view have briefly accommodated one another in this period, in the face of a common enemy? Did the Gnostics get the 'James and Peter rule' idea from the Jewish Christians, or did the writer of the pseudo-Clementine proto-novel take a tip from aspects of Gnostic propaganda? Was it possible to be a Jewish Christian and a kind of Gnostic as well? Had members of Jesus's family embraced aspects of Gnostic philosophy?

Within the Nag Hammadi collection there exist three works devoted, in their peculiar way, to James, the brother of the Lord. They are the Apocryphon of James, and the First, and Second, Apocalypse of James. These remarkable works are all related. They have been dated to the 3rd century or possibly to the late 2nd century at the earliest. They contain strong themes of coming to gnosis, but, interestingly, have nothing to say directly about radical Gnostic views about the folly of the world's creator or of the vanity of the law. Like the pseudo-Clementine literature, Peter and James are the chosen vessels to reveal the secret gnosis reserved for those fit to receive it. Paul does not appear. Do they have any connection to the missing family of Jesus?

The Lord's first message to James in the First Apocalypse should give us pause:

> See now the completion of my redemption. I have given you a sign
> of these things, James, my brother. For not without reason have I
> called you my brother, although you are not my brother materially.
> And I am not ignorant concerning you; so that when I give you a sign
> – know and hear.

This 'apocalypse', that is to say, the revelation of the hidden, is not interested in James as a member of Jesus's family. The work is concerned with James in two senses: first, James as an authority, as a leader and holder of true doctrine, close to Jesus; second, James as a *type* of the true, would-be redeemed Gnostic: 'my brother', that is, *spiritual* brother, one who is, and who has seen what Jesus is and has seen.

The idea of the authority of James, the Lord's brother, was probably familiar to the author of the Apocalypse of James from at least two sources: Jewish Christianity, prominent in Syria where the apocalypse is thought to have been composed, and the Gospel of Thomas (dated AD 50–140), the most famous 'Gnostic Gospel'.

In logion 12 of the Gospel of Thomas, the disciples ask: "We know that You [Jesus] will depart from us. Who is to be our leader?' Jesus said to them, 'Wherever you are, you are to go to James the righteous, for whose sake heaven and earth came into being."

You are to go to James the righteous… Apart from the primacy given unequivocally to brother James, the meaning of that last phrase is unclear. Did heaven and earth come into being for the sake of 'righteousness' (*zedek*), that is to say, was the world waiting for the revelation of the 'true Prophet', the upright man of righteousness? Was creation's purpose the manifestation of righteousness, or the righteous 'sons of God', or, alternatively, was it that heaven and earth appeared for the sake of James the righteous *himself*? This last interpretation seems a trifle excessive, unless James too had his supporters as a redeemer figure in his own right.

From the Gnostic point of view, James was such a figure. First, James the righteous stands as the perfected Gnostic. This is the radical, revisionist interpretation of the word 'Just' inherent to the work. James is a spiritual role-model: one to identify with. That is to say that while heaven and earth would pass away, the *One who Knows Himself* will stand forever: he is the true, ripe, full fruit of the tension of heaven and earth.

Alternatively, the logion or saying may preserve something authentic of the real relationship between Jesus and his brother. That is, Jesus was enjoying a joke at the expense of his brother's weaknesses: James, the voluble brother – so big for his boots, in fact, that he thought heaven and earth 'were made just for him!' Surely, we have all met people of whom this might be said! It is a homely touch and may lie at the root of this isolated saying. However, we may be sure the saying was not interpreted this way by Gnostic apologists. They would certainly have gone for the former interpretation.

What makes James 'righteous', what makes him 'stand', what makes him a pinnacle or pillar of creation is that Jesus had imparted to him directly his divine gnosis. *This* is what made James his 'brother'; it was not his relationship to his earthly mother, but to his heavenly mother, the divine *Sophia* or Wisdom Tree, and, of course James's relationship to *He who is*. The previous logion (no.11) encapsulates the point: 'This heaven will pass away, and the one above it will pass away. The dead are not alive, and the living will not die.' James becomes a paragon of how to die, how to follow Jesus; how to identify with him.

So, have these Gnostic writings preserved actual information about Jesus's family?

There is no doubt that both the First and Second Apocalypses of James contain passages which show familiarity with stories about what happened in Jerusalem to James, the brother of the Lord.

> James said, 'Rabbi, you have said, 'They will seize me.' But I, what can I do?' He said to me, 'Fear not, James. You too they will seize. But leave Jerusalem. For it is she who always gives the cup of bitterness to the sons of light. She is the dwelling place of a great number of archons. But your redemption will be preserved from them.
>
> (First Apocalypse of James, codex V, 3, p.25)

The 'archons' are the villains of Gnostic mythology. The word *archon* means 'ruler' and may here denote the pro-Herodian high-priesthood of the 1st century, or the power which Gnostics perceived *manifesting* in them: the dark angels who served the 'lord of this world' and who could take over the souls of their unconscious servants. Thus Jesus could say, 'Lord forgive them for they know not what they do'. Unconscious, Jesus's perceived enemies are but tools, puppets and putty, in the hands of the real spiritual enemy, the demon demiurge, ruler of the dark, fallen angels.

Also apparent and perceived, but not real, in some Gnostic literature is Jesus's suffering. When Jesus describes his sufferings to James, he says they were only 'in appearance', not real: 'I am he who was within me.' Death has released *Him*. The people who scourged and crucified him 'existed as a type of the archons', James is told. Jesus was not distressed; he had seen through the show and begged James also to see through the show when *his* time came to be persecuted by the blind:

> James, behold, I shall reveal to you your redemption. When you are seized, and undergo these sufferings, a multitude will arm themselves against you, that they may seize you. And in particular three of them will seize you – they who sit as toll collectors. Not only do they demand toll, but they also take away souls by theft.

> (Apocalypse of James, codex V, 3, p.33)

The story of James's death is used by the Gnostic author to illustrate this point about reality and illusion. James is told that the three who will seize him are mere tools of the archons, 'toll collectors' who will try to hold his soul when the time comes to ascend in spirit to the Father. The world is the Devil's hotel, follows his law, and the Devil takes his charge. This is *meta*-history on a terrifyingly intimate level.

The Second Apocalypse of James purports to be a true record: 'This is the discourse that James the Just spoke in Jerusalem, which Mareim, one of the priests wrote. He had told it to Theuda, the father of the Just One, since he was a relative of his.' Sounds promising. However, as the apocalypse unfolds, we quickly see that this James the Just is himself a Gnostic redeemer figure, a stand-in for his brother in a visionary setting:

> I [am the] first [son] who was begotten.
> He will destroy the dominion of [them] all.
> I am the beloved.

I am the righteous one.
I am the son of [the Father]

I speak even as [I] heard.
I command even as I [received] the order.
I show you (pl.) even as I have [found]

The author of the apocalypse is aware of a tradition that *James* was the 'beloved disciple'. This is an interesting, late identification of the 'disciple whom Jesus loved' from St John's gospel, to whom Jesus entrusts his earthly mother, and it is not the first time that we have observed this identification. We may recall how James as the beloved disciple makes sense of Jesus's words in John, 'Woman, behold thy son!' followed by Jesus's words to 'the disciple standing by, whom he loved': 'Behold thy mother!' The writer of the apocalypse has taken this exchange and provided its solution: the beloved disciple was James. Now you know.

James is presented in his Second Apocalypse sitting on the especially exalted fifth step of the Temple, preaching to the multitude. His message is a Gnostic one. Gnosis will come forth from the flesh: 'I am surely dying, but it is in life that I shall be found.' Here the author is reflecting on the Church tradition that James prayed for those who were killing him, as Jesus forgave his crucifiers, but he gives the tradition a thoroughly Gnostic twist. James does not blame the blind, violent servants of the archons: 'I hasten to make them free and want to take them above him who wants to rule over them [the false god].' 'If they are helped, I am the brother in secret, who prayed to the Father until he...'

That's a powerful phrase, is it not? *The brother in secret*. James can be *your* brother!

The manuscript has holes in it from its long-suffering beneath the sands of Egypt, but it appears that the author is familiar with the story told in the writings of Hegesippus (fl. AD 165–75) of how James prayed for his killers even at the point of death, 'Father, forgive them, for they know not what they do.' The reference in the following quotation to Jesus opening the door certainly shows knowledge of Hegesippus's account, for in that account of the death of James the Just, prior to their murdering him, the high priests ask James what is meant by the 'door of Jesus':

> Once when I [James] was sitting deliberating, [he] opened [the] door. That one whom you hated and persecuted came in to me. He said to me, 'Hail, my brother; my brother, hail.' As I raised my [face] to stare at him, [my] mother said to me, 'Do not be frightened, my son, because he said 'My brother to you [singular]. For you [plural] were nourished with this same milk. Because of this he calls me 'My mother.' For he is not a stranger to us. He is your [step-brother…]'

He opened the door… This is all deeply allegorical and it would be unwise to try to jump to historical conclusions. This 'same milk' for example refers to what nourishes the Gnostic: spiritual food, as well as hinting at the familial relation between Jesus and James inherited from the canonical record. The spiritual message is what counts.

Those who make much of the supposition from a damaged text of the apocryphal Gospel of Philip that Jesus kissed Mary Magdalene on the mouth, allegedly denoting a sexual relationship, should look at Jesus's visionary approach to his brother:

> And he kissed my mouth. He took hold of me, saying, 'My beloved! Behold, I shall reveal to you those [things] that [neither the] heavens nor their archons have known.'

In Gnostic writings, spiritual gnosis, deep understanding and common mind is communicated by Jesus through breath directly. The spirit of the Lord is expressed in the love of the Lord, by a kiss. (Judas's famous kiss of Jesus did not go unnoticed by Gnostic commentators either).

Having kissed James, Jesus then comes out with a radical Gnostic message. James will be taught things that the one who 'boasted' that there was no 'other except me' does not know. This can only be a reference to the God of the

Mosaic Law and covenant, the God of the world, the artificer of matter, the Big Ego, the dungeon-guard of time and space. Reference to this being means that whatever historical material might underlie the allegorical and symbolic message, the pitch of the message itself is not authentic to the historical James.

What has happened is that the Gnostic literary mind has taken characters from the canonical record and radically interpreted elements of their traditional identities, finding in James, for example, a special interpretation of what it means to be 'just'. This process was much at work in other Gnostic writings, including the now-famous Gospel of Judas (*see* my book, *Kiss of Death* for a description of how its author used canonical material to build a Gnostic tract). I suspect there were very few 'Gnostic' writers indeed. They had a genius and a formula which they used over and over again. This suggests a brilliant coterie, not the works of a 'religious movement'. What 'movement' there may have been was, I am sure, kicked off and nourished by a handful of bright sparks.

Returning to the 'brother in secret' of the Second Apocalypse of James, we see that James and Jesus are one, but not by flesh. They are one by spirit and vision:

> He was that one whom he who created the heaven and the earth,
> And dwelled in it, did not see.
> He was [this one who] is the life.
> He was the light.
> He was that one who will come to be.

The living Jesus will come forth from the Gnostic. Then, he is ready to die:

> '[On] that day all the [people] and the crowd were disturbed, and they showed that they had not been persuaded. And he [James] arose and went forth speaking in this [manner]. And he entered [again] on that same day and spoke a few hours. And I was with the priests and revealed nothing of the relationship, since all of them were saying with

one voice, 'Come, let us stone the Just One.' And they arose, saying, 'Yes, let us kill this man, that he may be taken from our midst. For he will be of no use to us.'

'And they were there and found him standing beside the columns of the temple beside the mighty corner stone. And they decided to throw him down from the height, and they cast him down. And they [...] they [...]. They seized him and [struck] him as they dragged him upon the ground. They stretched him out, and placed a stone on his abdomen. They all placed their feet on him, saying, 'You have erred!''

'Again they raised him up, since he was alive, and made him dig a hole. They made him stand in it. After having covered him up to his abdomen, they stoned him in this manner.

'And he stretched out his hands and said this prayer – not that [one] which it is his custom to say:'

James then says a mighty prayer to his God and Father who saved him 'from this dead hope'. 'Deliver me from this place of sojourn!' (*the world*) 'Bring me from a tomb alive, because your grace – love – is alive in me to accomplish a work of fullness!' (Perfection.) This is the prayer of the Gnostic redeemed. It redeems the Gnostic but leaves the world condemned.

The Apocryphon, or 'secret book' of James bursts upon the reader's consciousness with a similar message to the Apocalypses. The secret book is sent to a person whose name has dropped out of the papyrus with time. In James's letter of purported remembrances to its unknown recipient, he makes it plain he is one of the twelve, but not all of the twelve were given the message. The book is a discourse with the Saviour given 550 days after the Resurrection to James and Peter alone. One almost has the feeling that the author has read the pseudo-Clementine material. The theology of the Apocryphon contains a fairly mixed bag of Christian commonplaces delivered with enthusiasm not by James, but by the Saviour, anxious to depart this world and be on his way: 'I shall go to the place from whence I came. If you wish to come with me, come!' The Saviour cannot understand, after all that has happened, and after all that he has already said, that Peter and James are still afraid of death:

> 'Do you dare to spare the flesh, you for whom the Spirit is an encircling wall? If you consider how long the world existed before you, and how long it will exist after you, you will find that your life is one single day and your sufferings one single hour. For the good will not enter the world. Scorn death, therefore, and take thought for life! Remember my cross and my death, and you will live!'

The Lord is going to prepare a special house for those who 'hasten to be saved without being urged', a special house for those 'whom the Lord has made his sons'.

There is some homely wisdom in the secret book, echoes of James's teaching in his (?) canonical epistle perhaps: 'Come to hate hypocrisy and the evil thought; for it is the thought that gives birth to hypocrisy; but hypocrisy is far from truth.' But this is not James's teaching, this is the risen Lord's that James and Peter are expected to give to those able to hear it. It is James and Peter's job to sow the seeds of the spirit. The canonical James's teaching about 'works' being vital for righteousness is spiritualized:

> Become earnest about the word! For as to the word, its first part is faith, the second, love, the third, works; for from these comes life. For the word is like a grain of wheat: when someone had sown it, he had faith in it; and when it had sprouted, he loved it because he had seen many grains in place of one. And when he had worked, he was saved because he had prepared it for food, [and] again he left [some] to sow. So also can you yourselves receive the kingdom of heaven; unless you receive this through knowledge, you will not be able to find it.

Without gnosis, there can be no spiritual harvest. The fruit is the 'filling' of the disciple; once 'filled' or made perfect, he is ready, willing to leave this world and return to the fullness of the Father.

The secret book ends with an ascent vision vouchsafed to James and Peter. They ascend in the spirit to heaven, hearing the sounds of things prefigured to take place on earth (war), as well as angelic singing and benediction. They are only 'brought back to earth' by voices breaking in, those of anxious disciples, crying to know what the 'Master' has told the inspired pair.

All we can say for sure is that the Gnostic writers saw the gnosis in 'James', as other Gnostic writers would find the gnosis in Judas too, for he, Judas, saw what others could not; Gnostics observed how Judas 'kissed' Jesus when the Lord was 'handed over' to his enemies.

But James's job was to make more 'brothers' of the Lord and move from a House of David to a House in the heavens.

———

I think there is another factor in the choice made by Gnostic writers to show a special interest in James, the brother of the Lord, and I think this factor presents to us a luminous key to opening the secret chest of Gnostic lore.

The Second Apocalypse of James depicts James at the Temple delivering a Gnostic redemption message to the people, which they reject. It is too much for them; they stone him. Certain Gnostic writings show a powerful interest in the psychological reactions of people to the supposed raw truth of Gnostic spiritual liberation. Jesus's less-than-intimate disciples are sometimes singled out to demonstrate the idea: the worldly man's fear of vision. That is to say, the unenlightened disciples' fear of the Word is expressed in an uncontrollable desire to stone the speaker. Unable to share the vision, they are peevish, conspiratorial, resentful, dominating. This idea is in part a reflection on the canonical story of the disciples trying to keep children away from Jesus. Gnostic writers noticed this and made children and the idea of the child important in their narratives, not unaware of the prophecy: 'A little child shall lead them.' In The Gospel of Judas, Jesus actually appears as a child to the adult disciples. Similarly, in the Gospel of Philip, the Gnostic writer perceives an anti-feminine bias in the canonical treatment of women; they are sometimes rebuked and kept at a distance from the main action. Thus, the apocryphal gospel has the disciples complaining to Mary Magdalene as to why Jesus loved her more than them. The reason, of course, is that she did not reject the spiritual visionary experience that Jesus opened her eyes to.

According to the Gospel of Thomas, Jesus offers intimate spiritual teaching to chosen Thomas, identified in the gospel as Didymos Judas Thomas, Jesus's twin brother: 'Jesus said, 'He who will drink from My mouth will become like Me. I myself shall become he, and the things that are hidden will be revealed to him.'' We have the drinking-from-the-mouth idea, also expressed in the spirit-giving kiss of Jesus to James the beloved, and possibly to Mary Magdalene, in The Gospel of Philip.

When, in the Gospel of Thomas, Didymos Judas Thomas returns from instruction to the disciples, they ache to know what things have been passed on to him by the Master. Thomas has this to say to them: 'If I tell you one of the things which he told me, you will pick up stones and throw them at me; a fire will come out of the stones and burn you up.' Precisely the same scheme is employed in the 'Sethian Gnostic' Gospel of Judas (I shall explain 'Sethian' in due course). After Judas in that gospel has received high spiritual instruction from Jesus, Judas suffers a nightmare in which the disciples stone him.

Surely this 'stoning' metaphor is significant; the mind of the world cannot bear the truth. 'He who has never sinned cast the first stone.' So much for the righteous! If the Gnostics shared the common view of identifying Mary Magdalene with the 'woman caught in adultery' who was threatened with stoning, we have yet another example of the stoning theme that curiously alerts the Gnostic writer to unseen spiritual potential. It would have been obvious to the Gnostic writer that when Jesus stopped the stoning self-righteous in their tracks, he would then impart spiritual wisdom to her. What was encapsulated as 'Go and sin no more' in the canonical account was expanded to full sermon length in Gnostic writings. However, the wisdom is *always more or less the same* in Gnostic apocrypha, whether the recipient is James, Peter, Judas, Thomas, or Mary.

Writers adept at employing the Gnostic composition formula saw the rejection of Judas Iscariot by the disciples, the rejection of James by the 'people', and the implied reaction to Didymos Judas Thomas, and of course the archons' attempt to annihilate Jesus, as a perennial truth, even an *archetype* which began with the rejection of Adam and Eve from Paradise. *What the world rejects, the Gnostic values.* If the family of Jesus had been more explicitly rejected in the canonical gospels, we may be fairly sure there would have been a Gnostic Gospel according to Jesus's Family. But, in a certain sense, that is exactly what we do have!

Let us look at the first lines of the Gospel of Thomas: 'These are the secret sayings which the living Jesus spoke and which Didymos Judas Thomas wrote down. And he said, 'Whoever finds the interpretation of these sayings will not experience death.''

Who is this Didymos Judas Thomas? The canonical gospels give us a Thomas, and a Didymus, but not a Didymos Judas Thomas. The only other place where we find Didymos Judas Thomas is in the apocryphal Acts of Thomas (*c.*AD 200–25). The Acts of Thomas is an apocryphal text believed to have been written, we should not be surprised, in the Syriac Christian Church based in Edessa, 250 miles north-east of Damascus. The church of Edessa was established by messengers sent out by James, first Bishop of Jerusalem. That community, far to the north of Galilee, held Judas Didymos Thomas in high esteem. Indeed, in the Acts of Thomas, Thomas is explicitly Jesus's *twin brother*!

'Thomas' is Aramaic for twin. *Didymos* is Greek for twin. So we have the Twin Judas the Twin. This idea was clearly very attractive to the Gnostic interpreter. Working with the tradition that Jesus had a brother called Judas, and a disciple called 'Thomas', The Gospel of Thomas works on the idea that Jesus is the 'twin brother' of the redeemed, formerly hidden Gnostic spirit, for the 'living Jesus' is, according to Christian Gnostics, the hidden identity, the spiritual *daimon* of Man. Man must 'bring forth' the 'twin brother' or be destroyed. There was no *Doubting* Thomas; he was a *Knowing* Thomas, and did not need to feel the wounds of Jesus to see the truth. He looked into, and beyond, himself.

Another work from the Nag Hammadi Library builds on the Gnostics' 'twin' identification with Jesus and with Judas, his brother. The Syriac Book of Thomas the Contender is also thought to come from Edessa in the first half of the 3rd century. It contains a conversation of 'secret words' between Jesus and 'Brother Thomas' – Judas Thomas – written down by one Mathaias (Matthew). The book teases the reader with the idea of a complete fulfilment of spiritual aspiration. It is possible to 'become the twin', to reach the spiritual level of the Master so that the aspirant himself is no longer mastered, taking the holy words direct from Jesus's mouth into himself:

> Now since it has been said that you are my twin and true companion, examine yourself that you may understand who you are, in what way you exist, and how you will come to be. Since you are called my brother, it is not fitting that you be ignorant of yourself. And I know that you have understood, because you had already understood that I am the knowledge of the truth. So while you accompany me, although you are uncomprehending, you have [in fact] already come to know, and you will be called 'the one who knows himself'. For he who has not known himself has known nothing, but he who has known himself has at the same time already achieved knowledge about the Depth of the All. So then, you, my brother Thomas, have beheld what is obscure to men, that is, against which they ignorantly stumble.

The last line on perceiving what has been obscure to men, is an intriguing reference to a little-known saying of Jesus from the gospels:

> And he beheld them, and said, What is this then that is written, The stone which the builders rejected, the same is become the head of the corner? Whosoever shall fall upon that stone shall be crushed; but on whomsoever it shall fall, he shall be winnowed.

> (Luke, 20:17–18)

It is not the stone that falls from heaven that will crush the ignorant, but the one the blind cannot see in their way, and thus trip upon. As Jesus says to Judas Thomas: you have seen that 'against which they [unenlightened men] ignorantly stumble'. We note again the all-important 'rejection theme'. And we may further note with emphasis that in the Apocalypse of James, James addresses the people standing next to the 'mighty cornerstone' of the Temple; he is with the Lord! And he is rejected, as Gnostics felt themselves to be rejected by the blind, as the gnosis is rejected by the earth and the earth-bound. The *Stone* is unavoidable: bring it forth or be crushed by it. When Jesus renames Simon, he calls him Cephas: *stone.*

The stone from above, the 'rejected stone' 'winnows' the one on whom it falls; it separates the wheat (goodness/gold) from the chaff (darkness/low matter), an alchemical image perhaps. The one who knows himself has been 'hit by the stone'. And it is worth mentioning here that it is from an account in the Acts of Thomas that Thomas became the patron saint of *masons*, after Thomas built a church for an Indian king on his missionary journey to the east, described in the apocryphal Acts of Thomas. There is a statue of Thomas with his set-square outside Lichfield Cathedral; perhaps he learned how to do it from his father.

Thomas too was close to the cornerstone – the Stone of the Philosophers.

Had the Gnostics believed that Jesus Iscariot and Didymos Judas Thomas were the same person, they would likely have made much of it, but they do not. They *were* aware however that Jesus had a family whose members had not been valued or understood by orthodox teachers. But Gnostic interest was not genealogical, at least not in the ordinary sense of the word.

The Gnostic writings show interest in those with intimate and profound access to the mind of Jesus; their interest in brotherhood is spiritual and symbolic. That may have been Jesus's own position, but as to whether Jesus's brothers were granted instruction in spiritual knowledge, or of what that might *originally* have consisted, must remain open questions. The Gnostic writings were satisfied that their traditions derived from source by, literally, oral transmission. On the other hand, most Gnostic writing is presented in terms of revelation, access by mind of the writer to a timeless level where events in time may be seen imprinted. Nevertheless, a clear itinerary of Gnostic interpretation dominates, and the schemes of interpretation are consistent with the insights of people in the period in which the works were composed. It is pointless to speculate as to whether Jesus's familial descendants would have endorsed the visionary gospel. Certainly, no Gnostic writing claims any link with any extant *descendant* of Jesus's 1st-century family, and this fact is surely significant.

There is however, one genealogical interest of a number of Gnostic works that cannot be denied. They may have had little interest in the House of David (by the 3rd century, Judea as a political entity had been obliterated), but they *were* interested in a certain holy line of descent: the real 'blood-grail', if you like, of Gnostic interest.

In The Gospel of Judas, Judas does not want an eternity on earth, he wants to join the 'great and holy generation' in their more beautiful 'house'.

What House is this?

This is the House of 'the immovable generation'. In The Apocryphon of James, Jesus says to James and Peter: 'I am revealed to you building a house which is of great value to you since you find shelter beneath it, just as it will be able to stand by your neighbours' house when it threatens to fall.' This House will stand when all else has gone. Whose House is this?

This is the House of the generation of Seth.

Remember how in Luke's genealogy, the writer traces Jesus's lineage back through *Seth*, to Adam, 'the son of God'. This detail was not lost upon Gnostic commentators. When Adam's children Cain and Abel fell out, Abel was left dead and Cain was marked with the mark of wickedness. The human race was sullied. A new beginning was needed. Adam had a new son, Seth, a name not unlinked I suspect with the Egyptian god of the burning sun and of victory, of the same Greek name.

In Genesis, Seth stands as a pure new beginning for the human race. Seth is holy. His seed was regarded in esoteric circles as unique. According to historian Josephus, the 'children of Seth' were the fathers of science; two ancient pillars of knowledge that survived the Great Flood were called the Pillars of Seth, and were linked in Gnostic traditions to the wisdom of Hermes, the Thrice Greatest, progenitor of antediluvian knowledge and wisdom.

We know that some Gnostics saw Jesus as a kind of manifestation of the 'great Seth': a pure being of primal knowledge direct from the Source. The Nag Hammadi Library contains at least two 'Sethian' works: The Second Treatise of the Great Seth, in which Seth only appears in the title and 'Jesus Christ' does the speaking, and The Three Steles of Seth, which does not refer to Jesus but purports to be the revelation of the 'son of Seth', father of 'another race', 'another seed'. The Gnostic tract Allogenes, which can be translated as 'The Alien' also deals with the theme of belonging to a unique lineage of spiritual men, continuing the tradition of the primal revelation of God to Adam. Jesus is regarded as coming from this mighty spiritual stock, able to make new 'sons of God'.

These Sethian works were probably written in the early 3rd to mid 3rd century and show the influence of Neoplatonic, pagan philosophy and esotericism. We have come a long way from the 'House of David' to this entirely esoteric family of Jesus in which Jesus's real relatives seem to be absorbed altogether in high fallutin' philosophy, losing their – and Jesus's – humanity completely. It can only be said that in the apparent absence of Jesus's real family from these writers, speculation about the family grew, and nearly always in an unearthly direction. One might have supposed that the missing family of Jesus had all been assumed to heaven.

Found in History

Having examined the spiritual interpretation of Jesus's family in Gnostic writings, we now look at the work of two early historians who left records concerning Jesus's family. The historians are Josephus, a 1st-century Jew, and Hegesippus, a 2nd-century Christian. Both historians share an interest in Jesus's brother, James. We discuss the shocking possibility that Paul was an Herodian or Roman stooge, an enemy of Jesus's family. We find that the primitive Church was centred on the Jerusalem Temple and was an essentially priestly organization in conflict with richer, ruling priests.

Let's 'come down to earth' from the Gnostics' spiritual affirmation and other-worldly philosophy and return to plain historical records. In doing so, we should remember that historical records are seldom entirely plain and may themselves grow from speculation, guesswork and bias. At least in this case we need not say 'the victors write the history', for the record we now approach was written by a person who, while at the time confident of the *end* of things, had every reason to be uncertain about his own future. I refer to the 2nd-century Christian chronicler Hegesippus. But before we enter Hegesippus's remarkable and controversial testimony, we should first look at the work of an earlier historian.

Flavius Josephus chose the winning side – eventually. A patriotic Jew, he fought in the Jewish Revolt of AD 66–73, but at a critical moment, sickened by the conduct of the war among his more extreme countrymen, Josephus threw his lot in with the Emperor Vespasian, hailing the Roman conqueror as the prophesied master of the world who would emerge from Judea, and went to live in comfort in Rome.

Josephus was a brilliant and exacting historian. Writing of the Jewish War in about AD 75, Josephus declared that what had made the revolutionaries undertake a war against the vastly superior Roman force was:

> an ambiguous oracle that was also found in their sacred writings, how, 'about that time, one from their country should become governor of the habitable earth.' The Jews took this prediction to belong to themselves in particular, and many of the wise men were thereby deceived in their determination. Now this oracle certainly denoted the government of Vespasian, who was appointed emperor in Judea. However, it is not possible for men to avoid fate, although they see it beforehand. But these men interpreted some of these signals according to their own pleasure, and some of them they utterly despised, until their madness was demonstrated, both by the taking of their city and their own destruction.
>
> (*Jewish War*, 6.5.4)

It is interesting to hear a contemporary speak of what to us are well known messianic prophecies in this cool and political manner. He speaks of the practical effect of the messianism familiar to most of us only through its accretion to the story of Jesus and his followers. Josephus was of a moderate party and recognized a moderate when he saw one.

Writing in about AD 95, the 56-year-old Josephus recounts the events surrounding the death of James, brother of the Lord. Since Josephus marks James's death with respect and the opposition to it as coming from 'equitable citizens', we may infer Josephus did not see James as one determined to instigate political storms or violence. By his references to the death of Procurator Festus and the arrival of Procurator Albinus, we can safely date these events to AD 62–3. Some 30 years after the crucifixion of his brother, the venerable James the Righteous was in charge of the 'Nazarenes' in Jerusalem, clearly a man of high repute among Jewish leaders of the country:

> And now Caesar, upon hearing of the death of Festus, sent Albinus into
> Judea, as procurator. But the king deprived Joseph of the high priest-
> hood, and bestowed the succession to that dignity on the son of Ananus,
> who was also himself called Ananus. Now the report goes, that this elder
> Ananus proved a most fortunate man; for he had five sons, who had all
> performed the office of a high priest to God, and he had himself
> enjoyed that dignity a long time formerly, which had never happened
> to any other of our high priests. But this younger Ananus, who, as we
> have told you already, took the high priesthood, was a bold man in his
> temper, and very insolent; he was also of the sect of the Sadducees, who
> are very rigid in judging offenders above all the rest of the Jews, as we
> have already observed: when, therefore, Ananus was of this disposition,
> he thought he had now a proper opportunity [to exercise his authority.]
> Festus was now dead, and Albinus was but upon the road; so he assem-
> bled the Sanhedrin of judges, and brought before them the brother of
> Jesus, who was called Christ, whose name was James, and some others,
> [or, some of his companions]. And when he had formed an accusation
> against them as breakers of the law, he delivered them to be stoned; but
> as for those who seemed the most equitable of the citizens, and such as
> were the most uneasy at the breach of the laws, they disliked what was
> done; they also sent to the king, [Agrippa] desiring him to send to
> Ananus that he should act so no more, for that what he had already done
> was not to be justified: nay, some of them went also to meet Albinus, as
> he was upon his journey from Alexandria, and informed him that it was
> not lawful for Ananus to assemble a Sanhedrin without his consent.
> Whereupon Albinus complied with what they said, and wrote in anger
> to Ananus, and threatened that he would bring him to punishment for
> what he had done; on which king Agrippa took the high priesthood from
> him, when he had ruled but three months, and made Jesus the son of
> Damneus high priest.

(Antiquities, 20.9.1)

Ananus the younger clearly hated the followers of James's brother. Eisenman, who identifies this Ananus with the 'wicked priest' of the Dead Sea Scrolls, reckons that James was murdered in retribution for the murder of Ananus's brother, high priest Jonathan, by 'Sicarii' or dagger-men, Zealot assassins. This supposes James was in sympathetic touch with the 'men of violence'. It is possible, but unproven.

Ananus probably thought he would enjoy the tacit approval of Rome for dealing with those, such as James, who looked for the Messiah to end the calamities that had befallen God's people, for less than two years after James's death, a terrible fire in Rome was blamed by the Emperor Nero on what Roman historian Tacitus, writing between AD 115–20, described as a sect of people in Rome 'who were held in abhorrence for their crimes and called by the vulgar 'Christians" (*Annal.* Book XV, 44). This was not the first time 'Christians' in Rome had raised the imperial ire. According to Suetonius's *Life of Claudius*, written in about AD 120, the Emperor Claudius had expelled Jews from Rome because 'the Jews at Rome caused continuous disturbances at the instigation of Chrestus' (presumably an error for 'Christus'). Claudius ruled from AD 41–54. These messianic-inspired Jews may not necessarily have been followers of Jesus; they may have been messianic preachers of the 'Sons of light' type familiar to the Qumran 'War Scroll' and other works, but the Romans would not have been too fine about distinctions between troublesome Jews.

Ananus, in having James killed, may have been in cahoots with Agrippa. Herod Agrippa, now co-ruling in Judea, had already put to death John the Baptist and James the brother of John. Ananus doubtless calculated that finishing off Jesus's brother, coupled with a vicious crackdown on all around him, would extirpate at least one wing of the 'Christus' problem before the arrival of the procurator. As Josephus tells it, Ananus severely misjudged the issue of authority. Young Ananus should have secured the procurator's authority for a death sentence of this magnitude. Even Agrippa, it seems, was party to the reactionary challenge to High Priest Ananus. While James clearly had influential friends, they were too late to save him. It is possible that unrest followed the judicial murder of Jesus's brother. In the event, the new procurator permitted Agrippa to strip Ananus of the high priesthood. A new high priest was appointed. His name was Jesus.

The canonical epistle of James may have been composed by James during this trying period, at the eve of his own murder. The epistle addresses fellow sufferers of persecution: 'Do not rich men oppress you and bring you before the judgement seats?' Josephus reports that it was the wealth of the ruling high priests that allowed them to overthrow the plans of the poorer priests, among whom Eisenman believes we must include James, Jesus's brother.

Similar statements in the canonical epistle of James ring true in the context of a Sadducean plot to wipe out the 'Nazarenes':

> behold the judge standeth before the door [note that tell-tale reference to 'the door' again]. Take, my brethren, the prophets, who have spoken in the name of the Lord, for an example of suffering affliction and of patience. Behold, we count them happy which endure. Ye have heard of the patience of Job, and have seen the end of the Lord.

The Messiah will return; hold on.

That curious reference to 'the door' will reappear in the most detailed account of James's death.

We may ask where Paul was at the time of this shock to the Church. *Elsewhere*, cometh the uninformed reply; possibly in the western empire, though Eisenman is of the opinion that the attack on James was provoked, if not led, by Paul the Roman citizen with friends in the Herodian court. Paul had written in his epistle to the Galatians (1:9) that 'if any other man preach any other gospel unto you than that you have received, let him be accursed'. Even if he be 'an angel from heaven', 'let him be accursed'. James's gospel was certainly at odds with Paul's. Josephus, however, is plain: James was killed by an enemy of the whole movement; Ananus may have wished to kill Paul as well.

Nevertheless, Josephus may be the place where we find the absent Paul, and not in good odour. Shortly after James's death, Agrippa invited the hatred of Judeans when he took beautiful objects from Judea to adorn his rebuilding of

Caesarea Philippi. The city was to be renamed Neronias, in honour of *Nero*, a city far from Judea on the northern border with the province of Syria. Furthermore, the king's replacement for Ananus, Jesus, son of Damneus, was succeeded by *another* Jesus, this one the son of Gamaliel. The appointment of Jesus, son of Gamaliel, outraged the high priests, causing what Jospehus calls, 'a sedition'. This development would have made immediate sense to Paul, wherever he was. Paul had as a youth sat at the feet of the great rabbi Gamaliel. He would have known his sons; they were present when, according to Acts, Paul was brought before the Sanhedrin *c.*AD 54, accused of undermining the law of Moses.

The high priests gathered their own rowdy supporters. The rival parties began throwing stones at one another, causing a tumult quelled only by Ananias who had more money than the rest and was thus assured of beefier support. Josephus's next statement gives us some idea of the internal politics of Jerusalem at the time, the real world in which Jesus's followers' assembly assembled: battles of rival priests for control. Josephus's account may also tell us something about the whereabouts of Paul, or *Saul*, as he was known in Judea:

> Costobarus also, and Saulus, did themselves get together a multitude of wicked wretches, and this because they were of the royal family; and so they obtained favour among them, because of their kindred to Agrippa: but still they used violence with the people, and were very ready to plunder those that were weaker than themselves. And from that time it principally came to pass, that our city was greatly disordered, and that all things grew worse and worse among us.

> (*Antiquities* XX.9:4)

We know very little of the real causes of this disruption, or whether this 'Saulus' was the same person as the Christian saint whose extant epistles advocate patient long-suffering and love for one's enemies, as well as curses for doctrinal opponents. What we do see, however, is the beginning of the slide that, with the arrival of the new and very severe procurator Gessius Florus, would lead to the Jewish Revolt and the collapse of the world familiar to Jesus's immediate family.

That Paul was familiar with the Herodians and with Roman authority is plain even from the pro-Pauline, pro-Gentile, arguably anti-Jewish, Acts of the Apostles, however unpalatable such a scenario may be to Christians who view the origins of the Church through the rose-coloured spectacles of orthodox teaching. While Josephus writes of a 'Simon' who demanded that Herodians be banned from the Temple (a demythologized 'Simon Peter' according to Eisenman), Paul seems, by contrast, fairly cosy with the authorities who regularly executed threatening Judeans. Take a look at the following scenario.

In Acts 24:24, Felix and his wife Drusilla, an Herodian princess described curiously as 'a Jewess' by the author of Acts, ask for Paul, whom Felix is holding in custody for his own good, to come and tell them about his 'faith in Christ'. Having heard Paul's view, Felix would have released Paul, but hoped Paul would obtain money to buy his way out. Felix met with him often and only kept Paul in custody 'to shew the Jews a pleasure'. Amazing that Paul is distinguished plainly in Roman eyes – or Luke's – from 'the Jews'. It is the old story, except here it is *Paul* that is presented as 'rejected of his own', a group again that includes Jesus's family. While this scenario is almost certainly post-Jewish Revolt anti-Jewish propaganda, it is likely to be based on some authentic relations of Paul to the governing factions of the time, relations that would not have seemed embarrassing at all to Gentiles unfamiliar with the realities of Judean and Galilean politics at the time, but which constituted outrageous and insufferable treason to patriotic Jews.

Drusilla's sister, the Herodian princess Bernice, was rumoured to be enjoying incestuous relations with her brother Agrippa II, king of Galilee from AD 54–68 (Josephus's *Antiquities* 20, 145). This princess is the same Bernice who will become mistress to the Emperor Vespasian's son Titus, the Roman commanding the destruction of the Temple in AD 70. Bernice appears with Agrippa II in Acts 25:13–26. They ask the new procurator, Festus, about getting Paul out of the bonds in which he had been placed by Festus's predecessor, Felix. Agrippa's reasoning is that the 'chief priests and the elders of the

Jews' demanded judgement against Paul. Paul's enemies were Jews. That seems to be quite enough rationale to fix Paul up with the liberty to have his case brought before Caesar. After a preliminary hearing of Paul's entire career and beliefs, Agrippa, Bernice and Procurator Festus retire to conclude:

> **This man doeth nothing worthy of death or of bonds. Then said Agrippa to Festus, This man might have been set at liberty, if he had not appealed to Ceasar. (Acts 26:32)**

Paul was the Romans' friend; their enemies were his enemies. By the 2nd century, an unbreakable prejudice had emerged in the western Christian Church: Paul's enemies, and the Church's enemies were 'the Jews'. For 'they' rejected Jesus; the Romans did not. Can Jesus really have been a Jew: all-Jew, at any rate? But as Luke's genealogy had it, Jesus's genealogy went back to Adam, to all men, and on this did his divine 'Sonship' rest, not on the House of David alone. According to this view, Jesus's 'own' were his enemies. Jews favoured sedition. This alone could explain why Luke cannot bring himself to accord James, the brother of the Lord, his genuine position in the early Church. James had opposed Luke's hero, Paul. The destruction of the Temple demonstrated emphatically whose side God was on, and He was not on the side of 'the Jews'.

Should you find this presentation a little shocking, examine Paul's advice about Roman authority in his epistle to the Romans, chapter 13, and try to put yourself in the position of a patriotic Jew, hearing that advice.

A Jew was taught from the cradle that the Promised Land was a divine gift; to render its fruit to a foreign unbeliever was treason to the Lord. What should one then think of the Romans, who regularly crucified Jews for fighting for their land, who beat them and humiliated them for non-payment of taxes, taxes that would be given to a man who called himself a god, a man indifferent to the God of the Jews, whose soldiers plundered the homes of one's countrymen?

Paul is comfortable with Roman taxes: 'For this cause pay ye tribute also: for they [the Romans] are God's ministers, attending continually upon this very thing.' There you are. The Romans who murder the 'saints' are God's ministers; those who resist are clearly not working for God. As for executions, they too do God's work against evil: 'For rulers are not a terror to good works, but to the evil.' The Romans are not the problem; the law is. Romans govern because Jews have rejected their prophets; they deserve to be punished, and governed, until they learn.

And stop all this nonsense about not paying tribute to Caesar! Taxes are good. Why? Not paying taxes leaves you owing that money to the one who has God's sanction for demanding it: 'Owe no man any thing, but to love one another: for he that loveth another hath fulfilled the law.' (Romans 13:8) *Note that*: loving the Romans fulfils the law! Paying taxes to Rome is fulfilling the law! This compound of ideas would have been simply, incredibly, jaw-droppingly outrageous to practically every patriotic Jew, while Paul, in that mood, would probably reply to such incredulity: 'And that's why your keep getting hammered!' *Submit! Your oppressors are God's own instruments.* It is arguable that a Jew who was content to see his Messiah crucified as a rebel by the Romans, and was himself regularly in Roman custody while also seeking Roman protection, would tolerate practically anything from them.

Again, living in his own world, Paul casts aside Jewish legal requirements over purity of food. Food at Gentile tables had often been first offered to idols before being sold in the markets. A Jew recognized such food as being tainted by its association with idolatry; Paul says such scruples indicate the person holding them is 'weak', and by extension the teacher of such scruples is 'weak' also. That teacher was James, brother of the Lord. To Paul, all idols are obviously just wood and stone; there was nothing to get excited about. Foolish Man made the idols; God made the food, so eat it.

If James teaches another doctrine, let him be accursed (Galatians 1:8–9).

———

That the brutal killing of James the brother of the Lord was no minor political event is evinced not only in Josephus but in two extracts from the writings of Christian theologian Origen (*c.*184–254), composed in about AD 230. While Christians after the war were encouraged to make a connection between prophecies attributed to Jesus foretelling the disaster of AD 70 and the event itself, Origen, a learned and careful man, wished his readers to know that many at the time of the wasting of the Temple attributed the calamity to God's judgement for the murder of Jesus's brother, not for those responsible for Jesus's crucifixion.

> **This James was of so shining a character among the people, on account of his righteousness, that Flavius Josephus, when, in his twentieth book of the Jewish Antiquities, he had a mind to set down what was the cause why the people suffered such miseries, till the very holy house was demolished, he said that these things befell them by the anger of God, on account of what they had dared to do to James, the brother of Jesus, who was called Christ: and wonderful it is that, while he did not receive Jesus for Christ, he did nevertheless bear witness that James was so righteous a man. He says further, that the people thought that they suffered these things for the sake of James.**
>
> (Origen, *c*.230, *Commenary on Matthew*)

Origen repeated the story in Book One of his work against Celsus, a sharp critic of Christianity (*Contra Celsum*, *c*.AD 250), in which work Origen also makes the point of saying that James was only Jesus's brother by 'agreement of manners and preaching'. Origen here interposes his own doctrinal reasons for denying the plain sense of Josephus's text with regard to the familial relation. Origen is also mistaken in his reference. There is nothing in Book XX of Josephus's *Antiquities* attributing the destruction of the Temple to the murder of James. Origen was perhaps confusing an inherited tradition to that effect with an account in *Antiquities* Book XVIII, chapter five. Josephus writes that the defeat of Herod the Tetrarch's army by Aretas, king of Arabia Petrea, was seen by observers as punishment for having John the Baptist unjustly executed. Josephus presents John as a 'good man' who commanded righteousness towards one's fellows and piety towards God. This commendation of righteousness in John presumably confused itself in Origen's mind with his knowledge of James the Righteous. So we cannot be certain that James's death was seen by anyone *at the time* as the retributive cause for Jerusalem's destruction.

We now come to Hegesippus's hair-raising account of the death of James, written some 110 years after the event. According to Thomas Lewin's scholarly *Life and Epistles of St Paul* (2 vols, London, 1874), Hegesippus's account should be treated with caution, since 'the details which he [Hegesippus] has given are so mixed with fable, and so manifestly absurd, that we forbear to insert them. They prove only that legendary fiction, even in that early age, had already begun to germinate.' Lewin's caution was not shared by Eusebius of Caesarea, writing in about AD 300 (*Ecclesiastical History*, Book II, ch.23). Eusebius also quotes a passage he believes to be from Josephus asserting that 'these things happened to the Jews [the destruction of the Temple] to avenge James the Just, who was the brother of Jesus the so-called Christ, for the Jews killed him in spite of his great righteousness'. Eusebius may have taken this on trust from Origen's account.

By the time Eusebius was writing, Hegesippus was judged not as a figure too late for a sitting at the 1st-century table, but as a fairly established authority on the early Church. That which made Oxford scholar Lewin dismiss Hegesippus's account is probably that which made it useful to Robert Eisenman, radical scholar of the James tradition. Hegesippus furnished Eisenman with supporting evidence for his contention that James was probably the Qumran 'Teacher of Righteousness', and that James was a major historical figure with more 'Josephus-space' than Jesus. Let us hear what Hegesippus had to say about the brother of the Lord:

> James, the Lord's brother, succeeded to the government of the Church, with the apostles. He has been called the Just by all men, from the days of the Lord down to the present time. For many bore the name of James; but this one was holy from his mother's womb. He drank no wine or other intoxicating liquor, nor did he eat flesh; no razor came

upon his head; he did not anoint himself with oil, nor make use of the bath. He alone was permitted to enter the sanctuary: for he did not wear any woollen garment, but fine linen only. And alone he used to go into the temple: and he used to be found kneeling and praying, begging forgiveness for the people, so that the skin of his knees became horny like that of a camel's, by reason of his constantly bending the knee in adoration to God, and begging forgiveness for the people. Therefore, in consequence of his pre-eminent justice, he was called the Just, and Oblias, which signifies in Greek 'Rampart of the people and righteousness', as the prophets declare concerning him. [Possibly referring to the 'high gate of the house of the Lord' and the 'wall of Ophel' built by King Jotham in II Chron. 27:3; Oblias may be an inaccurate transliteration of the Hebrew for 'bulwark' or 'rampart of the people'.]

Thus some of the seven sects existing among the people, which have been before described by me in the *Commentaries*, asked him: 'What is the door of Jesus?' And he replied that he was the Christ. Owing to this, some believed that Jesus is the Christ. But the sects before mentioned did not believe, either in a resurrection or in the coming of one to reward each according to his works; but as many as did believe, believed because of James. Now, since many even of the rulers believed, there was a tumult of the Judeans and the scribes and the pharisees, saying that the whole people were in danger of looking for Jesus as the Christ. So they assembled and said to James, 'We beseech you to restrain the people since they are straying after Jesus as if he were the Messiah. We beseech you to persuade concerning Jesus all who come for the day of the Passover, for everyone obeys you. For we and the whole people testify to you that you are righteous and do not respect persons. [Truth is truth regardless of personalities or status of persons concerned.] So do you persuade the crowd not to err concerning Jesus, for the whole people and we all obey you. [This unlikely idea that everyone obeyed James would be one of the things to make Lewin regard the work with caution.] Therefore stand on the battlement of the temple that you may be clearly visible on high, and that your words may be audible to all the people, for because of the Passover all the tribes, with the Gentiles also, have come together.' So the scribes and the pharisees mentioned before made James stand on the battlement of the temple, and they cried out to him and said, 'Oh, just one, to whom we all owe obedience, since the people are straying after Jesus who was crucified, tell us what is the door of Jesus?' And he answered with a loud voice, 'Why do you ask me concerning the Son of Man? He is sitting in heaven on the right hand of the great power, and he will come on the clouds of heaven.' [The 'great power' is a phrase associated with Simonian proto-Gnosis.] And many were convinced and glorified at James's testimony and said, 'Hosanna to the Son of David.' [Lewin probably felt this was impious since the title was applied to Jesus.] Then again the same scribes and pharisees said to one another, 'We did wrong to provide Jesus with such testimony, but let us go up and throw him down that they may be afraid and not believe him.' And they cried out saying, 'Oh, oh, even the just one erred.' And they fulfilled the scripture written to Isaiah, 'Let us take the just man for he is unprofitable to us. Yet they shall eat the fruit of their works.' [The first part of the quotation is from the Wisdom of Solomon.] So they went up and threw down the Just, and they said to one another, 'Let us stone James the Just,' and they began to stone him since the fall had not killed him, but he turned and knelt saying, 'I beseech thee O Lord, God and Father, forgive them, for they know not what they do.' And while they were thus stoning him one of the priests of the sons of Rechab, the son of Rechabim, to whom Jeremiah the prophet bore witness, cried out saying 'Stop! What are you doing? The Just is praying for you.'

Rechabim is only the plural of Rechab. The Rechabites were a tribe of Kenites adopted into Israel (*see* I Chron. 2:55; Jer. 35:19). Epiphanius (*Haer.* 78:14) replaces the mysterious Rechabite by Simeon of Clopas, a relative of Jesus. Eisenman notes Josephus's reference in this period to hymn-singing Levites who had taken to wearing the linen of the priesthood, being so sick of the corruption of the sacerdotal office. These hymn-singing Levites may not have been alone among lower ranking religious persons to seek the linen. Jeremiah had praised the Rechabites for keeping the commandments of their father Jonadab, who pleased the Lord, and promised they should never be in want of one to stand for them before the Lord.

Hegesippus's account now reaches its climax:

> And a certain man among them, one of the laundrymen, took the club with which he used to beat out the clothes, and hit the Just on the head, and so he suffered martyrdom. And they buried him on the spot by the temple. He became a true witness both to Jews and to Greeks that Jesus is the Christ. And immediately Vespasian began to besiege them.

> (*c.*AD 170, Hegesippus, *Commentaries on the Acts of the Church*,
> Book V paraphrased in Eusebius, *Ecclesiastical History*, Book II, 23)

Vespasian did not immediately besiege Jerusalem. That event lay ahead some years yet, but clearly the author implied that the one catastrophe was caused by the other, and this causal connection apparently got lodged into the written tradition.

Eisenman spotted something interesting in the account and, as we have seen, considered that Luke, in framing the Acts story of Stephen's martyrdom, already knew what Hegesippus knew about the event. So, to hide Paul's true role in events and to obscure the true primacy of James in the Church, Luke concocted a version of the facts whereby it was not *James* who was martyred for declaring the Temple's demise, but Stephen.

According to Eisenman's hypothesis, Hegesippus's reference to the laundrymen and the fuller's club was transformed by Luke into Paul's holding the *clothes* of those stoning Stephen/the Just, while Stephen's name, meaning 'crown' is somehow cross-linked to James's alleged 'crown' of uncut hair as befitting a keeper of the Nazarite vow, or was a general appellation for the 'crown of martyrdom' or 'crown of thorns', or a reference to the gold-decorated linen 'crown' or head-dress of an officiating priest of the Temple (recall the shining 'petalon' of the Anna-Joachim apocryphal story).

Eisenman's deconstruction/reconstruction of Luke's Acts is arresting. It has the virtue of inserting James well into Temple politics, eruptions about which had so much to do with fomenting the Jewish Revolt. It also puts Josephus's 'Saulus' and his crowd on the spot, angrily fighting priests, conceivably those who insisted on circumcision for Gentile believers in the Messiah.

But all this is a very great deal to put upon the shoulders of the Hegesippus account as transcribed by Eusebius some 250 years after the event. I am not convinced that Eisenman's 'Enigma machine' for decoding the New Testament does not have a design fault. We cannot be sure of Eusebius's own motives for including the account, and we know nothing of Hegesippus's own *bona fides*, or the provenance of his account. However, as so often in this investigation, we have to deal with what we have been given. We should remind ourselves that these events happened a very, very long time ago and we may be assured that while the quantity of information we have is, frankly, astonishing for the period, it is very far indeed from a sufficiency to give us an accurate historical picture. We are certainly not in the position of being able to offer a forensic interpretation of the evidence, in spite of the excitements of archaeological finds such as ossuaries bearing familiar names from the New Testament. The names are familiar from our New Testament because they were familiar, common names of the period: Mary, John, Joseph, Jesus, James, Judas, Matthew, Simon.

Eisenman is greatly reliant on Hegesippus's description of James. That this James was 'holy from his mother's womb', for example, appears to be echoed as a jibe-return of Paul's in his epistle to the Galatians: 'But when it pleased God, who separated me from my mother's womb, and called me by his grace, To reveal his Son in me…' (Gal.1:15–16). Paul seems to punch straight into the Jamesian jugular with this phrase. *If you think, you're special, get this!* Paul appears to ridicule James in the most personal, destructive, sarcastic way.

Paul found those who demanded circumcision of Gentiles awaiting the return of the Lord, and those who insisted on 'works righteousness' in keeping with the law and prophets as the way to salvation, intolerable. He cursed them, or thought God cursed them. Either way, they should be cursed! What does that mean? It means cut off and damned; Paul says he knows better than they. He can equal the most exalted state, namely of being *'holy from his mother's womb'* – and, incidentally, Paul never claimed this dignity meant that his mother was a perpetual virgin! He was consecrated, separated for God: Yahweh's exclusive property before birth.

Eisenman is minded that this phrase may be the origin of the 'virgin birth' narrative in conjunction with the famous 'Christmas' prophecy that 'a virgin shall conceive and shall bring forth a son, and he shall be called Immanuel' (Isaiah 7:14).

If, as seems to be the case, James's followers did indeed claim their leader was holy from his mother's womb, Paul slams back: *so am I*! His use of the phrase occurs shortly before telling his Galatian readers of how he had the briefest dealings with the Lord's brother, James. As a preamble, Paul asserts that he 'profited in the Jews' religion above many my equals in mine own nation, being more exceedingly zealous of the traditions of my fathers'. Paul admits to being pretty fanatical as regards his pre-conversion self. 'But when it pleased God, who separated me from my mother's womb, and called me by his grace, to reveal his Son in me…immediately I conferred not with flesh and blood'. Indeed, Paul did not bother to present himself to the acknowledged leaders of Jesus's followers, people he had been trying to kill shortly before. No, Paul was going to the top. Paul says he went into Petrean Arabia, then to Damascus for three years before troubling himself to be acquainted with James and Peter, his former enemies. Were they still enemies, in his heart?

Paul's reference to his mother's womb, to being consecrated for divine service may be compared to Mary the mother of Jesus's dedicated slavery to God's Temple. The 'womb' phrase appears in Jeremiah 1:5 when God ordains Jeremiah as a prophet to the nations, as well as in Isaiah 49:1: 'The LORD hath called me from the womb.' Eisenman sees this calling as evidence that the con-secration of Jesus to exclusive divine service properly and historically belongs to James, the sanctified 'brother of the Lord'. Paul considered it belonged to *him*: the prophet to whom Christ had appeared 'in person' on the road to

Damascus, as he marched to finish off Jesus's followers, accompanied by armed Herodian troops ready for a bloody bust-up.

Hegesippus's descriptions of James's restraint in matters of wine, liquor, bathing, hair-cutting as well as his vegetarianism mark him as a Nazarite devotee, a man of righteousness and piety. Clearly, the idea of the Temple's holy sanctuary being reserved exclusively for James cannot be correct, though James may have experienced an opportunity to enter the Holy of Holies in the manner of Zechariah and those of the priestly courses drawn by lot to seek a blessing for the people. That James wore linen almost certainly denotes him as a priest. Had he always been so, or was James, like the Levite holy hymn-singers, anxious to take up the linen and replace a corrupt senior priesthood? We do not know, but given James's parents' background, we may be inclined to think the priestly role and dress were no novelties.

———

Robert Eisenman, who has made the study of James his own, is convinced of two things. First, that James's authentic doctrine was that contained within the Dead Sea Scrolls under the authority of the 'Teacher of Righteousness' and second, that this same doctrine represents the authentic proto-Christian doctrine. The 'Nazarenes' and the New Covenanters were one and the same. 'Jesus' probably did not exist as an individual human personality. Material about James was, according to Eisenman, curiously confused with a 'brother' who was in fact a sectarian ideal, the 'Lord' or 'the Salvation'; this ideal was then romancified in the Jewish diaspora, using a copious quantity of messianic *testimonia* from the Hebrew prophets, in time generating a Gentile-friendly biography, heavily influenced by Paul and constructed to a great degree out of the matters at issue in a prior, obscured but nonetheless authentic conflict between Paul and James. Paul worked from his 'inner Christ' vision; James worked from the law, the New Covenant rules and the promises made on behalf of the Messiah.

Thus, Jesus's vaunted communion, if that is the right word, with the lame, the blind, the crippled, prostitutes, tax-collectors, sinners; his famous flouting of Sabbath observance regarding work, his eating 'freely' and drinking wine, his love for the outcast, his tolerance of menstruation, his closeness to the dead and the sick, all of this picture of generous and Pharisee-outraging goodness, the whole lot was, according to Eisenman, created out of the fact that it was these very sympathies that were held in abhorrence by the messianic New Covenanters. The gospels are the Gentiles' answer to authentic Jewish messianism. Paul's war was with the representatives of the dangerous New Covenanters. In this war, he was aided and abetted by the Herodians and by the Romans. They were his protectors. Paul, in this picture, was a stooge, an *agent provocateur*. It is an incredibly radical picture, backed up by passages such as the following, from the 'Qumran' War Scroll:

> No boy or woman shall enter their camps, from the time they leave Jerusalem and march out to war until they return. No man who is lame, or blind, or crippled, or afflicted with a lasting bodily blemish, or smitten with a bodily impurity, none of these shall march out to war with them. They shall all be freely enlisted for war, perfect in spirit and body and prepared for the day of Vengeance. And no man shall go down with them on the day of battle who is impure because of his 'fount', for the holy angels shall be with their hosts.

> (Vermes, *Dead Sea Scrolls*, p.172)

Eisenman reveals his contempt for anti-Semitic Christianity in no uncertain terms in the following passage of *James the Brother of Jesus* (p.300): 'What fun it must have been to portray the Messiah in Palestine as keeping company with such persons [prostitutes, tax collectors, sinners], knowing full well the opposite was true and how much types like those at Qumran abhorred them. This is not to mention the latterday satisfaction they would have derived from having people actually believe it for nearly 2,000 years had they but been around to enjoy it.'

Eisenman gives a potent example of the kind of manipulation he is talking about: 'The Son of Man came eating and drinking...a glutton and a wine-bibber, a friend of tax collectors and sinners.' (Mtt 11:19; Luke 7:34). But we see, to make his point, Eisenman must cut out a few key words, which, when restored, change the sense completely: 'The Son of Man came eating and drinking *and they say, Behold*, a glutton and a wine-bibber, a friend of tax collectors and sinners.' The remarks about gluttony and wine-bibbing constitute the substance of a jibe made at Jesus's expense. Jesus does something perfectly innocent and his opponents exaggerate it to suit themselves: '*They say...*' It is not good to claim a text is manipulative of the truth when you manipulate it yourself.

Luke, by the way, adds the words 'bread' and 'wine' to the quotation, so the Son of Man eats bread and drinks wine – no crime, according to the Torah, save in the context of special vows, or when entering the Holy of Holies in the Temple. Eisenman also omits to mention the verse previous to the quotation from Matthew, the all-important qualifier of what follows: 'For John came neither eating nor drinking, and they say, He hath a devil.' (v.18) John, holy from the womb, consecrated to God, probably a permanent Nazarite, or 'Essene', forebears wine and meat (being an eater of 'herbs', a vegetarian like James) – and still his enemies say he is possessed!

Furthermore, while it is fair to say that if you were lame, blind, a prostitute, someone with a skin disease, or a person who collected tribute for Rome, you would be well advised to keep out of a 'New Covenant' enclosure, for fear of tarnishing its 'holiness', documents within the Dead Sea Scrolls show that the messianic age would not mean automatic rejection for those whom Jesus was said to have healed. According to a 'Messianic Apocalypse' (4Q521), the Messiah is 'He who liberates the captives, restores sight to the blind, straightens the b[ent]. And f[or]ever I will clea[ve to the h]opeful and in His mercy... And the fr[uit] will not be delayed for anyone And the Lord will accomplish glorious things which have never been as [He...] For He will heal the wounded, and revive the dead and bring good news to the poor. ...He will lead the uprooted and make the hungry rich...' The gospels could have been compiled with an eye to illustrating this text, as they might any discourse of Paul's.

Again, Jesus in the gospels gives vent to much apocalyptic prophecy that a New Covenanter would recognize and favour, nor would such a one fail to notice Jesus's respect for the law, such as in this famous stark, if not typical, injunction: 'Whoever shall break the least one of these commandments and teach men to do so shall be called least in the kingdom of the Heavens.' (Mtt.5:19–20) The Paulinists do not seem to have been able to get round to twisting that one! No, it must be that to attack the existence of Jesus, using James as the club, is to misrepresent James's own position, as far as it can be discerned from the surviving texts. James, no less than the Jesus of the gospels, appears to have quoted from Daniel 7:13 concerning the 'Son of man' who in Daniel's vision 'came with the clouds of heaven'. According to the John the Baptist of Matthew 3:11–12: the one 'that cometh after me' (Jesus) 'will burn up the chaff with unquenchable fire'. That's pretty rough stuff for the sinners. Indeed, the Jesus of Mark 13: 26–7 might at first sight find little to quarrel with certain passages from the Qumran War Scroll. According to Mark:

> And then shall they see the Son of man coming in the clouds with great power and glory. And then shall he send his angels, and shall gather together his elect from the four winds, from the uttermost part of the earth to the uttermost part of heaven.

The War Scroll only adds the, admittedly vital, detail that the new holy warriors will join the angelic hosts, or rather, the emphasis seems more towards the idea that the 'Heavenly Host' will march with the consecrated, holy soldiers. This is a vital distinction from Hegesippus's record concerning James and the coming of the Son of Man in judgement. James is not recruiting 'Sons of Light' for the final Conflict; he trusts to the Messiah and his angels to do what is required. The War Scroll is plainly of the view that holy warriors are necessary:

> Valiant [warriors] of the angelic host are among our numbered men, and the Hero of war is with our congregation; the host of His spirits is with our foot-soldiers and horsemen. [They are as] clouds, as clouds of dew [covering] the earth, as a shower of rain shedding judgement on all that grows on the earth.

One thinks immediately of the brother disciples known as 'the sons of thunder', or *Boanerges*. Jesus *recruited* from the New Covenanters; he did not join them. If James had advocated armed insurrection, Josephus would almost certainly have noted it with the great disdain he habitually reserved for the armed Zealot, and it would most likely have been not the high priest who ordered James's death, but the Roman authorities. They had had plenty of time to 'find him out'. According to Church Father Jerome (AD 348–420) James 'ruled the Church of Jerusalem for thirty years' until the 'seventh year of Nero and was buried near the Temple, from which he had been cast down'. Jerome follows Eusebius in noting that James's tombstone with its inscription was well known until the siege of Titus and the end of Hadrian's reign (c.AD 138), when Jews were expelled from Jerusalem. It is unlikely that the Romans would have permitted an inscription to James if James's name was an incitement to armed struggle against the Roman invader.

———

Hegesippus's account of James's death served later generations with knowledge concerning Jesus's brother, but later commentators added their own information. The aforementioned Jerome, for example, wrote in his commentary on Galatians that 'this same James, who was the first Bishop of Jerusalem and known as Justus, was considered to be so Holy by the People that they zealously sought to touch the hem of his clothing'. Readers will be familiar with the story of the woman 'with an issue of blood' who sought to touch the hem of Jesus's garment, whereupon he felt 'power' had gone out of him and turned to her, much to her surprise. At first sight, Jerome's reference to James's hem seems to be a similar case, but it need not be. Numbers 15:38–9 has the Lord speaking to Moses, telling him to require of the children of Israel to make themselves fringes in the borders of their garments. These were so that they may look on it 'and remember all the commandments of the Lord, and do them, and that ye seek not after your own heart and your own eyes, after which ye used to go a whoring: That ye may remember, and do all my commandments, and be holy unto your God.' If James had such a fringe on the hem of his garment, it would itself be seen as a holy sign, and therefore, on the garment of a holy man, a source of sacredness, to be respected.

———

There can be little doubt that James was a priest, wearing linen. According to both Jerome and Epiphanius (AD 367–404), James wore the high priest's mitre and entered the Holy of Holies to make atonement. Epiphanius's *Panarion* also tells us that James was a vegetarian, an eater of 'herbs' and practised sexual abstinence. Epiphanius also adds a detail of great interest concerning Jesus's family.

Whereas Eusebius repeats Hegesippus's account that at the martyrdom of James, one of the witnesses to James's fate was 'one of the priests of the sons of Rechab', Epiphanius, writing around a century later, reports that the witness who defended James against his enemies was Jesus's cousin, Simeon bar Cleophas: 'Thus, even Simeon bar Cleophas, his [James's] cousin, who was standing not far away, said, 'Stop, why are you stoning the Just One? Behold, he is praying the most wonderful prayers for you.' Was Epiphanius implying that Simeon bar Cleophas was a priest of the 'sons of Rechab'? This would seem unlikely, for otherwise he should have mentioned it. But Eusebius's account looks faulty too, since he repeats Hegesippus's description of the witness, namely, that he was a priest of the sons of Rechab. Who were these 'sons of Rechab'?

According to I Chronicles 2:55, Rechab's House was of the tribe of Kenites, there described as 'scribes'. There is nothing solid to indicate 'Rechabites' ever being priests, though Eisenman cites rabbinic sources to show that the sons and daughters of 'Rechabites' did marry sons and daughters of the high priests, and performed services at the altar. According to Nehemiah 3:14, set in c.450 BC, 'Malchiah' 'the son of Rechab' was given the task of repairing the 'dung gate', a poor gate of Jerusalem, but Eisenman's attempt to link this 'Malchiah' with the 'Malchijah' given the fifth priestly course in the reign of David (I Chronicles 24:9) carries no conviction.

The 'priestly connection' would appear to stem from Jeremiah, chapter 36. There the Lord tells Jeremiah to go to the House of the Rechabites and 'bring them into the house of the LORD'. Jeremiah does so and the Rechabites are offered cups of wine. But they refuse: 'We will drink no wine' say the Rechabites, 'for Jonadab the son of Rechab our father commanded us, saying, Ye shall drink no wine, neither ye, nor your sons for ever. Neither shall ye build house, nor sow seed, nor plant vineyard, nor have any: but all your days ye shall dwell in tents; that ye may live many days in the land where ye be strangers.'

Keeping the commandments commended the Rechabites to God; their eschewing of material benefits strikes us as exemplifying the holy man of all time, the one with nowhere permanent on earth to lay his head. The reference to the Rechabites living in tents is particularly significant in a period of wilderness camps erected by those awaiting the Day of the Lord.

Since priests were forbidden to drink wine when entering the inner court of the Temple, it would be an easy error to make, when reading the text of Jeremiah and seeing the Rechabites entering the house of the Lord, to presume some special kind of priesthood. On the other hand, would not a righteous critic of the priesthood note the superiority in holiness of the Rechabite to a supposed corrupt priesthood who claimed entry to the Holy of Holies as a right? Would it then be unjust to conjecture the existence of a group of perhaps *would-be holy priests* within the Temple, and attached to James's assembly, who had taken vows of like kind and called themselves, in honour of past keepers of the law who eschewed possessions, 'sons of the Rechabites'. They may themselves have been Levites already. Certainly, such an idea fits neatly into the angry tumult recorded by Josephus that was rapidly sowing chaos in the Temple, as rival priestly parties sought to make up for the deficiencies and corruption of the richest priests. That James was one of these poorer priests, perhaps in the tradition of his late relative, Zechariah, a 'keeper' of the law and a watcher for the Lord, would be perfectly consistent with the evidence. Whether or not Jesus's 'cousin' Simeon bar Cleophas was a member of the 'sons of Rechab' fraternity, if there was such a thing as Hegesippus refers to, cannot be known. However, when we see that it is Simeon bar Cleophas who will succeed James as second bishop of Jerusalem, we may regard such an idea as a reasonable inference from the evidence, such as it is.

This picture undoubtedly revolutionizes our conception of the origins of the Christian Church, and we should not have come to it had we not been in search of Jesus's real family. The authentic leadership of the primitive Church was more Jewish priestly than 'Christian apostolic'.

———————

One thing is indisputable. Hegesippus was convinced that James believed Jesus was the 'door' or 'way' to God; James's brother was the Messiah. If you try to take that conviction away from Hegesippus's account, you do so because you do not like it, not because it is not manifestly there. If Hegesippus is wrong about his central conviction, the peripherals may hardly be taken seriously. And it may be argued that we need to take Hegesippus reasonably seriously, for without his accounts, we should know nothing of other members of Jesus's family in the 50 or so years following the stoning of James the Righteous, brother of Jesus.

The Desposyni – Heirs of Jesus

Jesus was a man. His relatives survived the 1st century. How did his family understand Jesus and his work? What happened to Jesus's family members who supported his message and messiahship? We examine the persecution of the House of David by Roman intelligence in the late 1st and early 2nd centuries, including accounts of interrogation and murder. We explore the life and beliefs of Jesus's brother Judas's grandsons, and of the martyrdom of Jesus's cousin, the second bishop of Jerusalem. We look at the reappearance of Jesus's family in the 3rd century, proud of their genealogies and their link with their 'master', Jesus.

Once Christianity had been 'de-Judaized' and become an imperial religion, Jesus's family descendants were surplus baggage from the past; they disappear from history.

According to early Church Father Ignatius's Epistle to the Ephesians (ch.8) written about AD 105–15, 'Jesus Christ, was, according to the economy of God, conceived in the womb by Mary, of the seed of David, but by the Holy Ghost.'

Justin Martyr, a Gentile philosophy enthusiast from Samaria (AD 110–65) wrote in his *Dialogue* with Trypho, a Judean:

we know him [Christ] to be the first-begotten of God, and to be before all creatures; likewise to be the son of the patriarchs, since he assumed flesh by the Virgin of their family, and submitted to become a man without comeliness, dishonoured, and subject to suffering.

(*Dialogue with Trypho*, composed *c.*150–60)

A century earlier, Paul in his epistle to the Romans (I:3–4; AD 50–60) had nothing to say about Jesus's 'comeliness' or otherwise, but declared that God's son 'Jesus Christ our Lord' 'was made of the semen of David [*ek spermatos Daueid*] according to the flesh; And declared to be the Son of God with power, according to holy *pneuma* [spirit], by the resurrection of the dead'. The phrase 'according to the flesh' means: 'as far as the flesh is concerned'. As far as his body was concerned, Jesus was a man of David's House.

These quotations express the core of the earliest known traditions about Jesus held by his followers some two decades and more after his earthly lifetime. As for Jesus's flesh, he was of the House of David, a genetic descendant of the ancient fathers of Israel, and, before them, the patriarchs of mankind. The Davidic, monarchical dignity came, according to Justin Martyr, through his mother; Paul makes no distinction. Jesus's being the Christ or Messiah, the spiritual Son of God born before all created life, came by the power of holy spirit: the primal power of God that transcends creation, and therefore, death.

Now, theologians would come to bicker about the precise meaning of all this, as pundits will today, but at the beginning of the 1st century, many were satisfied with these statements and gloried in them. The question occurs: did Jesus's family share this outlook? Did they recognize that something unique had happened in their family? Did they recognize that God had separated one of their own for unique service?

There is no record of any objection being made by any member of Jesus's family in the 1st century as to Jesus's unique status in the history of his people's salvation. From what we may glean of the point of view of Jesus's brother James, Israel at last had the monarch, the holy Messiah foretold. Defeating God's enemies in the corrupt priesthood and monarchy by his mysterious death and resurrection, the holy king ruled not from a palace, as did Herod Antipas, but from the heavens, on God's right hand, over all, through his chosen ministers. His *spiritual* kingdom was established: the people had seen miracles, while the meaning of righteousness and mercy and knowledge and love had been declared to his closest followers. That message was now being declared openly: the time of salvation had come; the corrupt would be swallowed up in the fire of holy righteousness. In course of time, that heavenly house would come to replace the corrupt house on earth, and the seed of David would come to its full fruition in the spiritual redemption of Israel, through which mighty, apocalyptic events the Gentiles would also come to know God and His purpose, as all men had once known God before their ancient corruption into idolatry and the catastrophe of Babel divided the children of Noah into the nations.

God was calling forth His own: a grand atonement was in process.

That at least one member of Jesus's family not only accepted this core *kerygma* or proclamation, but worked with Jesus's other followers to promulgate it during the 1st century and beyond is attested by Josephus in the 1st century and by Hegesippus in the 2nd. As far as we can tell, the place of Jesus's family would come to be seen as an inconvenience, even an anomaly, to the Gentile Church. Attempts were made to distance Jesus's brothers from him, while elevating his mother beyond familial realities. Nevertheless, during the 1st century, it would appear there was something of a 'Jesus dynasty' being accorded respect in Jerusalem, at least until the time of the Emperor Trajan (AD 98–117).

We had better examine that word 'dynasty'.

Dynasty... It is an attractive word, especially today where we have seen it associated with family and business combined into a powerful nexus of wheeler-dealing and internecine strife. Our ancestors would not have thought about padded shoulders, neurotic children, domineering mothers and unscrupulous brothers – well, not entirely. They would have thought in terms of claims to the throne, power being passed on from generation to generation: status to inherit. And here lies the problem when we are asked to think of Jesus's family constituting a dynasty, or even 'Jesus Dynasty'. What *power* could have been conceivably passed on by members of Jesus's family? Unless, of course, the Church would itself become a power on earth. But that was a long way off from the situation of 'Christians' in the 1st century.

Surely, if we were speaking of a conventional Jewish royal House, even if in exile or deposed and discrete, they would have reason to strive for kingship and the highest priesthood. But there is no mention of James, for example, claiming the throne of a reunited Israel, or of the throne being claimed for him by messianically inspired followers. James is apparently content to play back-room Aaron to Jesus's on-the-mountaintop Moses, or greater-than Moses. James was content to work with Cephas, apparently a man of trade from Galilee. The Hegesippus account presents James in charge of the Church in Jerusalem *with the apostles*. One might dream of them as a 'court' of sorts, with James seated on an episcopal throne, but all the evidence points to their being sent out to do *work*, not bask in reflected regal or faded regal glory. This might equate strangely with the Knights of the Round Table, but the knights were only sent out for the Grail because they were getting lazy at Camelot! The apostles were sent to the synagogues of the world to announce the Messiah had come and been raised from the dead. The beginning of the end was nigh. It was time to enter the Kingdom. This kingdom had no end. That means it did not need a dynasty to keep it going. The fount was priestly, not monarchical.

There is absolutely no evidence whatsoever of any interest in Jesus producing an heir, or of having so produced an heir: the first object of a king in any dynasty. This is hardly surprising. What would such an heir inherit? He could hardly inherit his father's kingdom, since it was widely believed 'his Father' was ruling his kingdom and would always rule it, in heaven. If he wanted to claim *that* throne, he would have to die first! As a dynast, Jesus seems to have made the 'dynasty' redundant. It had reached its fruit *in him* and he was no longer about his dynastic forebears' business. If his mother thought she could advise him, as in most dynasties, she was mistaken. This dynasty had its roots in heaven.

Are there any grounds for thinking something of Jesus's unique powers could be inherited by other members of the family *because* they were members of his family? None whatever; the power of miracles came from faith in God, and inner holiness, not from blood. There was no point claiming Judea for the House of David because a messianic kingdom was on its way, and Jesus, its lord, had given no specific indication that even his closest followers were going to be accorded the highest places within it, or even if a hierarchy was intended. Those working in the kingdom were going to suffer and have to learn to glory in suffering. They must find their princely treasure not in chests of foaming gold, but in heaven.

It must have been very difficult being a member of Jesus's family.

You would hear all sorts of amazing things about the star of the family, but there was not much for relatives to do except follow instructions, work with the others, and go along with the whole thing, or, well, fade out of sight. It appears that at least some members of the family decided to go along with the spiritual adventure launched by their extraordinary relative. If they could do little else, they could at least give substance to the reality of their lord, and endorse Jesus's – and the family's – messianic credentials. He was of the House of David, and so were they. That should count for something, surely. And besides, in Jesus's terrestrial absence, there was an assembly to run, a dynasty of Herodian usurpers to keep an eye on, and a fight to be fought for all Israel's sake. Like any worthy royal House, they had best serve God, and be seen to serve God, to justify their position.

James himself was a holy celibate. This says quite a lot: not only that James had no intention of producing a genetic 'heir', any more than his brother Jesus, but also that the oft-repeated idea that a rabbi's duty, in all circumstances, was to marry and have children as a 'good Jew' was not true in every single case. In James's case, his virginity was counted for holiness, and we may suppose the same of Jesus, though, interestingly, we have no account of its ever being an issue; we never hear of the 'virgin Jesus' as we do his mother.

It should be made clear that any attempts to assert claims of terrestrial kingship would not only invite Herodian hit-men, but would be most unwelcome to Roman authority. As it was, the messianic claims were sufficient for the Sanhedrin to persecute the assembly in Jerusalem and elsewhere, led by super-zealous Pharisee, Saul.

The emperors had got used to the slimy ways of the Herodians: Herodians could be trusted to play the game, if not always very well. The Herodians were, at least, men of the world, unlike the righteousness brigade in its sundry forms, who refused to bend. The Romans, a fairly superstitious lot, were very sensitive about predictions and prophecies, especially where rulers were concerned. Judeans were not very popular in the Roman court at the best of times. Tiberius (AD 14–37), during whose reign as emperor Jesus was crucified, made this plain when, according to Suetonius's *Life of Tiberius*:

> He abolished foreign cults at Rome, particularly the Egyptian and Jewish, forcing all [Roman] citizens who had embraced these super-stitious faiths to burn their religious vestments and other accessories. Jews of military age were removed to unhealthy regions, on the pretext of drafting them into the army; the others of the same race or of similar beliefs were expelled from the city and threatened with slavery if they defied the order. Tiberius also banished all astrologers except such as asked for his forgiveness and undertook to make no more predictions.
>
> (*c*.119–22; *Life of Tiberius*, 36)

The predictions that really bothered the emperors were those with political ramifications. Roman historian Tacitus, writing *c*.AD 105–8, alluded to a story referred to by Josephus. Judean Zealots took a mysterious opening of a great brass door in the Temple as a sign of God's support for their, in part, messianic war against the Romans, 'a sinister interpretation' as Tacitus saw it, but nonetheless of a piece with the conviction that world domination was in God's, not Rome's hands:

> The majority [of Judeans] were convinced that the ancient scriptures of their priests alluded to the present as the very time when the orient would triumph and from Judea would go forth men destined to rule the world. This mysterious prophesy really referred to Vespasian and Titus, but the common people, true to the selfish ambitions of

mankind, thought that this mighty destiny was reserved for them, and not even their calamities opened their eyes to the truth.

(Tacitus, *Histories*, 5.6.13)

Astonishingly, this prophecy of men coming forth from Judea to rule the world would bring members of Jesus's family before an investigative committee. According to Eusebius, during the reign of the emperor Trajan (AD 98–117) popular uprisings in some cities issued in sporadic persecutions of Christians:

> We have learnt that in it Simeon, the son of Clopas, whom we showed to have been the second bishop of the church at Jerusalem, ended his life in martyrdom. The witness for this is that same Hegesippus, of whom we have already quoted several passages. After speaking of certain heretics he goes on to explain how Simeon was at this time accused by them and for many days was tortured in various manners for being a Christian, to the great astonishment of the judge and those with him, until he suffered an end like that of the Lord. But there is nothing better than to listen to the historian who tells these facts as follows. 'Some of these [that is to say the heretics] accused Simon the son of Clopas of being descended from David and a Christian and thus he suffered martyrdom, being 120 years old, when Trajan was emperor and Atticus was Consular.' [In Eusebius's *Chronicon*, he dates Simeon's martyrdom to AD 106 or 107.]
>
> The same writer says that his accusers also suffered arrest for being of the royal House of the Jews when search was made at the time for those of that family. And one would reasonably say that Simeon was one of the eyewitnesses and actual hearers of the Lord on the evidence of the length of his life and the reference in the gospels [John 19:25ff.] to Mary the wife of Clopas whose son the narrative has already shown him to be.

(*Ecclesiastical History*, Book III, ch.32)

This is remarkable testimony; one would like to know who were the 'heretics' referred to in Hegesippus's account who accused Simeon, but we only know Hegesippus's work from what Eusebius quoted from it; it must have been easy enough to get hold of in his day.

Apparently, Trajan was not the first emperor to 'have it in' for the House of David. There had clearly been a directed search made by Roman authorities for members of Jesus's family, that is to say, members of the House of David, a threat-source taken very seriously. The Romans were wary of an armed messianic movement; a pretender from the family could easily have ignited fresh revolt. Jesus's family had become a political intelligence target. According to Eusebius:

> Domitian [AD 81–96] gave orders for the execution of those of the family of David and an ancient story goes that some heretics accused the grandsons of Judas (who is said to have been the brother, according to the flesh, of the Saviour) saying that they were of the family of David and related to the Christ himself. Hegesippus relates this exactly as follows.
>
> 'Now there still survived of the family of the Lord grandsons of Judas, who was said to have been his brother according to the flesh, and they were delated as being of the family of David. These the officer brought to Domitian Caesar, for, like Herod, he was afraid of the coming of the Christ. He asked them if they were of the House of David and they admitted it. Then he asked them how much property they had, or how much money they controlled, and they said that all they possessed was 9,000 denarii [a few hundred pounds] between them, the half belonging to each, and they stated that they did not possess this in money but that it was a valuation of only 39 plethra [about 19 acres] of ground on which they paid taxes and lived on it by their own work.' They then showed him their hands, adducing as testimony of their labour the hardness of their bodies, and the tough skin which had been embossed on their hands from their incessant work.
>
> They were asked concerning the Christ and his kingdom, its nature,

origin, and time of appearance, and explained that it was neither of the world nor earthly, but heavenly and angelic, and it would be at the end of the world, when he would come in glory to judge the living and the dead and to reward every man according to his deeds. At this Domitian did not condemn them at all, but despised them as simple folk, released them, and decreed an end to the persecution against the church. But when they were released they were the leaders of the churches, both for their testimony and for their relation to the Lord, and remained alive in the peace which ensued until Trajan. Hegesippus tells this; moreover, Tertullian [*c*.160–221] also has made similar mention of Domitian. 'Domitian also once tried to do the same as he, for he was a Nero in cruelty, but, I believe, inasmuch as he had some sense, he stopped at once and recalled those whom he had banished.'

(*Ecclesiastical History*, Book III, 19–20)

Again, this is a remarkable account of the survival and status of Jesus's family. We may note that the force of their testimony appears to have had the extraordinary effect of ceasing a persecution and bringing accused Christians back from banishment. The banishment may refer to upper-class Christians such as, among others, Flavia Domitilla, niece (or wife, as Suetonius has it) of the Roman consul Flavius Clemens. Domitilla was banished to the island of Pontia for testifying to Christ. The Christian message had entered the imperial household.

It would have been nice to know where Jesus's relatives were living before confronting the imperial authority. Had they been banished too?

The account is full of interest. We have heard nothing from history of Jesus's and James's brother, Judas. This little bobbing up above history's waves of his grandchildren, preserved for us by Eusebius, undoubtedly conceals an iceberg of unknown history beneath. What was their grandfather like?

We have one little-read canonical epistle that might just be the work of Judas, brother of James and Jesus. The 'General Epistle of Jude' (Juda or Judas) in the New Testament, begins: 'Judas, the servant of Jesus Christ, and brother of James, to them that are sanctified by God the Father, and preserved in Jesus Christ, and called: Mercy unto you, and peace, and love, be multiplied.'

Judas addresses the 'sanctified', those set apart for holiness. He writes of a crisis in their world. 'Lascivious' men have crept into the Church 'unawares'. The sanctified must contend for the true faith; they must fight for it. Judas writes of the corrupters in terms of the Book of Enoch, a highly significant esoteric text, popular with Essenes: 'Raging waves of the sea, foaming out of their own shame; wandering stars, to whom is reserved the blackness of darkness for ever.' (v.13) Jude refers to the mythology of the fallen angels who have come to earth to frustrate God's work among men: 'And the angels which kept not their first estate, but left their own habitation, he hath reserved in everlasting chains under darkness unto the judgement of the great day.' (v.6)

The filthy men, blasphemers, atheists, denying 'the only Lord God, and our Lord Jesus Christ', give 'themselves over to fornication, and going after strange flesh, are set forth for an example, suffering the vengeance of eternal fire. Likewise all these filthy dreamers defile the flesh, despise dominion, and speak evil of dignities. [...] Woe unto them! For they have gone in the way of Cain, and ran greedily after the error of Balaam [a Gentile] for reward and perished in the gainsaying of Core.'

Judas, like his brother, or perhaps brothers (he may be addressing them), is sure he is living in 'the last time', a time when 'mockers' were prophesied, those who 'should walk after their own ungodly lusts. These are they who separate themselves, sensual, having not the Spirit.' (v.19) While, in the face of attack, the 'beloved' must build themselves up in their 'most holy faith, praying in the Holy Spirit', showing compassion on those in danger, 'pulling them out of the fire; hating even the garment spotted by the flesh', they may be assured that the wicked will come to judgement:

> And Enoch also, the seventh from Adam, prophesied of these, saying, Behold, the Lord cometh with ten thousand of his saints, To execute judgement upon all, and to convince all that are ungodly among them of all their ungodly deeds which they have ungodly

committed, and all their hard speeches which ungodly sinners have spoke against him.

(Jude, v.14)

The letter is striking, little known. But there it is: a lonely outpost in the New Testament, seldom visited. Positively fuming with the smoke of righteousness, the letter of Judas would hardly be out of place in the Dead Sea Scrolls. It speaks of an authentic Jewish faith in the 'only wise God our Saviour' before whom the saved soul will be presented 'faultless' and 'with exceeding joy' by 'him that is able to keep you from falling'. This language meshes in with the Jesus 'door' language attributed to James, and, bears the authentic aroma of mid to late 1st-century Palestine. It is usually dated, with no great certainty, to AD 90–120.

The epistle of Judas is certainly consistent in part with the fragmentary message attributed by Hegesippus to Judas's grandchildren, that when asked concerning the kingdom, they told the emperor that 'it was neither of the world nor earthly, but heavenly and angelic, and it would be at the end of the world, when he would come in glory to judge the living and the dead and to reward every man according to his deeds'.

Domitian's concern with the grandsons of Judas's worldly possessions suggests an anxiety about the dimensions of the 'dynasty' natural to an emperor on the look-out for revolt and pretenders to power. Also interesting is the account of the beliefs of Jesus's relatives concerning the spiritual kingdom. Domitian obviously knew well the prophecy of a mighty conqueror and saviour who would come from the east, probably Judea. The prophecy had lost none of its power to evoke resistance with the deaths of Domitian's brother Titus and his father Vespasian, whom Josephus declared to be embodiments of the prophesied victors. Domitian was right to be cautious; Judea exploded one last time behind a messianic pretender some 40 years after Domitian's death. The emperor may have flattered himself that it would be *he* who would yet emerge from the east as a saviour of the world. Domitian successfully led his army against the Sarmatians and the Dacians, rebellious peoples north and west of the Black Sea respectively. Suetonius writes that Domitian pined for military glory in the east.

While Domitian could on occasion exercise a passion for justice, fear of assassination and of bankruptcy manifested themselves in episodes of capriciousness and appalling, sadistic cruelty. Really, Judas's grandsons were very lucky to 'get away with it'. They were standing on most unstable ice before an intelligent emperor with an ear for every nuance of doubt or evasion. Suetonius recorded how Domitian would preface his most savage sentences with a 'little speech about mercy'. Hearing Domitian mention the word mercy was sign enough that something ugly was going to happen. Taking a dislike to some incautious allusions introduced by Hermogenes of Tarsus into a literary work, Domitian had the author executed and his copyist slaves crucified. Domitian, who loathed theatricals, executed one sickly boy because he was a pupil of the despised actor, Paris, resembling him in looks and mannerisms. Many senators were put to death on trivial charges, regardless of who they looked like.

Domitian was always eager to grab new estates. He secured one property on the basis of uncorroborated hearsay that its late owner had opined he would leave it to the emperor. The emperor took it. Perhaps that is why Domitian enquired after Judas's grandsons' estate!

Domitian had a particular dislike of Jews. His brother Titus had ordered that the Jewish Sanctuary tax due from every Jew throughout the world for Temple expenses should be collected for the empire, even though the Temple was destroyed, an act celebrated on the still-standing triumphal arch of Titus in Rome. Only those who paid the tax could practise their religion. Greek converts to the Jewish faith who would not be circumcised escaped the tax. Most Christians did all they could to prove they were not Jews. Resistance to circumcision saved hard cash *and* went some way to remove the believer from official suspicion; Paul's writings on the subject went down very well in this context. Judas's grandsons, on the other hand, would have been exceptional on this account. Hegesippus notes that they paid their taxes. Suetonius writes:

Domitian's agents collected the tax on Jews with a peculiar lack of mercy; and took proceedings not only against those who kept their Jewish origins a secret in order to avoid the tax, but against those who lived as Jews without professing Judaism [these were probably uncircumcised 'God-fearers' rather than Christians; though there might be a reference here to Jewish Christians, such as Judas's grandchildren]. As a boy, I [Suetonius] remember once attending a crowded Court where the Procurator had a ninety-year-old man stripped to establish whether or not he had been circumcised.

Perhaps Suetonius had, as a boy, witnessed the humiliation of Jesus's brother's grandson. It is plain anyway that Domitian did not treat members of the House of David like royalty.

One may presume that though set free, the grandsons of Jesus's brother Judas would have been warned to keep very quiet indeed, and out of all seditious company, to stick with the spiritual kingdom and not get any funny ideas about its realization on earth. They may also have been encouraged to vacate the sensitive region of Palestine and embark on husbandry elsewhere, if they had not, in fact, already done so. In the event of banishment, troublesome Judean leaders were usually sent to faraway France, or Gaul as it was known at the time. Herod's sons Archelaus and, eventually, Herod Antipas, for example, were both forced to take up residence at Vienne. In AD 177, there would be savage persecutions against Christians in Vienne and Lyons. Their bishop, Pothinos, 90 years old, perished in the torment. It seems likely that many of those persecuted would have been Jews. Perhaps Jesus's family's descendants were among their number; records of the persecution crisis are sparse.

In any event, according to Eusebius and Hegesippus, the descendants of King David continued as Church leaders after Domitian's interrogation, both on account of their testifying to Christ before the emperor at great risk to themselves, and because of the esteem that, at this period at least, was still accorded the Lord's family. If God chose that family to serve him, the Church should respect that. Just how much they should respect it is impossible to determine usefully.

Eusebius reports that Judas's grandsons were still alive at the beginning of Trajan's reign (AD 98–117):

> The same writer [Hegesippus] says that other grandsons of one of the so-called brothers of the saviour named Judas survived to the same reign after they had given in the time of Domitian the testimony already recorded of them in behalf of the faith in Christ. He writes thus: 'They came therefore and presided over every church as witnesses belonging to the Lord's family, and when there was complete peace in every church they survived until the reign of the Emperor Trajan, until the time when the son of the Lord's uncle [Clopas, Joseph's brother], the aforesaid Simeon the son of Clopas, was similarly accused by the sects on the same charge before Atticus the Consular. He was tortured for many days and gave his witness, so that all, even the consular, were extremely surprised how, at the age of 120, he endured, and he was commanded to be crucified.'
>
> (*Ecclesiastical History* III.32)

This sectarian opposition to the son of Simeon the son of Clopas, leading to ignominious crucifixion, is fascinating, but the character of that opposition remains a mystery. Eusebius elsewhere speaks of a number of sects of 'Ebionites', that is, the 'Poor'. They were Churches of Judean and Syrian-Jewish Christians characterized by differing degrees of severity in applying the law of Moses. They also held different convictions regarding the role of the Holy Spirit in Jesus's birth and being. Thus, Eusebius took the term 'Ebionite' as meaning they held 'poor' or 'mean' views of Jesus's nature, a mischievous pun perhaps. For all of them, Jesus was the Messiah, but he was a man; the virgin birth was dismissed. According to Epiphanius's account of 'Ebionites' made in *c.*AD 400, they believed that 'the Spirit which is Christ came into him and put on the Man who is called 'Jesus'.'

We have no evidence for supposing that these views were held by members of Jesus's family. If some of these groups shared the high levels of strict intolerance that we see in the discipline observed by the 'Qumran sectaries', such alone might account for the venom wherewith a Jew could condemn another Jew before a Roman. Nevertheless, such betrayal must be regarded as the least likely possibility. Alternatively, the opposition to Jesus's family might have come from fanatical *uncircumcised* Christians, followers of Paul perhaps. The possibility that it came from zealous Jews who did not accept Jesus at all, cannot be discounted. Whatever the truth, it will still come as a surprise to most readers to think of a time when Jesus's family members were persecuted for supporting him both by Jewish sects and by Romans.

Writing towards the end of the long era of Roman persecution of Christians, Eusebius has some more to tell us about Simeon, the son of Clopas, cousin of Jesus:

> After the martyrdom of James and the capture of Jerusalem which immediately followed, the story goes that those of the Apostles and of the disciples of the Lord who were still alive came together from every place with those who were, according to the flesh, of the family of the Lord, for many of them were then still alive, and they all took counsel together as to whom they ought to adjudge worthy to succeed James, and all unanimously decided that Simeon the son of Clopas, whom the scripture of the gospel also mentions, was judged worthy of the throne of the diocese there. He was, so it is said, a cousin [or possibly first-cousin] of the saviour, for Hegesippus relates that Clopas was the brother of Joseph, and in addition that Vespasian, after the capture of Jerusalem, ordered a search to be made for all who were of the family of David, that there might be left among the Judeans no one of the royal family and, for this reason, a very great persecution was again inflicted on the Judeans.
>
> (*Ecclesiastical History*, III, 11)

Once more, we are presented with a fascinating glimpse into early Church politics. We should be most struck I think by the indication of the authority held by Simeon, Clopas's son. James, Jesus's brother, is succeeded, after the destruction of the Temple, by Jesus's cousin. The authority structure is clearly a family affair. Simeon (or Simon) is given the diocesan 'throne'. He rules vicariously on earth for Jesus. Might one say he is Christ's vicar, that is to say his 'stand-in', on earth? He is the judge of right practice. Inevitably, he would have found opposition.

Eusebius could himself sympathize with Simeon's position. After AD 313, Eusebius became bishop of Caesarea. Twelve years later he would sit on the right hand of the Emperor Constantine as a moderate advisor in the formulation of the Nicene Creed, opposing the extremes, as he saw them, of Athanasius, on the one hand, and of Arius on the other. Eusebius sought comprehensiveness while maintaining what he considered the authority of the eastern, and especially Syrian and Palestinian Church, which he took as the inheritance of the first Church and bishops of Jerusalem. Jesus's cousin once occupied that throne and, for Eusebius, Simeon was an ideal exemplar of evangelical courage.

Since Constantine was occupied in moving the capital of the empire from Rome in the west to Constantinople in the east, it might have seemed a period of triumph for the eastern patriarchates. Politically then, as well as theologically, it was a good time for Eusebius to draw attention to the authority of the family of Jesus, though what had happened to them in the intervening 200 years is largely a mystery.

Not surprisingly then, Eusebius concludes his treatment of Simeon, son of Joseph's brother, by emphasizing, not altogether accurately I think, that until the times of Simeon, 'the church remained a pure and uncorrupted virgin, for those who attempted to corrupt the healthful rule of the saviour's *kērugmatos* [proclamation], if they existed at all, lurked in obscure darkness'. He then asserts that the heretics only slipped from the shadows when the 'holy band of Apostles' and those who had heard the 'divine wisdom' directly with their own ears began to die away. Then 'the federation of godless error', the 'false teachers' 'barefacedly tried against the preaching of the truth the counter-proclamation of '*gnosis* falsely so-called'. This last phrase – the false gnosis or knowledge – Eusebius has taken directly from Bishop Irenaeus of Lyon's books *Against the*

Heretics (*c*.AD 180) which deals with many heresies associated with teachers of false gnosis who decried the God of Genesis and of the law: manifest heresy to men like Eusebius who believed, apparently along with Jesus's close family, that the only 'false god' was the Devil or 'prince of this world' who, with his demonic servants and dark angels, perverted men from their salvation and obscured the divine wisdom that was as manifest in the universe as it was in the incarnation of that wisdom, Jesus. For Eusebius, the family of Jesus was undoubtedly 'on message'.

It would surely have helped Eusebius of Caesarea and indeed Hegesippus and many others if descendants of Simeon who held fast to the family tradition of Jesus could have added their weight to maintaining peace and harmony in the Christian Church. Imagine the impact such descendants might have made at Nicaea. Or are we mistaken? Two hundred years after the crucifixion of Simeon, did the Lord's family matter any more?

As far as we can tell, with the passing of Trajan's reign, Jesus's family went missing. It appears that they – whoever 'they' may have been – curiously and, mostly, inexplicably, become removed from the recorded development of the Christian Church.

Well, almost.

There survives a fragment of a mention in a letter to one Aristides by Christian geographer and historian Julius Africanus (*c*.170–245), an 'African' possibly from Libya but at the time of writing a converted inhabitant of Jerusalem and Emmaus.

Julius's pains to establish the correct genealogy for Jesus earned him considerable space in Book I, chapter seven, of Eusebius's *Ecclesiastical History*. In that chapter we find unique usage of the word *desposunoi* to describe Jesus's family descendants.

In Greek, a *desposunos* is one *belonging to the master or lord*, surely a peculiar way of describing Jesus's descendants as a collective. The lord, in Eusebius's quotation from Julius Africanus, is presumed to be the Lord ('despot', with no pejorative meaning) Jesus.

The 'desposyni' are mentioned because Julius wants to explain to Aristides that the genealogies of Jesus in Luke and in Matthew, however divergent they appear, can yet be reconciled. According to Julius, one only has to realize the existence of a practice among Judeans whereby if a brother died married but childless, the surviving brother might father children on his brother's wife, ensuing progeny taking the legal name of the deceased, so retaining the man's name for the general resurrection. Thus a child could have 'two' fathers. The African gives a complex account of how all this works which I shall not reproduce as it is confusing, except to say that, according to Sextus Julius Africanius, Joseph was *legally* the son of Eli, but physically of Jacob. This relation is further complicated by the record of Eli and Jacob being *half-brothers*, since they were the sons of the same mother, Estha, but while Eli was the son of her second husband, Melchi, descended from Nathan the son of David, Jacob was the son of her first husband Matthan, descended from David's son, King Solomon. Thus Matthew traces the descent through Jacob to Solomon, but Luke, giving the legal descent, traces it through Eli to Nathan. It is as simple as that, or so Julius Africanus thought:

> This is neither devoid of proof, nor is it conjecture, for the relatives of the saviour according to the flesh [that is, *as far as the flesh is concerned*] have handed on this tradition, either from family pride, or merely to give information, but in any case speaking the truth.

He then tells Aristides that while records of Jewish lineages had been maintained for generations, Herod the Great's jealousy over the Jewish nobility overcame him. Herod was an Idumean Arab whose only claim to rule Judea, other than the approval of Rome, and a strong will to do so, was that he had embraced the faith and married Judean Maccabean princess, Mariamme. He thought he could make himself more noble than the old nobility if he simply burnt all the genealogical records then staked his claim as one descended from 'the patriarchs or proselytes and to those mingled with them, the so-called geiōras [a Hellenized form of a Hebrew word for 'stranger' as in 'the stranger within the gates']'.

Nevertheless, members of the House of David could still boast:

> Now a few who were careful, however, having private records for
> themselves, either remembering the names or otherwise deriving
> them from copies, gloried in the preservation of the memory of their
> good birth; among these were those mentioned above, called *despo-*
> *sunoi*, because of their relation to the family of the saviour, and from
> the Judean villages of *Nazarōn* [which can be transliterated from the
> Greek as 'Nazara'] and *Kōchaba* [or 'Cochaba'], they traversed the rest
> of the land and expounded the preceding genealogy of their descent,
> and from the Book of Days [Chronicles] as far as they went. Whether
> this be so or not no one could give a clearer account, in my opinion and
> in that of all well-disposed persons, and it may suffice us even though
> it is not corroborated, since we have nothing better or truer to say: in
> any case the gospel speaks the truth.

(*Ecclesiastical History*, I, 7)

It is not entirely clear if Julius Africanus had actually met the desposyni
because his earlier reference to them has been lost, so we cannot be sure *when*
they were going forth from these villages in Judea. He puts the village of
'Nazara' in Judea, a region with which he was very familiar. Julius successfully
petitioned the authorities to rebuild the ravaged Emmaus, which would
become the Roman-style Nicopolis. However, Judea was no longer a political
entity in Julius's time, so the 'Judean' reference may simply be to 'Jewish'
lands.

Why the desposyni traversed the land with their genealogy is unknown.
Were they making a claim for dominance in the churches of Palestine in the
early to mid 3rd century when Julius was writing? We do not know. One
suspects their arrival in some Christian gatherings might have elicited a kind
of awe-struck horror. By AD 300, Jesus had been so thoroughly translated
from the earthly sphere into the supernal realm of the eternal trinity that the
sight of his kinsmen in the flesh might have been too much for some persons.

Sadly, Julius Africanus does not say whether the desposyni held any positions in the Church. All we really learn is that they were proud of their genealogy and that they were keen for their origins to be accorded recognition. This tiny glimpse into the life of the almost forgotten desposyni now appears rather sad. We had asked at the beginning of this chapter, what could the members of the 'dynasty' possibly inherit? Well, for over 200 years the answer to that might well have been hard work, persecution and awesome responsibility. By the end of the 4th century, the kingdom may well have been heavenly in essence, but in reality, it had now acquired a powerful, earthly counterpart. The representatives of 'King Jesus' were now close to the cusp of assuming the spiritual authority of the world's greatest empire; what need would they have, once that authority was in place, for the 'authority' of Jewish relatives of the crucified? The Church was now too big to be given away; its leadership, not its persecution, would in due course become an imperial political issue.

Had the desposyni been politically significant, we should have known their names, but Judea was now *Syria Palaestina*, and Sion was *Aelia Capitolina*, and Jesus was not really a Jew; he was God.

An Eternity in Provence

*Why were the Desposyni rejected? What became of the
Desposyni? Did Jesus's family descendants go to live in the
south of France? Did the descendants include the alleged offspring of
Jesus and Mary Magdalene? We examine the Gospel of Mary and
stories of the Magdalene as Jesus's 'lover' as told in apocryphal
writings and popular accounts.*

*Were Jesus's family descendants somehow linked to the Frankish
Merovingian Dynasty? Was there a Jewish principality run by
Jesus's family descendants in Languedoc in the 9th century? Is there
a royal bloodline from Jesus protected by the 'Order of Sion'?*

It is customary, we like to think, as we look back upon the history of our species,
to regard with favour those who have fought for their freedom. How the
English admire the Dutch who fought Spain, the Saxons who rebelled against
the Normans, the Finns who fought the Russians, and so on. But it would be
hard to get an Englishman to admire Irish Republicans, Indian nationalists or
the Egyptian President Nasser. The English are hardly unique in being selec-
tive over defining who is a freedom-fighter and who is a terrorist. No nation
admires those who seek freedom from their own rule. It is also a curious facet
of human nature that those who oppress frequently despise those whom they
oppress; however great the suffering, the cry itself creates contempt.

We should not be surprised that many who enjoyed the benefits of Roman rule in late antiquity despised Jews indiscriminately. Judean and Galilean warriors had risen against the legions named 'Kittim' in the Dead Sea Scrolls, those whom Western classical education describes as the world's great civilizers: the Romans. Perhaps the Romans themselves were in some sort of denial. Josephus claimed that the Roman commander Titus was sorry the Temple in Jerusalem was burned down in AD 70; it was not his intention: it was the fault of the bandits who had made it their base. When General Franco encouraged the German air force to bomb the undefended Basque town of Guernica during the Spanish Civil War, he laid the deaths of the women and children and men of the town at the door of the republicans. It was not bombed, he claimed, but set on fire by the enemies of Spain. Fascism would cleanse Spain of its enemies, town by town.

And what had the Jews done to deserve their fate? Sick to death, by and large, of their puppet governors, sick of sorties by Roman soldiers into their homes, their fields, their pockets, sick of crucifixions, sick of the armed constraints, foreign habits and bribes and corruptions and insults, they demanded to rule themselves. The Romans naturally understood this expectation of self-rule as sedition, gross ingratitude, rank insult to Roman pride and the gods of Rome and mankind. Through more humiliation, more taxation and an ever heavier yoke of oppression, Jews would be made to accept and be grateful for the *Pax Romana*. But the peoples of Judea and Samaria and Galilee and Perea and Decapolis remembered better times, golden ages, and they refused to forget them; they refused to give in. Would not the LORD of Hosts who had vanquished the Egyptian and the Assyrian, the Moabite, the Syrian and the Greek vanquish the Roman too?

By AD 140, when most of the killing and demolition was over, Jews, for their temerity, earned little but cordial dislike or contempt, except perhaps among those who felt equally marginalized. The children of Israel had not only been absorbed geographically into the empire, but by the middle of the 2nd century, much of their religion had been absorbed into Christianity, though pagans loathed 'Judaism' as much in the bosom of the churches as they had in the deserts and fields and towns of Palestine. It is a staggering irony that

Christianity, which began as something of a sect among a minority of Judeans and Galileans, would be considered in the 4th century as a *religion* suitable for the whole empire! But Jews-as-Jews were not included in the imperial feast. By a strange and terrible twist, the children of Israel were excluded from what was now the Gentile messianic banquet. Love one another; love your Emperor! The 'Christian' had become another oppressor of the Jew. No wonder many rabbis grew to hate the name of Jesus, of Yeshua, their own. In Iraq today, a baptizing sect that traces its lineage to John the Baptist, the 'Mandaeans' or 'Sabians' of Mesopotamia, hold to ancient writings that express a comprehensible disgust about a figure they call 'Christ the Roman'.

According to the Christian Church, the Jewish struggle for freedom from Roman rule was not a struggle of heroes fired by sincere messianic expectation and love of liberty and of holy law; it was a shameless crime against God and the empire. When Josephus came to write his history of the Jews and of the Jewish Revolt of AD 66–73, 20 years later, he blamed the war on a futile and wicked appropriation of Jewish culture and tradition by factions of 'robbers', 'innovators', 'bandits' and 'Zealots' – *bad Jews*, as it were. The destruction of Judea as a national homeland was a judgement of God for allowing good sense to be trampled on by ungrounded enthusiasm for holy war. Like St Paul and virtually the whole Church, it was held that the Roman Empire had been ordained by God to advance His purposes among the human race. The 'Jews' had stood in the way of the Lord. Bashing them, smashing them, crippling and crucifying them was God's will.

God had all but given up on the Jews.

Jesus was crucified: a Roman punishment for sedition. He was called 'King of the Jews' by bloodthirsty Prefect, Pontius Pilate, just to rub it in. Guilty or not, Jesus was crucified for sedition, by *Roman* soldiers. And yet, the gospels deny he had any argument with Rome; the guilt was laid at the door of the 'Jews', not some extremist faction of Jews, not a political cabal of Herodians and Judean priests, not his personal enemies. No, Jesus was crucified by 'the Jews', *all of them* (his disciples had fled), who persuaded Pilate that Roman rule required his assent to 'their' demand to 'Crucify him!'. Pilate, reluctantly, we are to believe, permitted an act that all Christians were taught led directly to the destruction of the Temple of the Jews, after which time, the new Temple began: *theirs*. His *own* ran away, but there was another, chosen by God, a citizen of Rome, waiting in the wings.

Paul provided the theology and history provided the lesson. The religion of Christ superseded the religion of the law, that is to say, the Jews.

To many Jews, not infrequently exiled, such a view was utterly incomprehensible, diabolical, a Satanic inversion of the facts. The Messiah would no more cuddle up to Rome than Moses would extinguish the Burning Bush. God long ago gave His law to cleanse His People and His Land from the scoffers of the nations about them. Now the Jews had to hear Gentiles quoting their own prophets to them, telling *them*, the Chosen, that they were being properly punished once more for rejecting their Messiah! But without a passionate belief in the coming – or return – of the Messiah, the revolt against Rome would hardly have got going. There was no lack of messianic faith in the resistance. The Messiah was surely one of their own; how could he now be riding the eagle of Rome? *Ah!* That was the problem, chided the arguably quisling Josephus: too much belief in messianic redemption! – while the Gentile Christians thought the Jews not messianic *enough*. Were there *two* Messiahs? – one for the Jews, one for the Christians?

Taunted by fellow Jews who saw Jesus as nothing but a blasphemous enemy to the people, a false Messiah, Jewish Christians must, in the circumstances, have held out the hope that Jesus would yet return on the clouds with power and angelic might to wipe away the stain and humiliation of Rome and all their enemies with judgement swift and certain, when, as Jesus's parables foretold, the unrighteous chaff would be burnt forever in the fires of righteousness. We may imagine the 'Revelation of St John the Divine' or the 'Apocalypse' coming from such a person, confused, traumatized, haunted by events that seemed to tear reality apart, revealing a fanatical war in the heavens to be unleashed any second on earth.

It did not happen.

We have seen that the emperors Domitian and Trajan took a serious security interest in the survivors of the House of David, from which the messianic redeemer would, or had, come. Hegesippus presents Domitian as finding the grandsons of Judas, Jesus's brother, beneath either regard or condemnation; they were just country simpletons on their uppers. Trajan, on the other hand, preferred to crucify the son of Jesus's cousin Simeon, to be on the safe side. How many other descendants of Jesus's once royal family survived the 2nd century we know not. There may have been violent purges aimed at them. We may suppose a certain amount of hiding or discretion being observed as to their identity.

According to Julius Africanus, self-aware 'Desposyni' seem to have survived in a couple of Palestinian villages, perhaps operative in some way c.220, proud of their genealogies. To what, if any, Church they belonged, or what cause, we cannot say. As far as both Rome as a political power and the Christian Church was concerned, the House of David was absolutely defunct. If it meant anything, it was theological, not genealogical or political. Jerusalem would never again, it was believed, be a Jewish city; the religion of Christ would never again be promulgated by Jews, it was believed. Already in the 2nd century, the old distinctions between the parts of ancient Israel, the distinction between a Judean and a Galilean, for example, were obliterated. There were only 'Jews', and the 'Jews' had crucified Christ. There was no room for nuance. The 'Jews' had rejected their own, which meant for most Christians, when the old Church of Jerusalem was forgotten and the life and testimony of James the 'Zaddik' was known only to a few historians, that Jesus was rejected by his family, 'his own' who 'received him not' *because they were Jews.*

Eternal life was for the Gentiles; they would be the 'sons of God'. The Jews had had their chance, and they had blown it. Those Jews who claimed to be Christians were fakes. Their views on the virgin birth and the significance of the law marked them out as heretics contemptuous of the apostles and of the saints. Josephus's caveats that Romans should not judge *all* Jews as being addicted to liberty and driven to oppose Roman rule, were views held only by liberals and intellectuals. God had obviously abandoned the Jewish people to their own devices and had instituted a new covenant, based on a new testament, for a post-Jewish era, to be led by Christian bishops and Roman emperors, as the will of God permitted.

The family of Jesus went missing because nobody wanted to see them.

Figures from the past have no power over how they will be used, or abused, by those who come after them. The dead make excellent propaganda for the living. They can speak volumes, but they do not speak. They may act on new stages; they do not object. They may be given new lines, new dress, new identities. They are cheap to run and easy to clean. Whatever individual merits or powers may once have been enjoyed, all the saints are given regulation-size auras, a neat and tidy nimbus and an established place in the pecking order, a hymn sheet to sing from, and a high place to look down from. High or low, be assured, the dead are anybody's.

Perhaps one of the most striking manipulations of the dead of recent times surrounds the alleged descendants of Jesus. A net of speculation has enmeshed hundreds of thousands of people around the world in a curious quest for a kind of salvation from history; but history it *ain't*. Well, it is *story*, and it concerns history, but if it was a table, I would not eat my dinner off it if I valued my carpet. This is not simply my opinion.

I imagine that most readers will be familiar with the outline of the story told in Lincoln, Baigent and Leigh's 1982 bestseller, *The Holy Blood and the Holy Grail*, without which, and sundry spin-offs, such as *The Templar Legacy* by Picknett and Prince, Dan Brown's *The Da Vinci Code* would never have graced our shelves. Here is a refresher of the story's outline as it concerns us.

Jesus had progeny from Mary Magdalene. Jesus's family ran the Church in Jerusalem, but as time went on, they found themselves marginalized by the burgeoning power and rival authority of the Roman Church, with whom Jesus's own differed in matters of doctrine, though the Magdalene herself and the all-important direct bloodline had probably left for France long before. Eventually, the *Desposyni* – or those of them that might have stayed behind in the east – were definitively given the order of the boot by Pope

Sylvester I in AD 318; the Church had no need of living relatives of the second person of the Holy Trinity.

Two lines are then pursued.

Mary Magdalene, back in the 1st century AD, might have escaped to France with Jesus's 'bloodline'. Alternatively and additionally both, over three and a half centuries later, the pagan royal House of the Sicambrian Franks, led in the early 5th century by semi-mythical King Merovée, held some kind of special blood that impressed such power as the papacy enjoyed in the first half of the 5th century. Merovée's great-grandson Clovis I (456–511) became a baptized Christian in AD 496 and, with the pope's support, the resulting dynasty went on to control half of France and a good slice of 'Germany' until Childeric III was deposed by Pepin 'the Short' with the pope's connivance in AD 751. The Merovingians, according to the story, had outlived their usefulness to the papacy, who shifted their favour to the Carolingians to produce the 'Holy Roman Empire', a theocratic imperialism and throw-back to the past.

So where are the Desposyni in all this?

Well, by a good deal of literary sleight of hand we are led to consider that the Merovingians might have had something to do with members of the tribe of Benjamin who left Israel for Arcadia, Greece, way back in Old Testament times. King Merovée himself was supposed the son of a human princess and a sea-creature called a quinotaur, which is taken to indicate symbolically that his lineage might have come from 'across the sea'. Merovée has the French word for sea, and mother, in it: 'Mer'; so does 'merry' and 'farmer', of course. This oceanic snippet is tied in, subliminally as it were, with the idea of Mary Magdalene arriving in France by boat, and the sojourn in Arcadia by ancient Benjamites: Jews-sea-Mother-Magdalene-Arcadia. The fact that Merovée was a pagan appears incidental. Many Jewish tribes had pagan tendencies – in Old Testament times at least.

ET IN ARCADIA EGO. 'Even in Arcadia I (Death) am.' What if idyllic Arcadia was in Languedoc? Well, painter Nicolas Poussin did kind of put it there, in a painting called *The Shepherds of Arcadia*, apparently, and I mean *apparently*, based on a tomb which used to stand by a road near Arques, some miles from a place called Rennes le Château, possibly the former Visigothic capital Rhedae, where Merovingian 'survivors' stayed with the Count of Razès, who left a treasure discovered, maybe, by a French priest who died mysteriously in 1917 after redecorating his church strangely at great personal expense, dedicating it to Mary Magdalene: Magdalene-secret-treasure-Masonry.

Back to the Merovingians...

Merovingian royalty was eventually Christianized, but the family's doctrine and attitude to Rome were troublesome. Merovingians made peace with Arian, or heretical, Visigoths, who knew Jesus only as a man adopted by the Holy Spirit. Added to this blurry picture of a doctrinally deviant royalty irritating the pope is a genealogical scheme, employed and manipulated by clever French surrealist hoaxers to tie in their supposed, virtual secret Order to ancient roots.

The line now acquires a new element: a Jewish 'princedom' operating in 'Septimania', or the Narbonne region of Languedoc and Provence in the 9th century. According to a source, these Jewish leaders operating in sunny France were descendants of the *House of David*. The authors of the Blood and Grail narrative encourage us to leap to the obvious conclusion.

The mingled Houses stemming from Merovingian, Carolingian and Jewish blood culminate in Godfroi de Bouillon (1061–1100), crusader and first Christian king of Jerusalem. As the narrative goes, Godfroi returned to claim what was duly 'his'. Godfroi also allegedly founded the hoaxers' hoax Order: the *Priory of Sion*. This fringe quasi-rosicrucian-masonic-chivalric order, established on paper in the mid 1950s, was supposed to hold a secret that could bring down the papacy. The secret is understood by the book *The Holy Blood and the Holy Grail* to be that Jesus's authentic bloodline, and doctrine, has been guarded as a sacred duty by the Order, after having coursed through the veins of a number of European royal and aristocratic Houses, beginning with the Merovingians.

Now we all know the secret, but it appears the papacy is still there, indifferent to the idea that the Tribe of Judah, its royal House, and royal promise would yet be unfolded among the godless, faith-wanderers of modern Europe. According to a speculative future that concludes the Blood-Grail adventure, a sacred monarchy, joined to a sacred France and a united Europe would rule again, well, for once anyway. Good news for post-hippy spiritual believers: this monarchy – or perhaps presidency – would be spiritual, non-dogmatic, thoroughly decent about human rights, a bit magical, somewhat esoteric (being the power behind Freemasonry, Rosicrucianism and Hermetic Philosophy, it ought to be), not a little astrological, somewhat Gnostic, fairly free-thinking, primal in authority, cosmic in outlook, sex-positive, archetypal in appeal, tried and tested through the vicissitudes of time. It would be a kind of delicious second coming: a new beginning perhaps, and certainly a colossal dream.

Who can deny that this story, this new myth, has not been influential? Yet again, the real Desposyni, the real Jewish brethren of Jesus, are excluded, having been dragged into another quasi-messianic banquet run by others in their name. If there were a *genuine* descendant of the House of David interested in his genealogy and its possible import, I should expect to find him or her campaigning in Israel, not in Brussells, for with the return of the Jews to Jerusalem, there would be, in fantastic theory, a political role once more for the, by now, possibly thousands or more bifurcated bloodline descendants of Simeon and Judas and Joseph and their sisters – or even, if you insist, against all the evidence, Jesus and Mary Magdalene. Would their 'own' receive them? It would make an interesting fictional challenge to the Knesset if the House of David appeared in Jerusalem to re-establish a Solomonic golden age while declaring Jesus was the Jewish Messiah for all Jews – and everybody else. This is the stuff of fiction.

What makes this author so confident in dismissing the Blood-Grail story? Do I know more than the not-so-secret 'society' behind all this? Behind all *what*? Trace the provenance of the source texts and you soon find, in this case, there is nothing much behind anything.

If we agree that medieval romances concerning the Holy Grail are not admissible as evidence for establishing historical facts, the entire edifice of the Jesus-Magdalene-Sion cult is revealed as a treacherous, if humorous, gaudily-decorated font, mounted on three pillars, all of them faulty. That is to say, they cannot take the weight of the hypothesis under normal conditions of gravity. If, however, we dream, then pigs might fly and I might be president of Europe, ruling from a branch with a pig as my deputy.

Those who feel that the fact that the 'Prieuré Documents' that include the Merovingian and post-Merovingian genealogies were faked in the 1950s and 1960s still does not extinguish the fire of which these documents are merely the smoke, should consider the following supports to the narrative.

The Messianic Legacy (Cape, London, 1984), the follow-up book to *The Holy Blood and the Holy Grail*, builds on the Desposyni story. At first reading, it appears as impressive testimony, coming, as it appeared to do from a 'Catholic authority'. The authors referred to a meeting between Pope Sylvester I and the 'Jewish Christian leaders' that allegedly took place in AD 318. The dating is canny; it would bring us to the period when Eusebius became bishop of Caesarea and came to acquaint the reading world with the relevant parts of Hegesippus's books on the early history of the Church and the place of Jesus's relatives within that history. Here is the source referred to by *The Messianic Legacy*:

> The vital interview was not, as far as we know, recorded [*note the caveat*: 'not recorded'], but the issues were very well known, and it is probable [*probable?*] that Joses, the oldest of the Christian Jews, spoke on behalf of the Desposyni and the rest. [...] That most hallowed name, *desposyni*, had been respected by all believers in the first century and a half of Christian history. The word literally meant, in Greek, 'belonging to the Lord'. It was reserved uniquely for Jesus' blood relatives. Every part of the ancient Jewish Christian church had always been governed by a *desposynos*, and each of them carried one of the names traditional in Jesus' family – Zachary, Joseph, John, James, Joses, Simeon, Matthias, and so on. But no one was ever called Jesus. Neither Sylvester nor any of the thirty-two popes before him, nor those succeeding him, ever emphasized that there were at least three well-known and authentic lines of legitimate blood descent from Jesus' own family. [...] The *Desposyni* demanded that Sylvester, who now had Roman patronage, revoke his confirmation of the authority of the Greek Christian bishops at Jerusalem, in Antioch, in Ephesus, and in Alexandria, and to name *desposynos* bishops to take their place. They asked that the practice of sending cash to Jerusalem as the mother church be resumed.

[...] These blood relatives of Christ demanded the reintroduction of the law, which included the Sabbath and the Holy Day system of Feasts and New Moons of the Bible. Sylvester dismissed their claims and said that, from now on, the mother church was in Rome and he insisted they accept the Greek bishops to lead them. [...] This was the last known dialogue with the Sabbath-keeping church in the east led by the disciples who were descended from blood relatives of Jesus the Messiah.

The authors of *The Messianic Legacy* were not at pains to indicate plainly to the reader that the *Desposyni*'s alleged rejection by the papacy derived from an outspoken claim made by controversial Irish priest, Malachi Martin. The source-note for the account in *The Messianic Legacy* did not indicate that Martin had no primary source to offer for his convincing-sounding story and had motives of his own for telling it (Malachi Martin, *The Decline and Fall of the Roman Church.* New York, Bantam, 1983, pages 30–1).

One controversial work stood on the back of another. It all seemed so plausible, but on closer inspection, in the context of the Blood-Grail-Messianic Legacy narrative, we can see that the story was employed to give a factual-sounding support to the idea that there existed historically a kind of established feud between Jesus's family descendants and the Roman Catholic Church: a justification for later alleged plotting against Rome by the imaginary 'Priory of Sion'. Of course, it is arguable that all the 'signs' point this way anyhow. Nothing could be more desirable then than to find that scholar's jackpot: hard evidence for such a feud. Had Martin been in a position to furnish such hard evidence, it would have been a truly controversial moment in the history of the Church: proof positive of the clandestine de-position of the family of Jesus by a Church with its eye on worldly power. But I'm afraid this is yet another example of the abuse of history: the narrative demanded the fact; the 'fact' was duly provided. Why is history 'abused'? Simply because by obscuring provenance, you get your 'point' out and lodge it powerfully in the reader's mind, without having to back it up; in other words, historical abuse is a form of propaganda.

We now move on to the most controversial element of the story of Jesus's 'bloodline', his *sang réal* or 'royal blood': the Grail Holy. Here the sources are straightforward, once we cut away the decorative foliage.

A possibly late 2nd-century apocryphal work, The Gospel of Mary, existing in Greek fragments and in a Coptic version with ten of its pages missing, presents a standard 'Gnostic' account of a revelation given by Jesus to Mary Magdalene. The revelation explains how to deal with the 'powers' encountered by the soul in its ascent to the heavenly soul-home. The setting corresponds to the context of a polemic about the role of women in the Church. In the 2nd-century Church, women could be prophetesses. That was an office of the Church, probably going back to the enthusiastic Pauline missionary churches among the Gentiles. In Gnostic communities, women could officiate at sacramental rituals. The idea of a priestess was familiar and natural to former pagans. However, Paul himself favoured controlling women in meetings, while the position of women in general was curtailed as the powers of orthodox bishops increased. Had not Jesus chosen only men as apostles; were women not there *to serve*? Well, so were the men! Some Gnostics took the name of Mary Magdalene and the presence of Mary the mother and her sister as sufficient testimony that Jesus not only permitted closeness to women, but found them more amenable to his 'inner teaching'. This was deduced from references to their presence in the canonical gospels. There is no other known source for the contention that Jesus loved Mary Magdalene 'more' than the disciples. The references to kissing on the mouth as a mode by which the 'spiritual Jesus' conveyed his spirit is extended that little bit further in the tiny Gnostic Marian *corpus* to suggest Mary Magdalene was Jesus's 'lover' in an undefined sense:

> Peter said to Mary, 'Sister, we know that the Saviour loved you more than the rest of women. Tell us the words of the Saviour that you remember – which you know [but] we do not, nor have we heard them.' Mary answered and said, 'What is hidden from you I will proclaim to you.'

After an account of the soul's ascent, Andrew, anticipating the neophyte's sceptical response to this non-canonical account, complains that 'certainly these teachings are strange ideas'. Peter asks: 'Did he really speak with a woman without our knowledge (and) not openly? Are we to turn about and all listen to her? Did he prefer her to us?' Leading and apposite questions, for sure:

> Then Mary wept and said to Peter, 'My brother Peter, what do you think? Do you think that I thought this up myself in my heart, or that I am lying about the Saviour?' Levi answered and said to Peter, 'Peter, you have always been hot-tempered. Now I see you contending against the woman like the adversaries. But if the Saviour made her worthy, who are you indeed to reject her? Surely the Saviour knows her very well. This is why he loved her more than us. Rather let us be ashamed and put on the perfect man and acquire him for ourselves as he commanded us, and preach the gospel, not laying down any other rule or other law beyond what the Saviour said.'

This is as clear a polemic against orthodox bishops using Jewish laws and masculine prejudice about the cleanliness, fitness, physicality and modesty of women to hold authority in the Church as could be imagined. Women were of equal importance to men in the lives of 'heretics'; therefore, suppress the women, suppress the heresy. Women, according to orthodox bishops, were too impressionable, romantic and sexually vulnerable: possibly corrupting and nearly always corruptible. On the contrary, said the heretics, women's capacity for intimacy, intuition, understanding, patience, loyalty and love made them fit companions for the Lord. The male disciples could be bullies – just like the orthodox bishops, pushing people around as if they were 'sheep'. The Gnostic learns from his or her own spirit: the inner 'perfect man'.

All this makes sense in the 2nd-century Church, but it does not make much sense of the original Judean and Galilean setting of the early to mid 1st century. The seductive Gospel of Mary was written to deal with a political problem in the 2nd-century Church.

Almost completely unknown until its discovery in the Nag Hammadi

Library, the strange, apocryphal Gospel of Philip offers the 'killer quotes' to the Jesus-was-married-to-Magdalene contingent. It is dated to the 3rd century and appears familiar with the contents of the Gospel of Mary:

> There were three who always walked with the Lord: Mary, his mother and her sister and Magdalene, whom they call his lover. A Mary is his sister and his mother and his lover.

The gospel is not really interested in positing an actual or banal relationship between Jesus and Magdalene, though there is the sense of a seductive tease to heighten the interest. Rather, the female reader may herself become a 'Mary', as with the Gnostic 'twin' idea, where the Gnostic may become a 'Judas Twin' or perceiving 'Christ':

> Since you have been called my twin and true companion, Examine yourself, that you may know who you are. And you will be called 'the one who knows himself' for he who has not known himself, has known nothing, but he who has known himself has achieved Knowledge, about the depth of the All.

> (Book of Thomas the Contender).

To fail to know oneself is to remain a mere animal, in love with the 'body'.

The Gnostic woman is mother-carer of, 'sister' of, and lover of, the 'Perfect Man' – Christ – that lives within her. The author posits a relationship between Mary Magdalene, the 'consort' of Jesus, and the Divine Mother, *Sophia*, that is, Wisdom, the 'real' mother of Jesus the Saviour, not the man. Thus 'Mary Magdalene' is a symbol for the woman's relationship to Christ:

> Wisdom, whom they call barren, is the mother of the angels, and the consort of Christ is Mary Magdalene. The [*here the text is damaged and has been reconstructed*: 'Lord loved Mary'] more than all the disciples, and he kissed her on the [mouth many times]. The other [women/dis-

ciples saw] ...him. They said to him, 'Why do you [love her] more than all of us?' The Saviour answered and said to them, 'Why do not I love you as I do her?'

Magdalene stands as his 'consort'; she symbolizes Wisdom, the heavenly power the Saviour enters the material world to express; Jesus is the 'fruit' of Wisdom. Mary Magdalene knows this power in herself. The Gnostic woman holds a spiritual-erotic secret; she is a gateway to God. The males are wrong to despise her, for they are not whole without her. The Gnostic Jesus knows this too: 'her price is far above rubies'. Through adoring the divine within the Magdalene, the man may come closer to God. We have here the theological essence for a cult of the Magdalene that seems to have flowered in 12th-century France, and may have flowered in the heyday of 2nd- and 3rd-century Christian gnosis.

Nevertheless, this is a very late spiritual commentary on clues perceived by the spiritual Gnostic from the canonical account. Did they think Jesus actually said these things? Well, the Gnostic was not particularly interested in the 1st-century historical figure, Jesus. That was a manifestation of the Lord, but the Gnostic could perceive him directly, as Paul claimed to do: a claim he considered superseded that of either Peter or Jesus's brother James! Christian Gnostics were taught to venerate and know communion with 'the living Jesus'. The living Jesus is a *post-resurrection*, utterly transfigured figure: that which the Gnostic may *become*. In this sense, 'the living Jesus' was still speaking to the Church through these writings which believers believed were inspired by the 'knowledge of the Truth', the Truth that the Saviour gave to his chosen after the Resurrection and which lay hidden within the Church, waiting for the times when the 'children of the resurrection' would grasp the gnosis, the secret spiritual truth that lay hidden in the revelation of Jesus to the apostles: Jesus was the perfect, divine being within every man and woman who had awoken from the sleep of the world. As the Gospel of Philip declares: 'He [Jesus] came crucifying the world.'

It will be observed that in none of these works is there any suggestion that Jesus and Mary Magdalene were married man and married wife, nor the slightest scintilla of a suggestion that Mary Magdalene bore a physical child or children to her 'lover'. The Gnostics who created these texts would have found such an idea completely meaningless, spiritually speaking, since the Jesus who communicates with Mary is a spiritual figure; their relationship is essentially visionary, not carnal. She was filled with his spirit, not his semen.

———

That Mary Magdalene was of great interest to men and women in the late Middle Ages is evinced by the *Legenda Aurea* or *Legenda Sanctorum*, better known as the 'Golden Legend'. This long, popular collection of hagiographies was compiled around 1250–60 by Jacobus de Voragine, the Dominican archbishop of Genoa. More than 1,000 manuscript copies survive. It was one of the first works to benefit from printing, appearing at the dawn of the printing age in every major European language; William Caxton's English version appeared in 1483 and it is from that version we shall be hearing.

You will not get from the *Golden Legend* any obviously heretical notions of a deep heretical cult around Mary Magdalene. Voragine was a Dominican. Dominicans ran the holy Inquisition and at the time he was writing, that institution was employed in the Languedoc region of the Ariège and Corbières, sequestrating the property of sympathizers to Catharism and interrogating 'Cathar' heretics, none of whom, incidentally, expressed any interest in a spiritual Mary Magdalene. Arguably, that could not be said with confidence of the aristocracy of the region who protected the Cathar Church of Good Christians. Familiar with the works of their local troubadours, the nobility were not out of tune with the idea of the spiritual-erotic, a 'pure love' or '*Fin'Amors*' that uplifted the soul of the lover before the ideal, but nonetheless rewardingly fleshly, lady. However, we have no evidence for the linkage of troubadour love philosophy to female religious figures during the heyday of the troubadours (*c.*1150–1230). Indeed, that linkage was made under Roman Catholic pressure subsequent to the crusades against the heretics, and it was the turning of erotic *cansos* into the service of Mariolatry and religious sainthood, rather than real women, and soulful-erotic satisfaction, that sterilized the troubadour movement at precisely the period when the rare spiritual teachers were being hounded into death and oblivion.

The nobility risked and lost their lives in the defence of their beliefs and the independence of their country. Had the 'lost family' of Jesus been current as a *symbol* of the 'true Church of Jesus', then we might have found Cathars and their sympathizers considering their number as a manifestation in time of such a 'lost family', but this is fanciful; no such identification took place at the time.

However, the *Golden Legend*, orthodox as it is, is employed to add colour and detail to the idea that Mary Magdalene brought Jesus's 'bloodline' to Provence, along with, arguably, other members of Jesus's family.

According to the text, Mary was a sinner, a repentant whore, a rich lady of the castle of 'Magdalo' who had offered her body and its delights to such knights as she fancied. Redeemed by Christ, she washed Jesus's feet and in so doing became an *illuminatrix*, showing forth the light of 'Christian service'. Catholic Mary Magdalene was almost eligible for the *Mother's Union*.

This presentation does rather suggest a bit of theological jiggerypokery. Magdalena must have had the reputation of being 'an illuminator' because she had been 'illuminated'. In other words, as Mary the Virgin was portrayed by Catholic iconography as the 'Morning Star', the Magdalene may have been already identified with the Morning Star – Ishtar-Venus, *Love* – rising above the waves, reflecting her astral power on the waters of creation and in the corn in spring. Not only is there the suggestion here of both pagan and Gnostic ideas, but also Jewish ones too. For in the wisdom-book of Proverbs, 'Lady Wisdom' (called Sophia in *Ecclesiasticus*) is compared to a whore that the wise man should follow through the streets in order to 'know' her, though he may find her costly: 'her price is far above rubies'.

Mary Magdalene was linked by Voragine and Church tradition with the 'fallen woman' whose costly spikenard was employed to anoint Jesus, as she washed his feet 'with the tears of her eyes' and dried his feet with her hair, preparing him for burial, and resurrection. All of this language suggests a cult with a powerful erotic and spiritual content. The fallen star would thus be the evening star dropping below the horizon, to rise like the Babylonian Ishtar at dawn. Thus she is in the garden of the Resurrection with her balm for the bleeding god, Love Rising; Life Rising.

The boat on the waters would be the crescent moon of the goddess.

It appears Voragine has sterilized much of this wondrous symbolism into a mere moral portrayal of the woman's service – to Jesus, and, of course, to the Catholic Church. Voragine says that Mary, aware of her sins, chose afterwards the 'path of contemplation'. That, he says, is why she is called an illuminator. I should think this must have sent a number of spiritual women off to the convent for further illumination: 'For then she was enlumined of perfect knowledge in thought, and with the light in clearness of body.'

> And this is she, that same Mary Magdalene to whom our Lord gave so many great gifts. And showed so great signs of love, that he took from her seven devils. He embraced her all in his love, and made her right familiar with him. He would that she should be his hostess, and his procuress on his journey, and he ofttimes excused her sweetly; for he excused her against the Pharisee which said that she was not clean, and unto her sister that said she was idle, unto Judas, who said that she was a wastresse of goods. And when he saw her weep he could not withhold his tears. And for the love of her he raised Lazarus which had been four days dead, and healed her sister from the flux of blood which had held her seven years. And by the merits of her he made Martelle, chamberer of her sister Martha, to say that sweet word: Blessed be the womb that bare thee, and the paps that gave thee suck.

Voragine goes on to tell that after the martyrdom of Stephen, many of the disciples left Jerusalem, one of whom was Saint Maximin, patron saint of the church of Marseilles. The Magdalene was entrusted to him for safety, along with other Christians, including her brother Lazarus and sister Mary. There is no mention in Voragine of two other women whom the legends of Saintes-Maries-de-la-Mer in the Camargue say arrived in a boat: Mary Jacobi (Mary of James) and Mary Salome, both of whom may be considered as relatives of Jesus.

> There was that time with the apostles S. Maximin, which was one of the seventy-two disciples of our Lord, to whom the blessed Mary Magdalene was committed by S. Peter, and then, when the disciples

were departed, S. Maximin, Mary Magdalene, and Lazarus her brother, Martha her sister, Marcelle, chamberer of Martha, and S. Cedony which was born blind, and after enlumined of our Lord; all these together, and many other Christian men were taken of the miscreants and put in a ship in the sea, without any tackle or rudder, for to be drowned. But by the purveyance of Almighty God they came all to Marseilles, where, as none would receive them to be lodged, they dwelled and abode under a porch before a temple of the people of that country. And when the blessed Mary Magdalene saw the people assembled at this temple for to do sacrifice to the idols, she arose up peaceably with a glad visage, a discreet tongue and well speaking, and began to preach the faith and law of Jesu Christ, and withdrew from the worshipping of the idols. Then were they amarvelled of the beauty, of the reason, and of the fair speaking of her. And it was no marvel that the mouth that had kissed the feet of our Lord so debonairly and so goodly, should be inspired with the word of God more than the other.

Mary had kissed the Lord; not his mouth, but his feet: an exceedingly low level of self-abasement in the east, that would surely have disgusted the apostles, and which may hold the key to the formation of the Gnostic story of a parallel annoyance with her having kissed Jesus on the mouth.

Voragine's sources are right peculiar. He claims Hegesippus's and Josephus's authority for his story of how Mary preached to pagans, converted them, then went into a barren place, dwelt in a cave on celestial nourishment administered by angels for 30 years, until the visit of a holy man marked the time of her blessed passing out of this world. No such accounts exist.

Hegesippus, with other books of Josephus accord enough with the said story, and Josephus saith in his treatise that the blessed Mary Magdalene, after the ascension of our Lord, for the burning love that she had to Jesu Christ and for the grief and discomfort that she had for the absence of her master our Lord, she would never see man. But after when she came into the country of Aix, she went into desert, and dwelt there thirty years without knowing of any man or woman. And he saith that, every day at the seven hours canonical she was lifted in the air of the angels. But he saith that, when the priest came to her, he found her enclosed in her cell; and she required of him a vestment, and he delivered to her one, which she clothed and covered her with. And she went with him to the church and received the communion, and then made her prayers with joined hands, and rested in peace.

Not a trace of any child or Desposyni. We have here all the materials for a romantic, pagan, Christian or Gnostic cult, but nothing to tell us about what happened to Jesus's family descendants. We may, I think, be assured that, whoever they were, they were not devotees of a Magdalene cult.

———

And so we come to the third pillar of the Blood-Grail font. *The Holy Blood and the Holy Grail* narrative needs somehow to tie in the Desposyni and/or the alleged Magdalene-Jesus bloodline with the *Prieuré Documents*' genealogies. This is achieved through a clever deployment of one book in particular. The book is Arthur J Zuckerman's *A Jewish Princedom in Feudal France, 768–900* (New York, Columbia University Press, 1972), a work which on its appearance was recognized as a 'radical re-interpretation' by Robert Chazan who reviewed it for the Indiana University Press in 1973.

According to Zuckerman, 'The Jews of Carolingian France stood under the authority of a *nasi* [Hebrew for leader], a prince or patriarch. The Jewish Patriarchate of the West was an institution comparable in its powers to the Exilarchate of Baghdad.' (p.1, Zuckerman.) This was some claim. The reconstruction was based on Zuckerman's observation that in AD 768, a deposed exilarch of Babylon, that is, the leader of Babylonian Jews, Makhir-Natronai, arrived in the west. The background was a feud over who was to be *nasi* of the Mesopotamian Jews. One Bustenai, marrying into Persian royalty, gained the upper hand, so Natronai ben Makhir left for the ancient Jewish community of Narbonne. The Babylonian Jews were the descendants of Jews who had been exiled there since the conquest of Jerusalem under Nebuchadnezzar in 587 BC.

Zuckerman leapt to the conclusion that this figure, Makhir-Natronai was to be identified with 'Theoderic', hero of a number of *chansons de geste*.

The political setting to Makhir-Natronai's appearance on the historical scene of Carolingian France was that country's war in 768 with Ummayad Spain. Jews in Barcelona helped the Carolingians take the city, in exchange for quasi-independent status in the Narbonnais. This was a reversal of the usual Jewish policy of supporting the Ummayads and then being left by the Arabs to administer the conquered territory. However, Abbassid Arabs were also at war with the Ummayads. They made a treaty with the Franks, a treaty requiring an Abbasid representative holding a court in Septimania (the *Narbonnais*). The person chosen was the deposed Jewish exilarch, Natronai ben Makhir.

Zuckerman reckoned the Babylonian-Jewish scholar took the name Theoderic, marrying into the Carolingian line to legitimate his rule. That rule required Septimania to stand as a buffer zone with Muslim Spain while serving as a base for attacking the enemy and defending Charlemagne's empire. According to Zuckerman, the presence of Jewish authority in a Christian empire was viewed with suspicion and the Church plotted to wrest control of Narbonne and Septimania from the Jews.

Zuckerman reconstructed an act of Charlemagne dated AD 791 whereby a Jewish client-patriarchate became a permanent institution. Natronai ben Habibi's son, identified as Isaac-William, a Carolingian warrior allegedly depicted falsely by Christian writers as going into a monastery, became the successor patriarch. Isaac-William's successor, Bernard, having been invited by Charlemagne to serve as imperial chamberlain in 829, was executed by the emperor's order in 844. Zuckerman traced the line through to the early 10th century when the 'traces finally get lost and disappear in the chaotic conditions which marked the decline and end of Carolingian rule'. (Zuckerman, p.378.)

A man named Makhir of Narbonne was certainly the leader of the significant Narbonne Jewish community at the end of the 8th century, and his descendants enjoyed the role of *nasi* or leaders of it, subject to fealty to the empire.

According to a tradition preserved by Abraham ibn Daud in his *Sefer ha-Qabbalah* (Book of the Kabbalah), written about 1161, Makhir was a descendant of the House of David:

> Then King Charles [Charlemagne] sent to the King of Baghdad [Caliph] requesting that he dispatch one of his Jews of the seed of royalty of the House of David. He hearkened and sent him one from there, a magnate and sage, Rabbi Makhir by name. And [Charles] settled him in Narbonne, the capital city, and planted him there, and gave him a great possession there at the time he captured it from the Ishmaelites [Arabs]. And he [Makhir] took to wife a woman from among the magnates of the town; […] and the King made him a nobleman and designed, out of love for [Makhir], good statutes for the benefit of all the Jews dwelling in the city, as is written and sealed in a Latin charter; and the seal of the King therein [bears] his name *Carolus*; and it is in their possession at the present time. The Prince Makhir became chieftain there. He and his descendants were close with the King and all his descendants.

This is a nice, intriguing story written over 350 years after the events, replete with fanciful details such as Charlemagne writing to the caliph requesting 'one of his Jews'. Whether the reference to the House of David has any truth in it at all, it will be observed that the Jews of Babylon had been in Mesopotamia since 587 BC when Nebuchadnezzar took Jerusalem and its nobility into exile. Apparently, not everyone of the house of David returned after Cyrus the Persian's edict of 538 BC permitted the exiles' return to the ruins of their city. This is plausible. However, it will be noted also that there is no reference whatsoever to these Jews being either Jewish Christians or, certainly, descendants of Jesus's family. That thought has been planted into the reception of this authentically Jewish material by the Blood-Grail hypothesis. It is not justified by the evidence at all. It has been imposed subtly upon the evidence. Admittedly, the authors of the Blood-Grail narrative do not make any such connection absolutely explicit, but the entire structure of the narrative leaves the reader to make this connection for themselves; the implied connection is intentional, not accidental.

Abraham ibn Daud ['Daud' means 'David'] is working on the level of legend. Makhir did not have a relationship with Charlemagne. It was Charlemagne's father, Pepin, king of the Franks, who, to gain the Narbonne Jews' support in his efforts to keep the Ummayads at bay, granted them wide-ranging powers in return for the surrender of Moorish Narbonne to him in 759. The Annals of Aniane and the Chronicle of Moissac, penned by monks, both concur that the massacre of the Saracen garrison was the result of an uprising of the Gothic leaders of Narbonne. In 768, Pepin granted Makhir and his heirs territory in the region. Pope Stephen III complained (Zuckerman, 'The Nasi of Frankland in the Ninth Century and the 'Colaphus Judaeorum' in Toulouse'; *Proceedings of the American Academy for Jewish Research 33*, 1965: 51–82), but in 791 Charlemagne confirmed the Jewish Principate's status, making the title *Nasi* permanent. 'Nasi' means 'leader' or 'prince', something of an honorific since the *nasis* ruled by grace of the Franks.

In 1165, Benjamin of Tudela visited Narbonne. Benjamin was much impressed by the status enjoyed by Makhir's descendants, while the 'Royal Letters' of 1364 (Doat Collection, pp.53 et seq., 339–53) record a *rex Iudaeorum*, a Jewish king at Narbonne. Saige's *Histoire des Juifs du Languedoc* (p.44) finds the Makhir family's home at Narbonne denoted in official documents as *Cortada Regis Judæorumis*, the court of the Jewish king. The family patronized a Talmudic school of international significance. But they never claimed to be the descendants of Jesus's family nor upholders of the identity of Desposyni. It is of course arguable that any such claim would have been most unwise, their protection coming from kings, not prelates. Any supposed hint of nervousness in the Vatican on such an account may be deemed wholly conjectural.

It is of course also conceivable that Jesus's family's descendants had at some point grown tired of a Church that had become alien from its roots and simply returned to the mainstream of Diaspora Jewish life, perhaps putting their collective experience and traditions into the study of Kabbalah, or Jewish 'Gnosticism' or mysticism which purports to reveal the spiritual mechanics behind all religious concepts. If such may be claimed of the Narbonnais Jews' leading family, then Jesus's descendants may be traced throughout many, many families throughout the world. The point, I suppose to raise here would be that the original family claimed no such descent for themselves, and none have come after declaring such a thing. To a Jew, the entire subject might appear, depending on the tradition in which he or she was raised, as a colossal embarrassment.

Furthermore, before any reader should get carried away, Zuckerman's work has come in for heavy academic criticism, none of which is reflected in the Blood-Grail narrative. For example, Zuckerman's identification of Makhir with Natronai ben Habibi, an exilarch exiled after a dispute involving two branches of the Bostanai family is uncertain. Zuckerman's identification of Makhir with a Maghario, Count of Narbonne, as well as with 'Aymeri de Narbonne', who appears in poetry married to Charles Martel's daughter, Alda or Aldana, thus siring William of Gellone is also insecure. Much is made of William of Gellone in the Blood-Grail narrative. He was a figure who appeared in numerous epics, including *Willehalm* by Wolfram von Eschenbach, author of the alchemical 'Gral' story in his *Parzifal*.

Zuckerman's identification of Makhir with Theoderic is likewise suspect. William of Gellone's more historical counterpart, William I, Count of Toulouse, distinguished himself commanding the Franks at Barcelona in 803. A Latin poem by Ermold Niger describes the conflict in terms of the Jewish calendar while at the same time depicting the count as an observant Jew. As Count William was the son of Theoderic, Frankish Count of Septimania, Zuckerman supposes Theoderic and Makhir were most likely the same person. Once this leap into the dark is allowed, a dynasty of Franco-Jewish 'kings' of Narbonne appears like magic out of Theoderic's genuine, documented descendants. Thus, when Christian chroniclers have Theoderic retiring to a monastery, Zuckerman considers them mistaken, obscuring a Jewish hero.

An alleged union of Martel's descendants with the supposed lineage of the exilarchs of Baghdad simply lights the blue touch-paper of an imagined 'Grail Dynasty'. N L Taylor's *Saint William, King David, and Makhir: a Controversial Medieval Descent* (*The American Genealogist*, 72: 205–23) has shown the flaws in Zuckerman's string of identifications taken on uncritically within the Blood-Grail narrative. Taylor is not alone; his negative judgement of the hypothesis is shared by other scholars, including Christian Settipani (*Continuité gentilice et continuité familiale dans les familles sénatoriales romaines à l'époque impériale: mythe et réalité*, Unit for Prosopographical Research, Linacre College, University of Oxford, 2000, p.78). Zuckerman's grand construction of a Jewish principality in Languedoc has been refuted by Aryeh Graboïs ('Une Principauté Juive dans la France du Midi a l'Époque Carolingienne?', *Annales du Midi*, 85: 191–202, 1973), while M L Bierbrier ('Genealogical Flights of Fancy. Old Assumptions, New Sources, Foundations'; *Journal of the Foundation for Medieval Genealogy*, 2: 379–87; p.381) opines unequivocally that the construction as a whole fails to merit serious scholarly attention. Bierbrier concludes: 'This view has been rejected by all specialists in the area as utter nonsense.'

I suppose they could all be wrong.

———

What have we got left? Not much really. And when we look at the narrative in terms of what it has to tell us about Jesus's family descendants, we have nothing concrete at all to walk on, only water, which is probably beyond most readers' scope, certainly mine.

———

We cannot leave our sojourn in Provence without drawing attention to the great attractiveness of the Blood-Grail, Priory of Sion story. It has the merit of bringing together virtually every strand of Western – and not a little Eastern – esoteric history and philosophy under a single umbrella. It appears to solve everything, while solving nothing. This is, I believe, because it continually asks the wrong questions; questions that the evidence is not fitted to answer. What we have in fact is a kind of prolonged allegory, full of symbols and metaphors. There is the archetypal link story: the 'invisible house' of secrets, only accessible to the Gnostic with the keys of understanding. We have a kind of simplistic code (that baffles experts!) and we have a genuine idea, that is to say, a transmission theory of gnostic liberation philosophy that has profoundly touched many individuals since ancient times. The real 'bloodline' is spiritual knowledge, suppressed by earthbound materialists who put all their treasure in earthly things and who have done so since Cain slugged Abel and the soon-to-be-drowned scoffed at Noah and his Ark.

This grand story is about loss, and it is about finding. It is about the hidden and the seen. It is about the buried and the raised, the body and the soul. It is about destruction of time giving birth to new hope. The Blood-Grail scheme is in fact a kind of prophetic vision, sparsely clad in history. From it may be learned something of what we suppose the wicked world can never tolerate for very long: the free spirit, the voice of truth, 'God', the dynamic hidden truth of man's inner potentialities, our magic to weave and wonder with, to make and break our destinies. It is arguable that such a story has as much validity as Isaiah's prophecy that a virgin shall conceive and bear a son and call his name *Immanuel*, God with us. But enthusiasts for such grand meta-histories might be warned.

It can be very dangerous to play with the Messiah, for as ancient kabbalah knows, the number or gematria of the Hebrew for 'Messiah' is the same as that for 'serpent'. It can, and does, bite.

The Watchers

– or the Mystery of Christianity Solved

When I began this investigation, I experienced a dim intuition that asking the key question 'Whatever happened to Jesus's Family?' might just reveal something new about the historical Jesus. The fact is, where Jesus's family has not been deliberately obscured, it has been transformed; the 'image-makers' have been at work. There is clearly a logical link between this fact and the idea that Jesus was who, or what, the dominant Churches have insisted he was. That is to say, knowledge of Jesus's family frustrates the Churches' efforts to produce a theological picture and impart it to converts and believers.

But it was not a theological picture that walked the roads and hills of Judea, Syria, Galilee and Transjordan in the 1st century of the Christian era. It was a man with a family.

The Christian Church has purloined the historical Jesus, repackaged and rebranded him. Had it been possible to assert copyright of his name, they would have done so, and there would have been nothing his family could do about it. They did not count. They, allegedly, rejected him, so the Church has rejected *them*. In losing the family, we have lost reality. If I were a Freudian, which I am not, I might suspect the Church is suffering from a deep-seated Oedipus complex. The paternity of Jesus has been, as it were, killed off or 'wiped out', and Mother has been penetrated by a dogma. Is there not something neurotic about Christian theology, always ready to explode at the hint of doubt?

We may add to this diagnosis a degree of schizophrenia, detectable in the tension between Jesus, James and the Family with their humane, spiritual righteousness, and the Pauline anti-law, atonement-dominated, 'evangelical' forensic mysticism. Paul was no friend of the Family. That is for sure. If Paul's real enemies were the 'New Covenanters', as Eisenman has asserted, the point of view of Jesus's family has got lost somewhere in the middle. The history of Christianity is largely written as a long theological row that shows no sign of abatement. They can't all be right; and they might all be wrong.

I have been amazed, speaking to people about my investigation, at how the knowledge that Jesus had brothers and sisters has transformed the level of their interest. Nowadays, a Jesus with a family gives him more immediate 'cred' than any high-in-the-sky theological dogma ever could. Jesus becomes someone you cannot easily dismiss simply by saying 'I'm an agnostic' or, 'I don't believe in any of that stuff'. He existed; he had a message. In such a visually-oriented era as ours, we are now in a position to say: once we were blind, now we can *see*. History may not always give us the truth, but it does give us colour, clear outlines and perspective. The trouble with, say, biblical movies, is that they *colour in* the whole screen. The viewer thinks they're getting a complete picture; they are not. It looks like 'reality', but it is not. It's just an image. If you want to film the Resurrection, you are going to need a time machine, and some heavy back-up.

———

The only time machine we are likely to have for the foreseeable future is our imagination. So it is time I came clean and gave you my best effort at reconstruction of the evidence, placed in what we can know of the social, religious and political setting in which Jesus's family appeared in history. It can be argued of course that this is only my interpretation of the evidence, and amounts to nothing more than opinion. Well, it is not *mere*, or uninformed, opinion, but it is not dogma either. I shall not be pleased if people simply take it on board as an approximation to 'the truth' without thinking. The reconstruction is offered as a stimulus to creative thought, above all. This change of perspective should enrich the mind and imagination of believer and non-believer alike. Vested interests will feel threatened; they should not. *Seek and ye shall find*, said Jesus, thus establishing the principle of science as an ethical imperative.

And if ecclesiastical authority says, as it oft does in these cases of knowledge *versus* dogma, 'We've heard it all before' – then, *why didn't you tell us?*

A RECONSTRUCTION

Jesus was born in 7 BC, the year recognized by the tribe of '*Magoi*' or Magi as holding significant astronomical indices for the appearance of a king in Israel (Mtt 2:2, 'we have seen his star in the east'). These regal indices have been confirmed by astronomers Joannes Kepler in the 17th century and by Professor David Hughes, astronomer of Sheffield University, in the 20th.

A party of these magi or 'natural magicians' hailing from somewhere between Edessa and Persia, consulted Hebrew prophetic writings. They would have read of a 'star' which came out of 'Jacob' (Israel) with a sceptre to rule by, and of a king who would bring God closer to mankind ('Immanuel') and of a place called Bethlehem. The child would be of the House of David, of the tribe of Judah. They correctly concluded a child could be found and 'worshipped', that is respected and recognized, at the city of Bethlehem in Judea. The Magi duly located a child in a house at Bethlehem. Unfortunately, in their enthusiasm, they seem to have alerted King Herod to the science, the birth and the prophecy.

The house in Bethlehem belonged to a man with close connections to the organization of the Temple in Jerusalem; he may have been a priest (he is reported to have had a priestly 'rod'). He may have been a widower. Joseph had recently been betrothed to a 16-year-old slave of the Temple, Mary. Priests took their wives from the virgins who were dedicated by their parents to God and made slaves of the Temple.

It is possible that each of the couple's fathers were brothers. According to this scenario, Mary's uncle Jacob and Joseph's uncle Yonakhir were twins, of the House of David. Jacob married Hadbhith and had at least two boys, Klopa (or 'Clopas') and Joseph (properly 'Yusef'). Yonakhir, a priest, married Hannah. They had a daughter, Mary (properly, 'Mariamme').

Mary's mother died when she was 12. Reportedly, she was put in the care of Zadok, another priest, and his wife, Sham'i, who died when Mary was 14. Mary must have felt lonely and vulnerable; she had no choice but to accept God's will, whatever it might entail. At 16, she had reached an age when a virgin should be married off, lest she be a source of impurity to the Temple on account of her menstruation. She was surrounded by older men who considered themselves holy. Imagine being surrounded by men in white, sacrificing animals all day long.

There appears to be something peculiar about the true father of Jesus. If Joseph was a priest, he was not supposed to marry a pregnant girl. According to Matthew, he was placed in a very embarrassing position. The earliest writings about Mary's relation to her newborn son indicate that as far as Jesus's flesh was concerned, Jesus was of the House and seed of David. We know that the creation of a human being requires sperm from a man and an egg from a woman. There can be no human body without a male and a female. This fact was not quite so obvious to people in the 1st century AD. A special child could be 'fathered' by a supernatural agent, a god or angel, the 'flesh' coming from the mother.

It was widely believed in Jesus's time by religious people that many sinful human women had, at the beginning of history, been impregnated by angels who lusted after them, descending from heaven to earth to have their wicked way, and producing a race of giants. It is highly likely that Mary would have heard such stories as she grew up, especially in the Temple. Indeed, as we shall see, such stories were very important to her family.

It is perfectly possible that the young girl became pregnant from a man without realizing the full biological facts, and, as a dedicated virgin, was terrified when she found she was pregnant – at least, to begin with. Being pregnant may have brought joy to a lonely girl: something precious of her own. At any rate, initial shock would surely explain her making her way to her relative, and possibly cousin, Elizabeth. Elizabeth was herself of the priestly line of Aaron and was married to a priest, Zechariah. She would know all about what went on at the Temple, and the life Mary lived. Elizabeth too, according to Luke, had conceived strangely. She was old, supposed barren, when she became pregnant with her son, John. Mary may have been informed by someone she trusted, such as Elizabeth, or even an angel that she was satisfied that she saw, that her condition was really the work of the Holy Spirit, and she had better offer herself up joyfully to the will of God, as she had been taught she must; a possession of the Temple until marriage, she was about to be the possession of Joseph.

If I was a police detective, and this was a crime, I should take an interest in step-father Zadok, or another priest of the Temple, especially since there were at the time ructions concerning the corruption of the priesthood. The Temple was a patriarchy; one does not imagine pregnant virgins would have had a leg to stand on if they were upset by those consecrated to divine service – like a molested boy in the hands of a Catholic priest in days, hopefully, gone by.

If one doubts, in all good faith, that the Holy Spirit can function as human sperm, one should first be looking at a member of the family for paternity, if, indeed, the true father was not Mary's betrothed all along, and Joseph had been having his cake and eating it before the marriage proper. Matthew does not think that was the case, and neither do I.

According to Matthew (Mtt.1:25), after Jesus's birth, Mary and Joseph had ordinary sexual relations as befitted man and wife, or priest and virgin. Mary was now safe, or thought she was, married to a man of means, securely fixed and respected in a family who carried the knowledge that they were of the chosen line of authentic Israelite monarchy, long since deprived, by the will of God and the force of usurpers. But from the House of David, from Jesse's 'stump', would come the 'Branch' of the Messiah, divinely anointed leader of the people.

The family hardly had time to settle into their Bethlehem house when Herod's men came looking for the born-to-be king of the Jews. The family fled to Egypt, possibly to Alexandria, where there was a sizeable Jewish community, some of whom were noted philosophers and holy men. Messianic beliefs flourished there along with philosophical versions of those beliefs.

In 4 BC, Herod died, succeeded by his son, Archelaus. Joseph had planned to return to his and Mary's homeland in Judea, but Joseph seems to have known enough about Archelaus and impending problems at the Temple to change his mind.

Jesus was about three years old, and may now have had two or three brothers or sisters, if two were twins. Mary was probably pregnant again. Insider-knowledge of the Herodian regime may have furnished Joseph with the option that Herod Antipas's territory in Galilee would be more stable and possibly more friendly than Herod's brother's kingdom in Judea, where a showdown between Archelaus and Judean religious leaders and their followers was about to erupt in Jerusalem with bloody consequences. As a family profoundly involved in the priestly Temple system, and as marked political enemies of Archelaus's father, Joseph may have known of a holy, priestly enclave in Galilee, perhaps secret, suitable anyway for the family to head to, to raise the family until the time was ripe for a full return to the Judean patrimony.

Alternatively, Joseph himself may have established the Galilean enclave or encampment, misleadingly called the 'city' of Nazareth in Matthew. I am minded to think that Joseph raised his children: Jesus, Judas, James, Joseph, Mary and Salome, to think of themselves as the *Natsarim*. Their encampment may have been called something like a *Natsarets*: 'keeper-land' or 'watcher-land'. The ideas around 'keeping' and 'watching' (from the Hebrew '*natsar*'), concern keeping the law of righteousness, and watching for the Day of the Lord (*Yom YHWH*).

More particularly, and potently, the term 'the watchers' (*Natsarim*), had at this time a specific esoteric meaning, revealed to the righteous who read the apocalyptic Book of Enoch (its parts dated *c.*100 BC–AD 70), a book familiar to the Essenes, to the 'New Covenanters' or 'Qumran sect', and, above all to Jesus and his brothers. The Book of Enoch provides much of the rationale and mythology for Jesus's message, though it is seldom read today, possibly because it has practically nothing to say to the Paulinist Christian.

Importantly, the term 'natsarim' occurs in Jeremiah 4:15–17. Key parts of

the Book of Enoch appear to be a *midrash* or expansion of this passage
in Jeremiah:

> For a voice declareth from Dan, and publish affliction from Mount
> Ephraim. Make ye mention to the nations; behold, publish against
> Jerusalem, that watchers come from a far country, and give out their
> voice against the cities of Judah. As keepers of a field, are they
> against her round about, because she hath been rebellious against
> me, saith the Lord.

Jesus's family had, according to Matthew, come from a far country. If based
near the place now called Natseret, they could have looked down from those
parts on the Plain of Megiddo ('Armageddon') and further southwards toward
Ephraim. The location had meaning within Jewish prophecy of the Day of the
Lord. Fifty miles north was Dan, with Mount Hermon to the north of Dan, in
the 'land of Damascus' where the Teacher of Righteousness's 'New Covenant'
was formed.

The Book of Enoch is illuminated by a series of visions concerning the condemnation of *evil* 'Watchers'. The evil 'Watchers' had come 'from afar' too:
corrupt angels who had quit heaven to sow the seeds of evil on earth.
According to Enoch, God punishes the evil Watchers by binding them to
earth, but in so doing, God's creation is corrupted. A showdown becomes
inevitable.

Generally speaking, the term 'the Watchers' denotes the angels of God,
imagined as stars, lights in the darkness. The Father of Lights declares to
Enoch: 'And whosoever shall be condemned and destroyed will from thence-
forth be bound together with them [the evil Watchers] to the end of all
generations.' Armageddon is coming:

> And destroy all the spirits of the reprobate, and the children of the
> Watchers, because they have wronged mankind. Destroy all wrong from
> the face of the earth, and let every evil work come to an end: and let
> the plant of righteousness and truth appear: and it shall prove a

blessing: the works of righteousness and truth appear: and it shall prove a blessing: the works of righteousness and truth shall be planted in truth and joy for evermore. And then shall all the righteous escape, and shall live till they beget thousands of children, And all the days of their youth and their old age shall they complete in peace.

(Enoch 11:15ff)

Imagine standing on the heights above the Plain of Megiddo, as perhaps your father recites these powerful words to you, knowing you have been consecrated for the Lord's work. Gazing from earth to sky and back again, you would soon become aware of what was involved in 'your Father's business'.

Significantly, we are told in chapter 12 of the book that before the end, 'Enoch was hidden, […] And his activities had to do with the Watchers, and his days were with the holy ones.' Enoch was about his Father's business, as his descendant Jesus was (Luke 3:37):

And I, Enoch, was blessing the Lord of majesty and the King of the ages, and lo! the Watchers called me – Enoch the scribe – and said to me: 'Enoch, the scribe of righteousness, go, declare, to the Watchers of the heaven who have left the high heaven, the holy eternal place, and have defiled themselves with women, and have done as the children of earth do, and have taken unto themselves wives: 'Ye have wrought great destruction on the earth…

(Enoch 12:3ff)

Imagine Mary, Jesus's mother, hearing about the fallen angels who have defiled women, and the evil men who follow the evil of the fallen Watchers, who will be bound to hell.

Azazel, prince of the fallen Watchers, begs Enoch to petition the Lord of Spirits, to intercede against their judgement. Here we can see Enoch tie in directly with the prophecy of Jeremiah above, for it is from *Dan*, in the far north, that Enoch will publish the judgement on those 'rebellious' against the Lord. This is the Dan that Jesus will visit, the Dan renamed and Romanized by Herodians *Caesarea Philippi*. This is where Peter declares Jesus to be the Messiah (Mark 8:27ff.), and where Jesus speaks of the 'Son of man' (a key figure of the Book of Enoch) only to be rebuked physically, that is to say *attacked*, by an enraged Peter for saying this figure must be rejected and killed – precisely the opposite of everything Peter was hoping for and trusting in. Jesus sees evil spirit working through Peter and casts this 'Satan' (or evil Watcher) aside. The defeat of the fallen Watchers, bound to them that do evil, requires a reversal of the world's expectation: Messiah must die!

Enoch shows that behind the fate of men who rebel against God, is a cosmic drama, played out between the Almighty and rebel angels whose evil spirits have possessed much of mankind: 'And I went off and sat down at the waters of Dan, in the land of Dan, to the south of the west of Hermon: I read their petition till I fell asleep.' (Enoch 13:7ff.) The book is clear: the 'evil spirits on earth' are the products of the evil Watchers enjoying the sins of men. Understanding this scenario helps us fully to understand Jesus's extensive operation of casting out devils. He knows who they serve, as in the case of the famous madman of Gadara, whose banished devils hop into the Gadarene swine and hurl themselves suicidally off a cliff, as many an enflamed Zealot would do, figuratively speaking. Was the Gadarene swine-suicide story originally a comment on the behaviour of suicidal Zealots sent mad by evil spirits?

Azazel is the 'prince of this world' whose legion of spirits Jesus and his fellow Natsarim will cast out. The enemies of God are *spiritual* enemies. Swords will not destroy them. The world needs the divine power of messianic exorcism: 'deliver us from evil', not phalanxes of self-righteous 'holy warriors' breaking the commandment not to kill.

It seems likely that Jesus's family became involved in some way with at least one 'New Covenanter' messianic encampment – if indeed 'Nazareth' was not itself one of these encampments – perhaps agreeing with much of their stance of piety and righteousness. However, Jesus was not by any account a slavish follower of anybody's manual of discipline. His stance on the pitfalls of obsessive external legal observance at the expense of true repentance and opportunity for forgiveness and self-knowledge would create a stumbling stone between him and the Teacher of Righteousness's followers, as surely as his father Joseph chose not to take his family to Jerusalem in BC 4 when *another* teacher of righteousness created a bloodbath in the Temple in the name of God.

As far as we can tell, Jesus did share a radical condemnation of the corruption of the Temple priesthood with the New Covenanters. One presumes the authors of the Qumran Manual of Discipline would have welcomed Jesus's inflammatory comments about the destruction of the Herodian Temple. However, Jesus's corresponding assertion that it could be raised again in 'three days' *in himself* would surely have outraged them. While to an outside observer, Jesus's position would have appeared very close indeed to the New Covenanters, as so often in radical circles, the smallest distinction may enflame radical groups to levels of hatred beyond even that reserved for declared opposite ideological enemies. It is obvious that Stalin hated Trotsky more than Winston Churchill, for example. Moderate Muslims enrage extremist Muslims even more than any pope. Heretics in interpretation have always been perceived as being more threatening to dominant religious ideologies than those who reject their beliefs wholesale.

Putting it mildly perhaps, Jesus differed with New Covenanters over issues of application of the law and the viability of waging messianic conflict by force of arms, unless, along with Eisenman, we discard the bulk of the canonical gospel record of Jesus as little more than Pauline propaganda. Jesus had found another door: *himself*. Furthermore, if the sectarians of righteousness had suspected for a second that Jesus knew himself, in himself, to be the promised Messiah, something he did not shout about, they would have dismissed him as a pretender fit for death by any means. According to their discipline, a blasphemous pseudo-Messiah Jesus was wholly outside of the mercy of God. Getting rid of him would have been a sacred duty. He was accursed: crucifixion was too good for him. In such circumstances, Jesus would only have had his family and, subsequently, any new Judean and Galilean followers to support him. In fact, he was supported, almost to the end by his followers, and right to the end by his family.

———

Once Jesus and his family had declared spiritual war on the leaders of Judean religion, as his relative and friend John declared war on the sins of the Herodians, the days of Jesus and his brothers were numbered, you might say, but so, as it turned out, were the days of the Herodian dynasty and the Temple system the Herodians had corrupted. Neither outlived the lifetimes of Jesus's family. And with the Temple and the Herodians went the New Covenanters or, if you prefer, 'Qumran sectaries' who were responsible for the more interesting texts of the 'Dead Sea Scrolls' and whose covenant, as it turned out, was not new enough.

———

We may be disposed to consider Jesus's operation a great success, even if its aims were limited to transforming the political corruption of God's religion by wicked priests and wicked kings. But of course a messianic programme inevitably goes much further than the kind of thing that gets reported on news channels or steals the headlines of newspapers.

Once we have grasped the point about the good 'Natsarim', the 'Watchers', God's agents on earth (rendered in Greek as 'Nazoreans'), in tune with the angels who did not fall, while yet doing battle with invisible powers that corrupt the soul, we can see that the fall of the old Temple and Herodian system was only the first wave of the new heaven and the new earth inaugurated by the Messiah of Israel.

How Jesus's brothers saw the Crucifixion or how they responded personally to the news of the Resurrection, is unknown, except to say that all the evidence points to them accepting that a miracle had happened. The Cross had not been the end of the story. The Jesus whose hideous cross was supposed to be the Roman prefect's last word on hopes for a 'King of the Jews', refused to lie down. Dead, it was as though he were alive. People were talking about him. Had he not risen, declared himself, then risen even further, to heaven? Was he not ruling from there? Did the family interpret Jesus's death this wise: that Jesus had outwitted the evil Watchers, the power behind the powers, by reversing the fundamental trend of humanity's self-love, opening thereby the door to resurrection and new life in the spirit of God, freeing up a path away from the paradoxes and fatality of worshipping the created, so that the holy children could more fully embrace the eternal spirit of creation?

Nice idea.

There can be no doubt that brother James, who led the Jerusalem assembly, preached not only righteousness in the legal sense but a present and coming salvation and judgement, foretold by the prophets of old. But this was all still well within the conceptions and traditions of prophetic Jewish life. It was normal for the prophets to be rejected; it would not have surprised Jesus's closest supporters that the 'Son of Man' was likewise too difficult for the wicked and the earth-bound to accept. When has the materialist embraced the divine? Answer: when he can see the material advantage.

It is notable that James, according to Hegesippus, echoed his Lord Jesus's words at his own death: 'Lord, forgive them, for they know not what they do.' Man does not know who he is. He sees not the covenant of love inside himself between himself and his Maker and Lord. He flounders, and is soon the tool of evil spirits, wasting himself and everything around him.

Understanding the essentially spiritual nature of the conflicts of the world freed Jesus and his family and friends from the narrowness of self-righteousness evinced in the 'Damascus Document' and other texts we now call the 'Dead Sea Scrolls'. Those texts represented the dominant thought patterns of messianically minded Jews in Jesus's lifetime, that is to say, messianically *committed* Jews. Their commitment was to a cleansed nation, a holy people, free and beloved of God. The aim was admirable, but the method was, as events demonstrated, unsound. Both Paul and Jesus would have agreed on this principle, I think. 'First clean the inside of the cup.' External law-keeping is possible for a person who keeps his true soul wrapped up and silent, looking 'good' on the outside, ticking all the boxes of righteousness, but inside remains the same old being. Eisenman is absolutely right to see the sharpest division of the era and the place as that between Paul and the New Covenanters. Paul was sure that the law could not make people good, where it counted. But he took a step beyond that to a position that I do not think the teaching of Jesus and his friends could possibly support: the abandonment of the law. The new covenant fulfilled the old; it did not abolish it. The call was to join, or re-join the holy beings of God. Paul's approach was schismatic from the beginning.

It seems likely that Jesus took his operational models from various sources, especially the scriptural accounts of the organization of the priesthood under David and Solomon. I see no reason why he could not have taken, or indeed shared, the idea of a high council of 12 men and 3 priests from the eschatological (end-of-the-world) operation of the New Covenanters (the so-called 'Qumran community'). The evidence suggests he removed what he would have considered the vices of this system, its perpetual judgemental pomposity and impossible ideal of human conduct, necessitating its tedious, dispiriting casuistry of legal penalties for backsliding.

Jesus's message conforms to authentic documents such as the Book of Enoch, the hottest text perhaps of Jewish esotericism in his lifetime. The Book of Enoch delineates the saving role of the figure known as 'the Son of Man' who had appeared in the inner being of Jesus as it had in the soul of Ezekiel over 500 years before. In Jesus, the vision of the divine form of Man seems to have been self-realized to such a degree as to inspire spiritual visions of him transfigured and witnessed by close followers, taken out of their ordinary selves and opened to the infinite worlds of inner vision.

The Son of Man is Man made in the image of God, the door for the human individual's progress: the proper end of that ancient injunction to 'know thyself': that part of the psyche that was not swallowed up in matter, and which, though obscure to ordinary consciousness, nonetheless reflects the pure light of the 'Father of Lights', as the Book of Enoch describes the Father in Heaven. In order to receive the Light, one must purify the inner part. Then, Jesus promised his pupils, powers of perception and exorcism would follow. Jesus let 'his own' loose on the world.

The inner circle of Jesus's extended family appears to have consisted of himself, the king, his brothers Judas, James and Joseph, his cousin Simeon, or Simon,

Klopa's wife Mary, Jesus's sisters Mary and Salome, family friend Mary Magdalene, Peter ('Stone') and John. This was the messianic power-pack launched upon a deeply suspicious and darkened world.

Even after the misery of the revolt of AD 66–73, messianic movements were perceived as threatening to Rome; Rome was correct. The Jewish fantasy of defeating Rome by force of arms would not crash finally until Bar Khochba was defeated over 60 years after the mass suicide at Masada ended the Jewish Revolt, considered by some who came after as a judgement on the wicked of Judea for murdering James, the brother of Jesus.

Before Shimon Bar Khochba reached his ignominious end, Roman intelligence services were seeking out members of the house of David, as intelligence services today will keep tabs on the relatives of Osama Bin Laden. It was the *religious* character of Jewish revolt that so enraged and exasperated the Romans, leading them to extremes of cruel suppression. The Romans were not immune to the fear of God. Jesus's family became victims of such fear, politically motivated, we may say, but which would have appeared entirely spiritual in origin to those who suffered most under it.

Simeon, son of Klopa died around AD 106–7 in such a purge, martyred under the rule of Trajan, another stooge of the wicked 'Watchers', as his relatives may have seen. Simeon, a very old man indeed, had survived the attack on the House of David that had taken place under the Emperor Domitian AD 81–96. Domitian's persecution had netted two of the grandsons of Jesus's brother Judas. We may imagine that these men had received the doctrines that appear in the canonical epistle of Judas, seldom read, but which contains direct reference to the prophet Enoch and the character of spiritual warfare. It is fascinating that in both of these cases, Hegesippus refers to their being specifically informed upon by 'heretics', prepared to pull in the Roman authorities to see the family of Jesus wiped out. Could these heretics, I wonder, have been the survivors of the 'New Covenanter' movement whose unforgiving testimonia have come down to us in the Dead Sea Scrolls? A tantalizing idea; their approach could well represent the authentic butts of Jesus's comment that a prophet was not dishonoured save among his own, a saying that Paul perhaps took very much to heart.

As history has shown, the Gentiles have claimed to be the biggest fans of Jesus, so long as he is not too Jewish.

After Julius Africanus's intriguing reference to the *desposyni* of c.AD 220, the family of Jesus effectively disappears, at least by AD 300, since Eusebius of Caesarea mentions no living member, unless he was protecting them, an idea with no evidence to support it.

It is possible that the family, which may have been very extensive by that time, found the credal absolutes of the Nicaean faith, cooked up under the eye of the Emperor Constantine, unbearable. Their kinsman Jesus had become a theological, christological concept, his humanity so rarefied that no one could call it human without subtle, intense caveats. Their delightfully human apocalyptic beacon had been made to join the *Pax Romana*, long after he had transcended it. He was welcome to rule in heaven but the emperor and his appointed bishops ruled on earth. His kingdom may not have been of this world, but there was still enough of this world left in the theological equation to provide ample scope for emperors and armies and merchants and nobles hungry for the status and wealth eschewed by the Natsarim.

Perhaps the family simply departed in disgust – to France, possibly, or even Babylon. The world was not exactly their oyster, but there were plenty of places in the Diaspora where they might find the burning inner fire of true Judaic holy mysticism – and peace and quiet. Perhaps they stayed put and simply minded their own business in Syria, content, that as a family, they had done their bit. New generations may have felt very differently to past generations.

Seventeen hundred years ago is an exceedingly long time ago. Jesus walked the earth a thousand years or so before the battle of Hastings. Our records from the Dark Ages are appallingly inadequate to the cause of tracing individual, non-noble families, especially when we have no names and no nuffin'.

It would be nice to think a providential hand kept the surviving families in safety and free from the peril of the night, but we have no evidence for it – probably the greatest security there is. If I wished to survive the 'information generation' intact, I should wish there to be no information. If you are out there, brothers and sisters, keep it a secret; this world has nothing to offer you, but trouble.

A great reparation is in order: the price for the rejection of Jesus's family has been the dislocation of spiritual civilization and the fragmentation of the world.

Really?

Yes, think about this.

———

If Jesus's family had continued leading the messianic assembly or 'Natsarim', and Paul had submitted to James and not pursued a doctrine at odds with that of the first bishop of Jerusalem, giving ammunition to the anti-Jewish direction of the faith after the Jewish Revolt, then, arguably, the western Church would not have become so detached from its Jewish heritage as to move towards an elevation of Jesus from metaphor to pseudo-physics, that is, from flesh to apotheosis.

The extravagance of christology (beliefs about Christ) that luxuriated with the attempted amalgam of Jewish thought with Greek, Egyptian and Asiatic thought not only provoked one 'heresy' after another, but would in the 7th century provoke the prophet Muhammad, for one, to a wholesale rejection of trinitarianism in all its orthodox forms, leading to an insistence on the isolate Godhead who can, or will, only deal with humanity from a position outside of created nature, which, being created, can only submit to the will of its creator, the sovereign unity, Allah. The impersonal deity was reasserted and the life of the creature relegated to the status where the human form in sacred contexts would be condemned as blasphemous.

The western Catholic Church, inheriting a christology that grew in external grandeur, unapproachability and spiritual vagueness as it inflated itself to imperial size, set itself up for more than the usual share of bitter internal struggles with 'heretics'. The Church militant would in time fall headlong into the sickness of the medieval crusades where the 'enemies' each claimed 'God' as their private backer: an absurd situation that persists in various forms with regrettable consequences for civilization; spiritual religion being its first, if not intended, victim.

It hardly bears underlining, for it should be so obvious to readers by now, that the anti-Judaic position of significant tracts of Christian tradition, leading to pogrom, suppression, expulsion, ridicule, and ultimately holocaust, of the children of Israel, would probably never have occurred had the family of Jesus remained in the frame. The rulers were able to attack Jews because the Church would not defend their own, for the Jew, as a Jew, was no longer in the divine family.

It is hard to imagine the split of Judaic monotheism into three 'distinct religions' had Jesus's nearest and dearest not been alienated from their own movement. There would have been no Reformation, no split between Catholic, Protestant and Orthodox believers; there would have been no reason to reformulate monotheism in terms of Islam; followers of Jesus would not have regarded Judaism as a distinct and altogether separate religion so there would have been no Nazi holocaust – all of this and so much more of our history and our present's disquiets stem from the rejection of Jesus's family.

They are not 'missing' for nothing.

In simpler terms, we may conclude that had Jesus's family not lost control of Jesus's spiritual operation, our species' entire history would have been very different, unimaginable. Arguably, religion would have evolved differently, perhaps into a war waged with exclusively spiritual rather than flesh-and-blood opponents, that is, a 'jihad' or struggle that is internal, personal, and not something to be manipulated from outside of the soul by pseudo-savants claiming God as their backer and authority, false prophets, or politicians vulgar, bourgeois or aristocratic.

In short, the rejection and loss of Jesus's real family has created the protracted religious crisis through which both East and West have trudged, rarely catching the light and holding it, for the past 1,900 disgraceful years.

Is it not time we found the missing Family, before the *Watchers*, as it were, find *us*?

Further Reading

Augustine, St, *City of God*, Penguin Classics

Baigent, Michael, Richard Leigh and Henry Lincoln, *The Messianic Legacy*, Cape, 1986

The Bible. Yes, the Bible. King James Version reads best in English.

Charles, R H (trans.), *The Book of Enoch*, SPCK, 1994

Churton, Tobias, *Kiss of Death, The True History of the Gospel of Judas*, Watkins, 2008

Churton, William Ralph, *Uncanonical and Apocryphal Scriptures*, J Whitaker, 1884

Ehrman, Bart D, *Lost Scriptures, Books that Did Not Make It into the New Testament*, OUP, 2005

Eisenman, Robert, *James the Brother of Jesus*, Watkins, 2002

Epiphanius, *Panarion*, Trans. Frank Williams, E J Brill, Leiden

Eusebius, *Ecclesiastical History*, 2 vols, trans. Kirsopp Lake, Loeb, 1975

Ignatius, *Epistle to the Ephesians*, (*The Ante-Nicene Fathers*, Erdmans Publishing Co., 1981)

Josephus, *Antiquities of the Jews*, trans. William Whiston, Nimmo, 1865

Josephus, *The Jewish War*, trans. William Whiston, Nimmo, 1865

Sextus Julius Africanus, Letter to Aristides, chapter 5

Justin Martyr, *Dialogue with Trypho*, (*The Ante-Nicene Fathers*, Erdmans Publishing Co., 1981)

Lewin, Thomas, *Life and Epistles of St Paul*, 2 vols, [n.p.], 1874

Martin, Malachi, *The Decline and Fall of the Roman Church*, New York, Bantam, 1983

May, Herbert G and John Day (eds), *Oxford Bible Atlas*, OUP, 1975

Robinson, James M (ed.), *The Nag Hammadi Library in English*, E J Brill, 1984

Suetonius, *The Twelve Caesars*, trans. Robert Graves, Folio Society, 1964

Taylor, *Christians and the Holy Places*, Oxford, 1993

Taylor, NL, 'Saint William, King David, and Makhir: a Controversial Medieval Descent', *American Genealogist*, 72: 205–23, 245

Tacitus, *Annals*, Penguin Classics

Vermes, Geza (trans.), *The Complete Dead Sea Scrolls in English*, Penguin, 2004

Zuckerman, Arthur J, *A Jewish Princedom in Feudal France, 768–900*, Columbia University Press, 1972

INDEX